Choosing a President DISCARD

DATE DUE

Choosing a President
The Electoral College and Beyond

Edited by

Paul D. Schumaker
University of Kansas

and

Burdett A. Loomis
University of Kansas

CHATHAM HOUSE PUBLISHERS
SEVEN BRIDGES PRESS, LLC
NEW YORK · LONDON

Seven Bridges Press
135 Fifth Avenue
New York, NY 10010-7101

Publisher: Ted Bolen
Managing Editor: Katharine Miller
Composition: ediType
Cover Design: Stefan Killen Design
Cover Art: Corbis; Eyewire
Map: Carto-Graphics
Printing and Binding: Victor Graphics, Inc.

Library of Congress Cataloging-in-Publication Data

Choosing a president : the electoral college and beyond / edited by Paul
D. Schumaker, Burdett A. Loomis.
    p.   cm.
    Includes bibliographical references and index.
    ISBN 1-889119-53-9 (pbk.)
    1. Presidents – United States – Election. 2. Electoral
college – United States.   I. Schumaker, Paul.   II. Loomis, Burdett A.,
1945- .
JK528 .C44 2002
324.6'3'0973 – dc21

                                                        2001005749

Manufactured in the United States of America
10   9   8   7   6   5   4   3   2   1

Contents

Figures and Tables

Preface

SHOULD THE ELECTORAL COLLEGE be reformed? Should it be abolished? As professors of political science, we were frequently asked these questions in the aftermath of the 2000 presidential election. Because the current rules and procedures of the Electoral College resulted in the elevation of George W. Bush to the presidency despite Al Gore's "victory" in the national popular vote, the students, friends, and reporters who asked these questions often presupposed an answer to them — the Electoral College is an anachronism that belongs in a museum rather than at the heart of the world's leading democracy.

As political scientists, we were not so sure. Despite our familiarity with the Electoral College, we had not viewed it as especially important in determining the outcome of a presidential election. Nor had we thought it one of the features of our political system most in need of reform. It was not clear that the discipline of political science had a conventional or consensual view of the merits and liabilities of the Electoral College. While political scientists had entered into debates on the topic, they could be found on both sides of the issue. Although scholars had conducted studies linking the Electoral College to various aspects of our political ideals and practices, no effort had been made to integrate these studies into an overall evaluation of the institution.

This book attempts such an evaluation. Our motivation in evaluating the Electoral College has never been to cast doubt on the legitimacy of the Bush presidency. From the outset, we recognized that democracy requires not adherence to any particular set of electoral rules, but rather adherence to whatever rules have emerged from fairly constructed previous agreements. We understood that the U.S. Constitution, our country's most basic political agreement, establishes that the presidency be contested through the rules of the Electoral College. We firmly believed that whoever won under the rules of the Electoral College in 2000 had a legitimate claim to the presidency, regardless of who received the most popular votes nationally. Our motivation for evaluating the Electoral College has been to prepare for future elections — to ask whether the Electoral College or some alternative is the electoral system that is best suited to preserve and promote

American democracy in the years to come. To address that question, we compare the Electoral College to six alternatives.

Three alternatives would retain the Electoral College but change it in important ways. Each state would still be given a particular number of electors, according to rules specified by the Constitution and as determined by the census. However, under two of the reform proposals, all of a state's electors would not be given to the candidate winning the popular vote within the state using the "winner-take-all" or unit rule that is employed by every state except Maine and Nebraska. Under the proposed district plan, most electors would be awarded to candidates winning particular districts within states. Under a proportional allocation plan, electors would be awarded to candidates based on the percentage of popular votes that the candidates received in each state. A third reform would keep the electoral college system intact (including the winner-take-all feature), but it would give the winner of the national popular vote a bonus of 102 electoral votes. This reform would practically ensure that the winner of the national popular vote would win in the Electoral College.

Three alternatives would abolish the Electoral College and replace it with various national popular vote schemes. The popular plurality system would give the presidency to whatever candidate receives the most votes. The popular majority system would institute a contingent runoff election between the top two vote-getters if no candidate achieves a majority in the initial balloting. An instant-runoff system would also require a candidate to get a majority of votes, but a runoff election would be avoided by determining a majority winner through a computerized analysis of voters' rank-ordering of three or more candidates.

Various critics of the Electoral College have proposed each of these alternative electoral systems, but is any of these alternatives better than the existing system? Answers to this question may depend on how these electoral systems affect our broader political concerns. For example, would an alternative system produce more political stability than the Electoral College? Would some alternative be more effective than the Electoral College at encouraging voter participation? Would another system do a better job than the Electoral College at producing a president whose party platform is relatively inclusive of the various interests in our country?

To answer such questions, we asked thirty-five colleagues in the field of political science to join us in a project designed to bring to bear their expertise about political stability, citizen participation, party coalitions, and other important aspects of our political life on an evaluation of the Electoral College and its alternatives. Nine groups composed of three to five political scientists were formed to analyze the impact of various electoral systems on our federal system of government, the functioning of our national governmental institutions, the conduct of presidential campaigns, and other matters.

The first chapter frames the central concern of this book, and differentiates our analysis from complementary analyses of other electoral problems, such as the errors in counting ballots, that became evident in Florida during the 2000 election. Here we make clear that our concerns are evaluative rather than explanatory. We are less concerned with why we have an electoral college system or why reform initiatives have so quickly receded from the public agenda than with reaching normative judgments about the Electoral College.

The second chapter describes the electoral college system, as it was initially conceived and as it has evolved. It also describes each of the alternatives to it. We also address analytical issues that must be resolved in reaching a collective judgment about a preferred presidential electoral system.

Chapters 3 through 11 provide the reports of each of the nine groups in the project. In these chapters, scholars use theories and findings from their areas of expertise to provide partial evaluations of the Electoral College. For example, in chapter 4 specialists in federalism consider how our federal system would be impacted by electoral reform. In chapter 8, experts on the media consider whether electoral reform would influence how television and newspapers report campaigns and the election. In chapter 11, specialists in racial and class issues in America consider how the electoral influence of minorities and other relatively powerless groups in our country is affected by the Electoral College, and how their influence might change under alternative arrangements.

Chapter 12 presents our collective judgments. After familiarizing ourselves with each others' findings and assessments, each participant in the project indicated their (degree of) support for the Electoral College and each alternative to it, and their votes have been compiled in various ways to provide quantitative measures of our overall support for each system. We also draw from each group's analysis to reach summary qualitative assessments of each system.

Unlike many scholars who write books, we didn't know what our conclusions would be until the project was nearly completed — until the various chapters had been received from each group, until we had assimilated each others' conclusions, and until we had voted. Many of the participants in the project are surprised by our results. Most of our acquaintances also have expressed surprise at the results. Our hope is that the results will prompt students, citizens, and public leaders to think more deeply about the matter than has often been the case.

We have incurred many debts in developing this project and producing this book. The Robert J. Dole Institute at the University of Kansas funded a useful conference at which we could discuss our findings. Our greatest debts are to our colleagues who have participated in this project. We appreciate their willingness to take time from their own research projects to participate in this collective endeavor. We hope the opportunity to participate in an issue of broad public interest and importance such as this is partial repayment on the debt that is owed.

Finally, we would be pleased to incur even more debts in the future, namely, to the readers of this volume. As teachers, we are interested in understanding how students and citizens analyze the issues under discussion here. Accordingly, we have developed a website at http://raven.cc.ukans.edu/~college. After you complete this book, we encourage you to go to this website and express your judgments about the Electoral College and the various alternatives to it. Your participation will enable us to develop a deeper understanding of citizen attitudes about how we choose our president.

CHAPTER 1

Bush, Gore, and the Issues of Electoral Reform

Paul Schumaker, *University of Kansas*

THE TUMULT FOLLOWING the 2000 presidential election has subsided. It began the morning of 8 November when we learned that Al Gore had received over 500,000 more votes than George W. Bush, but that the Electoral College would likely thwart his elevation to the highest office in the country. Since the American Constitution provides that the candidate with a majority of electoral votes in the College wins the presidency, the outcome hinged not on Gore's popular success but on who would get Florida's bloc of twenty-five electors and thus attain the necessary Electoral College majority. During the next several weeks — as the Florida votes were recounted (or not), as the lawyers and politicians maneuvered, and as the commentators pontificated — the legitimacy of a Bush presidency was often challenged and proposals to change our electoral system were plentiful. However, only mild, sporadic protests against the system were registered and, within six months, the issue of whether the Electoral College should be reformed or abolished vanished from the public agenda.[1]

How can we explain the failure of this issue to take hold? Four broad possibilities come readily to mind, based on *realism, elitism, pluralism,* and *functionalism*. The realistic explanation is that the Electoral College is part of our constitutional heritage and that the Constitution has placed such formidable hurdles to changing our electoral system that there is little to be gained by trying. The elitist explanation is that the Electoral College serves the interests of the powerful; having no reason to support changes in the system, party leaders in our political system have ignored or even suppressed a broader consideration of the issue. A pluralist explanation is that American citizens have diverse views about our electoral system, which prevent a broad social movement rallying around some alternative to it. A functional explanation is simply that Americans generally regard the Electoral College as a serving an important, useful role in our political system and thus see no reason to make an issue of changing our system for electing our president.[2] Let us take a closer look at each of these explanations.

The *realistic explanation* emphasizes the difficulty of changing our presidential electoral process because amending the Constitution is itself difficult — requiring supermajorities both in Congress and among the states. Realists understand that constitutional amendments to alter the Electoral College must win overwhelming support.

First, such amendments must be approved by two-thirds of the members of both branches of Congress.[3] Realists would recall that Congress has considered more than seven hundred separate proposals for changing the Electoral College, and these proposals have met with almost no success. Recently, Judiciary Committees in both the Senate (1992) and the House of Representatives (1997) conducted hearings on the issue, but no action was taken. In 1979 both the House and the Senate entertained but abandoned proposals to abolish the Electoral College. In 1956 and 1969, constitutional amendments calling for the direct popular election of the president passed the House but died in the Senate. We would have to go back to 1803 to find Congress passing an amendment directly modifying the Electoral College.

Second, even if Congress passed a constitutional amendment, it would require approval by three-quarters of the states. Such rules regarding the process of amending the Constitution make it easy for state legislators from small states to thwart changes in the electoral process that undermine their interests. Because the Electoral College provides each state with two electoral votes irrespective of its population, the relative voting power of citizens in small states is enhanced,[4] an advantage that both citizens and leaders of these states are loath to abandon. Realists would point out that George W. Bush won twenty of the twenty-nine smallest states, each overrepresented in the Electoral College and each decisive to Bush's narrow victory. If only thirteen of these states voted their interest in preserving an electoral system that advantages their voters, change would be thwarted.

The realist perspective derives from an institutional approach to explaining politics, which contends that political institutions and the rules governing them matter. As the most fundamental of all political institutions, constitutions create both the rules that govern political systems and the rules for changing these rules. The existing rules governing the process of amending the Constitution practically ensure the survival of the Electoral College as is.

The realist perspective has normative implications that are consistent with classical liberalism. At the time of America's founding, liberals viewed constitutions as articulating our social contract, or our most basic social agreements about our political community. A political process that sought widespread agreement about our governing institutions created the constitutional rules regarding the Electoral College. To found a nation at the constitutional convention, broad support was needed, and institutions such as the Electoral College achieved such backing. If we now wish to change our method of electing the president, we are morally (as well as legally) required to obtain roughly the same sort of supermajority to amend the Constitution that was required to create it. From a liberal perspective, the institutional rules for changing the Electoral College are entirely appropriate for ensuring that the agreements embedded in our Constitution will only be amended by supermajoritarian processes similar to those that created our republic. Reform of the Electoral College should thus succeed only as a result of a widespread social movement or broad political support for change. From a liberal perspective, citizens have little reason to become active and mobilize into a social movement to protest our electoral system unless that system egregiously violates citizens' equal political rights. That standard may not have been met in the wake of the 2000 election.

An *elitist explanation* would see the demise of the Electoral College issue as the result of how power is distributed and how powerful interests are represented in America. From this perspective the Constitution was created to serve elite interests, and the Electoral College was intended to obstruct democratic impulses such as having a direct popular election of the president.[5] Elite theorists would argue that throughout our history the Electoral College has helped shield presidents from popular and progressive impulses that threatened the most powerful economic, social, and political interests. They would claim that elites, particularly our political leaders, continue to use their power to thwart change in our electoral system. For the most part, our political leaders are Republicans and Democrats, and the Electoral College advantages our two major parties in the electoral process by shielding their office holders and candidates from third-party competition and pressure from other organizations outside the mainstream of American political life. Just as the Constitution presents substantial hurdles to electoral change, the interests of our elites — especially Democratic and Republican party leaders — dictate that political power will suppress the issue of electoral reform and defeat reform proposals that might reach our governmental agenda.[6]

The elitist explanation is also a structural one. While institutional explanations see political outcomes as greatly affected by the institutional rules, structural explanations see political outcomes as greatly affected by people's interests and their power resources. The structure of power in America makes it highly unlikely that any challenge to the system that undermines the interests of the powerful will be successful.

The elitist perspective has normative implications that are consistent with populism. Populists denounce the existing power structure and the institutions that support it. Populists face the dilemma of accepting an electoral college system they oppose or engaging in a difficult struggle to bring about change. Alienated populists would like to see the system change but opt for inaction because of their pessimism about the odds of successfully challenging the powerful. Activist populists would also like to see the system change, and they retain enough hope that they do challenge the powerful. But because of the institutional as well as the structural barriers to change, they often conclude that the Electoral College is not the best target of their challenges to the system. They seek more promising reforms that would undermine the current distributions of power and privilege in America.

The *pluralist explanation* focuses on the possibility of political change bubbling up from the citizenry, from the bottom of the power structure. Pluralists see the American political system as open to reform efforts, with Democratic and Republican public officials both competing and collaborating in political affairs. The competition between them means that our representatives must respond to citizens who are mobilized on behalf of popular causes. Given widespread support for change, perhaps expressed by a broad social movement, Democrats and Republicans may well incorporate the movement's demands into their platforms, if only to achieve partisan advantage. Pluralists would see the absence of a widespread social movement on behalf of change as explaining the failure of the Electoral College issue to take root.

Pluralists adopt a behavioral approach, which emphasizes that citizens' actions make a great difference in shaping the actions and outcomes of political life. Pluralists recognize that on most issues, citizen involvement in broad social movements is not essential for political success. Smaller groups of citizens can become active on routine issues, and, absent overt opposition, they can achieve their political goals in an open political system that responds to their demands. But on larger issues — such as a fundamental reform of our electoral system — a much broader mobilization of citizens into a social movement is required to bring about change.

Progressive social movements seek fundamental changes in economic, social, and political life, but such movements are often thwarted because the Left embraces many divergent points of view.[7] The splintering of the Left around different reform agendas leads to internal divisiveness, with different progressive factions criticizing one another's proposals. This dissension undermines the Left's capacity to generate popular support for its goals. From a pluralist perspective, the failure of the Electoral College issue to take hold does not mean that the Electoral College is beyond criticism. Rather, the progressive Left has failed to unify behind a single proposal for reforming or eliminating the Electoral College, thereby discouraging broad support for a more desirable alternative.

The pluralist perspective has normative implications consistent with progressivism. Progressives decry the early demise of any issue that can be addressed politically and that can promote democratic development and social progress. Progressives understand that diversity of opinion is a fundamental feature of political life and honor the rights of all to express their views, but they do not consider people's views as fixed or unchangeable. They judge political process as healthy when people present alternative views, deliberate on the merits of issues, and seek a resolution that best suits their collective needs. For those dissatisfied with current electoral arrangements, progressives urge careful evaluation of competing proposals. If one such idea merits their support, progressives would then attempt to use it in rallying a progressive movement to change the presidential election system.

The *functional explanation* argues that there simply isn't a good case for changing our electoral system. Functionalists regard the Electoral College as an integral part of the Constitution and see both the Constitution as a whole and its method for electing our president as contributing to more than two centuries of effective representative democracy, social stability, and economic prosperity. They look at the long history of American presidential elections and claim that the Electoral College serves well — or at least adequately — the fundamental purpose of any democratic election; it allows citizens to hold their presidents accountable, which enables them to remove those executives widely regarded as corrupt, ineffective, or out of sync with the public. Functionalists interpret the aftermath of the 2000 election as evidence that the Electoral College can guide us safely through political crisis and bolster the legitimacy of our government. Moreover, functionalists are cautious about changing or eliminating the system because the Electoral College performs "latent functions" for the system that are only dimly appreciated. An alternative electoral method might well have unfavorable, often unforeseen, consequences for our political system.

The functional explanation incorporates a cultural approach to understanding politics, as it stresses that political events are greatly influenced by the dominant beliefs, norms, and expectations held by citizens and leaders. Thus, in the wake of the 2000 election, most Americans have judged — consciously or not — that our inherited Electoral College is an acceptable aspect of our political culture.

This functional explanation has conservative normative implications. Conservatives take the occasion of the 2000 election as an opportunity to reaffirm the role of the Electoral College, to recognize the legitimacy of those who win under its rules, and to encourage our presidents to use their authority to govern in the public interest. Having celebrated the virtues of the Electoral College, conservatives want to bury the issue of electoral reform.

Perhaps the Electoral College issue (or nonissue) provides an excellent opportunity to analyze the validity of institutionalism, structuralism, behavioralism, and functionalism as frameworks for explaining political outcomes. But this is not the task that we have set for ourselves here. We suspect that constitutional rules, the distribution of power, the lack of a united social movement, and a political culture that accepts the role of the Electoral College each contribute to keeping the issue of electoral reform off the public agenda.

The more interesting and challenging task is to address the normative questions that arise from the views of liberals, populists, progressives, and conservatives. Is the Right, composed of conservatives and (classical) liberals, correct to regard the Electoral College as a functional system for electing our president? Is the Right correct to claim that our existing electoral method has produced no egregious injustice requiring a revision of our initial social contract? Or is the Left, made up of populists and progressives, correct to regard the Electoral College as an unfair system that privileges those at the top of the power structure? Is the Left justified in seeing a need to discover some alternative electoral arrangement that promotes democratic development and can rally a progressive social movement on behalf of a new method of electing our president? In short, should the Electoral College be reformed or abolished?

FRAMING THE ISSUE

This book takes up the challenge of evaluating the Electoral College and the major alternatives to it. We recognize that no electoral method is perfect. All methods embody certain values and produce distinct consequences. We simply wish to assess the strengths and weakness of the Electoral College and its major alternatives as methods for translating the preferences of over 100 million American voters into a collective choice among candidates for the presidency. Once citizens have cast their ballots, what is the best method for adding up these votes?

This restricted issue ignores many other elements of the presidential electoral process that are worthy of analysis and possible reform. The issue of recounting ballots in Florida points to the importance of ensuring that each voter's preferences are accurately recorded. Complex ballots like the infamous "butterfly ballot" used in Palm Beach County can confuse voters by prompting them to mark their ballots in ways that betray their intentions. Voting machines that fail mechanically, leaving "hanging chads" and "dimpled ballots," can result in an "undercount" of votes. These are serious technical problems that can and should be remedied. In this book, we assume that all citizens who intend to vote have their preferences accurately recorded. Our concerns lie with how these accurately recorded preferences should be counted.

Other important issues include questionable, sometimes illegitimate practices that hinder (or facilitate) the access to vote for some people. Cumbersome registration procedures in some states could be eased. Holding elections on a Sunday or holiday may make it easier for many citizens to vote. Keeping certain citizens from voting through obstruction, intimidation, and unsubstantiated allegations of criminal records clearly violate democratic rights.[8] Giving workers of one party access to public offices to ensure that their voters, but not voters registered to the competing party, properly return absentee ballots strains our conception of a fair electoral process. Such issues should be addressed if we want to ensure a fair democratic process, but these are not the issues discussed here. Our concern is how to aggregate the votes of all citizens who want to express their preferences.

Voter fraud also remains an important issue, especially in light of the 2000 election. *Miami Herald* investigative reporters noted that hundreds of illegal ballots — some for dead people — were cast in Dade County.[9] Lax voter registration procedures sometimes enabled students to register and vote in more than one place, and the growing use of absentee ballots requires that authorities address issues of forgery or fraudulent use.[10] It is even alleged that software used to compute vote totals may be manipulated without detection.[11] We believe that any such practices must be discovered and curtailed, but here our focus on fraud only addresses its likelihood using different electoral systems.

Perhaps the most important issues in presidential elections concern the bases of citizens' expressed preferences. Ideally, people's votes coincide with their political aspirations, principles, and interests, yet many other things influence their voting decisions. The enormous sums of money spent on elections to manipulate people's preferences, the deceptive ads employed to mislead voters, and the "horse race" (rather than issue-oriented) media coverage of campaigns are just a few practices that may undermine the capacity of voters to express their real values at the ballot box. Although these sorts of issues need to be addressed, they are not our *immediate* concern, which is how best to sum up citizens' individual preferences into a collective choice.

The issue that is our direct concern — how best to aggregate individual votes into a collective choice — may seem obvious and trivial. We have all participated in many elections that almost always produce a collective choice by giving all citizens one vote, letting them cast that vote for any of the nominees (or for no one at all), and pronouncing the nominee who gets the most votes as the winner. Because this method is so straightforward, many analysts advocate choosing the president by a direct popular vote with a plurality rule — awarding victory to the candidate with the most votes in a national election. A moment's reflection, however, gives most people pause that this is the best method. What if this scheme encouraged a proliferation of candidates, which led voters to split their votes among these candidates so that the highest vote-getter received only a small percentage of the votes? We might then adopt the familiar practice of majority rule: if no candidate gets 50 percent plus one of the popular vote, we would have a runoff election between the two top vote-getters in the initial round of balloting.

The difference between plurality rule and majority rule methods of determining a winner from our individual choices is not trivial. On seventeen occasions since 1824 (when popular vote totals were first reported) no candidate for the presidency achieved a majority of the popular vote. If rules required the winner to attain a popular-vote majority, five of the last seven elections would have had runoffs. It is not clear that the candidate with the most votes in the initial balloting would have won the majority. For example, in 1960 John Kennedy was attributed 49.7 percent of the popular vote and Richard Nixon was attributed 49.3 percent.[12] In a direct election with a runoff, if Southern Democrats who were skeptical of Kennedy and who had previously cast their ballots for "states rights" slates strongly supported Nixon in the runoff, a Kennedy presidency would not have occurred. Likewise, in 1992 Bill Clinton won only 43 percent of the popular vote. Those who supported Ross Perot might not have moved sufficiently to Clinton in a second round to deliver him a majority, and the Clinton era might not have happened.

Further examples could show over and over again how different methods of aggregating votes could have led to different results, but such examples would *underestimate* the overall impact of having alternative voting systems. Different voting methods can profoundly change the entire electoral processes. For instance, different electoral rules might encourage candidates who lost primary battles for their party's nomination to form "splinter parties" to pursue success in November. If we employed a popular vote with the plurality rule, perhaps John McCain, Bill Bradley, and other aspirants would have continued their campaigns into November, radically changing the popular vote totals received by Bush and Gore. Under such scenarios it is impossible to know what the results would have been. In short, alternative electoral systems do not only provide different ways of counting votes but they also change the distribution of individual votes that are to be aggregated. More generally, we can safely assume that methods of aggregating votes matter greatly, not only to who wins particular elections but also to how our political process functions.[13]

NOTES

1. Critics of the Electoral College did not anticipate this quiescence. See, for example, David W. Abbott and James P. Levine, *Wrong Winner: the Coming Debacle in the Electoral College* (New York: Praeger, 1991).

2. Most public opinion polls show considerable support for abolishing the Electoral College and instituting the direct election of the president. For example, a Gallup poll taken on 10 November 2000, showed 61 percent of the public favoring the direct election of the president, while 35 percent favored retaining the Electoral College. A Hart/Teeter poll conducted shortly thereafter reported 57 percent of respondents supporting the direct election of the president. See Ben Wildavsky, "School of Hard Knocks: The Electoral College: An Anachronism or Protector of Small States," *U.S. News & World Report,* 20 November 2000, 52. Defenders of the Electoral College refute the significance of such polls, claiming that the questions are "loaded" and that most Americans accept the institution.

3. The Constitution does permit the bypassing of Congress in the amendment process, but only when the legislatures of two-thirds of the states call a convention for the purpose. As indicated below, the likelihood of using this route to challenge the Electoral College is very small.

4. Lawrence D. Longley and Neal R. Peirce, *The Electoral College Primer 2000* (New Haven: Yale University Press, 2000), 151.

5. Charles A. Beard, *An Economic Interpretation of the Constitution of the United States* (New York: Free Press, 1986). Originally published in 1913.

6. The theory that many issues are suppressed from the political agenda by the application of power by those interests that dominate political life has its roots in the work of Karl Marx and has been developed by Peter Bachrach and Morton Baratz, *Power and Poverty* (New York: Oxford University Press, 1970).

7. See, for example, Richard Rorty, *Achieving Our Country* (Cambridge, Mass.: Harvard University Press, 1998), esp. 41–71.

8. Kevin Phillips, "His Fraudulency the Second? The Illegitimacy of George W. Bush," *American Prospect* 12, no. 2 (29 January 2001): 24.

9. Manny Garcia and Tom Dubocq, "Unregistered Voters Cast Ballots in Dade," *Miami Herald*, 24 December 2000, 1.

10. Norman Ornstein, "It's Not in the Numbers," *Washington Post*, 26 November 2000, B01.

11. Jonathan Vankin, "Vote of No Confidence," www.conspire.com/vote-fraud.html.

12. Such attributions may be leading. Voters in Alabama actually cast several votes for electors, some pledged to Kennedy and others to unpledged Democratic electors. It is likely that many voters who favored Harry Byrd cast ballots for both unpledged and Kennedy electors, but the method used to achieve a Kennedy popular victory over Nixon attributes all votes cast for Democratic electors as Kennedy votes. Other methods using plausible assumptions of voter intentions attribute fewer votes to Kennedy and provide Nixon a narrow popular margin over Kennedy. See Longley and Peirce, *Electoral College Primer 2000*, 46–59.

13. An important body of research in comparative politics has analyzed this topic. See Douglas Rae, *The Political Consequences of Electoral Laws* (New Haven: Yale University Press, 1967); and *Electoral Laws and their Political Consequences*, ed. Bernard Grofman and Arend Lijphart (New York: Agathon Press, 1986). The uniqueness of the Electoral College has prevented its systematic analysis in this literature.

CHAPTER 2

Analyzing the Electoral College and Its Alternatives

Paul Schumaker, *University of Kansas*

TO CONSIDER HOW electoral reform would affect our politics, thirty-seven political scientists have been assembled to bring the theories and findings of their discipline to bear on the issue. In the chapters that follow, these scholars discuss and analyze how various proposed reforms would affect such things as:

- the role of states in our federal political system and the authority of state and national government in our lives;

- the legitimacy of whoever wins the presidency and his capacity to provide leadership in a separation-of-powers government;

- our two-party system, and the roles of third parties and interest groups within that system;

- the organization and conduct of presidential campaigns;

- media coverage of elections;

- the participation of citizens;

- the stability of our political system; and

- the capacity of minorities and other relatively powerless citizens to exercise more equal power in our political system.

Most prior discussion of the Electoral College has come through debates between those who would retain the system and those who would change it.[1] Ironically, Al Gore is reported to have been an active participant in such debates — and a vociferous opponent of the Electoral College — while in high school.[2] But Al Gore's approach is not our approach.

For this project, we sought to avoid those political scientists who have participated in such debates and whose position on the issue seemed clearly entrenched.[3] This was not difficult. During the prolonged election of November (and December) 2000 we were struck by both the diversity of political scientists' views on the Electoral College and their lack of firmness in these views. The contributors to this volume fit this description.[4] They teach and have conducted some of the discipline's most important research on specific aspects of our political system (e.g., federalism, the presidency, political parties). They are experts on how different aspects of our political process work. They are more interested in analyzing how various electoral reforms would affect the political system than with defending some preestablished position.

Like most Americans, these contributors began the project with some opinions about the Electoral College and various alternatives to it. In a preliminary expression of these opinions — retaining the Electoral College, reforming it in some manner, and abolishing it — each received substantial numbers of "approval votes" from the participants in the project.[5] Retaining the Electoral College without any modification was the first preference of eleven of our participants and the last choice of at least three.[6] Each of the reforms that we shall consider was the first choice of at least one of the thirty-seven participants, and at least a quarter of the participants thought they could support each alternative. In short, our analysis did not begin with people united in their commitment to a particular position.

Thus, in conceiving this book, we did not know what our conclusions would be, but we were confident that important conclusions would emerge. As our contributors engaged in dialogues among themselves, they identified some of the most important effects or implications of reform on various aspects of our political system. These findings are the basis for our ultimate conclusions — reported in chapter 12 — regarding the desirability of the Electoral College and alternatives to it.

How did we decide which system(s) to endorse? We voted, employing electoral methods that are presented in this book. We cast our ballots under ideal conditions that are generally not available to the American electorate in voting for the president. First, our votes were informed by extensive deliberations and conclusions about the implications of electoral reform, as provided by our disciplinary expertise. Second, we cast our votes in ways that allow the most accurate aggregation of our views and preferences as possible. By casting "approval ballots" and by indicating our preferences through a "Borda count" — by indicating which alternatives are ultimately supported (or not) by each participant and by having each person provide a rank-ordering of their ultimate preferences — we have been able to aggregate our preferences in various ways to yield our collective judgment.[7] As a result of our final votes and the deliberations that preceded these votes, we can indicate the degree to which we support or oppose alternative electoral systems and explain the basis for our views.

In the remainder of this chapter, we describe the Electoral College and its most important alternatives. We then consider two alternative methods for analyzing different electoral schemes. We show that a deductive mode of analysis —

a mode used by public choice theorists — demonstrates that there is no one best method for selecting a president. We argue that this finding means that the best approach to evaluating electoral reform is to use the inductive mode of analysis presented here. The best way to think about electoral reform is to ask about its implications for how our political system works.

THE ELECTORAL COLLEGE

As presently practiced, the Electoral College aggregates votes in two stages. The first stage comprises popular votes in each of the fifty states and Washington, D.C. Except for Maine and Nebraska, which use congressional districts to choose electors, the candidate getting a popular plurality in each state wins all the electoral votes that constitutional provisions grant.[8] The second stage consists of a national count of the electoral votes won by candidates in each state. If one candidate gets the majority of the electors in the College, that individual becomes president.

Each state receives the same number of electors that it has senators and members of the House of Representatives. Of course, each state has two senators and the number of representatives that is proportional to its population. Since almost 12 percent of all Americans live in California, that state has 52 (12 percent) of the 435 members of the House. Since less than 1 percent of all Americans live in Kansas, that state has 0.9 percent (4) of all House members. California thus has 54 electoral votes at stake in the popular vote for president, while Kansas has 6. In the election of November 2000 Al Gore won the California popular vote, so 54 electors from California cast their votes for Gore, while the 6 electors from Kansas cast their votes for Bush, the popular winner in that state.

There are a total of 538 electors, with 100 based on the composition of Senate and 435 dependent on the composition of the House. The remaining 3 come from the District of Columbia under the Twenty-third Amendment to the Constitution (1961). The Constitution requires the winning candidate to amass a majority (270 votes) in the Electoral College. Bush collected 271 electoral votes; if he had won two fewer votes and Gore two more, each would have had exactly 50 percent of the electoral votes, not a majority. Had this been the case, a third stage in the electoral process would have kicked in: the House contingency election as provided for in the Constitution.

In this instance, the results of the state-by-state popular votes and the national Electoral College vote would have been set aside, except for the fact that the House of Representatives would have to decide among the three candidates with the most electoral votes. During a House contingency election, each state has one vote, and the winning candidate needs a majority of the states' votes. This procedure has not been required since 1824 when the Electoral College vote was split four ways, and the House finally selected John Quincy Adams over Andrew Jackson (the leader in both popular and elector votes cast). Had the House contingency procedure been used because of the failure of the Electoral College to yield a majority in 2000, Bush probably would have prevailed because Republicans had majorities in twenty-seven of the state delegations in the House of the new 107th Congress.[9]

This general description of the Electoral College mixes constitutional provisions with historical adaptations and ignores some troubling possibilities. In the remainder of this section, we provide some historical details to fill in this sketch. Chapter 3 provides a more thorough assessment of the founding and development of the College.

Our founders adopted the Electoral College as a compromise between two alternative methods for selecting the president. Initially, some delegates to the Constitutional Convention wanted Congress to select the president, while others favored a direct popular election. But those who wanted a president independent of the legislative branch and thus a greater separation of powers opposed congressional selection. Meanwhile, those who feared that this method left less populous states with an inferior role in presidential selection opposed a direct popular vote. As the Constitutional Convention proceeded, the founders established a "Committee of the Eleven" to work out an acceptable compromise for selecting the president. The method they proposed, centering on the Electoral College, won broad acceptance.[10] Little debate or controversy surrounded their proposal, which led to Alexander Hamilton's famous verdict about it: "The mode of appointment of the chief magistrate of the United States is almost the only part of the system, of any consequence, which has escaped without severe censure.... I venture somewhat further and hesitate not to affirm that if the manner of it be not perfect, it is at least excellent."[11]

The founders anticipated that the Electoral College would work as follows. Unlike Congress, the College would be an ad hoc and dispersed body, constituted by different members every four years. It would never convene collectively. Rather, state delegations would meet within their states, deliberate among themselves, and vote as individual electors. Such geographical dispersion would prevent national cabals or foreign powers from tampering with the selection process. State legislatures held the power to determine the method for selecting the electors. Some legislatures might directly choose electors, but others, in states where populism was strong, might select electors through a popular vote. However selected, the founders assumed that the electors would be prominent citizens, though not federal officials (such as members of Congress). They also expected the electors to vote for a variety of prominent individuals. Though it was generally presumed that George Washington would be named president by most electors in 1788, as he was, the founders thought it unlikely that subsequent nominees would obtain a majority of the electoral vote. Because parties did not yet exist, electors could not simply chose among the leaders of a few parties. Instead, the founders assumed that the electors would exercise independent judgments about who, among notable figures, was most qualified to serve as president. They would normally distribute their votes among several experienced leaders, with no one person gaining a majority of electors. The House contingency process was thus thought to be far more vital than it has become. In short, the founders expected that the Electoral College would nominate various candidates for the presidency to the House. The Constitution originally specified that the top five vote-getters in the Electoral College would be the nominees from which the House would make its selection, but the Twelfth Amendment, adopted in 1804 to remedy some of the difficulties that occurred in 1800, reduced this number to three.[12] Still, the House would make the ultimate selection. Again, each state delegation would have one vote, and a candidate would have to attain the votes of a majority of states to be selected as the president.

This procedure was a deft compromise in several ways. It gave the large states more electors in the College, which might allow them to dominate the nomination process. But it provided small states both a bonus in the Electoral College and equal power in the final House determination. Congress gained a role in the selection process, but could not impose its will in the determination of the president. The process allowed for the possibility of popular election selection of electors, but it created several barriers that would prevent some popular demagogue from ascending to the presidency.

Several developments changed how the Electoral College now works — indeed, how it has worked throughout most of the past two centuries. First, congressional caucuses and then mass-based party organizations arose to support particular nominees and electors pledged to their candidate. Between 1796 and 1828, parties increased their role in selecting electors, which resulted in choosing electors who were pledged and faithful party members, not persons exercising their independent judgments. Second, the development of a two-party system with partisan electors meant that the Electoral College vote was normally decisive; as the candidate of one party received the required majority of electoral votes, the House contingency procedure became dormant, unused since 1824. Third, the spread of democratic norms and practice (such as the expansion of the electorate) during the first half of the nineteenth century resulted in states increasingly choosing electors by popular vote. Fourth, by 1836 each state had adopted a "winner-take-all," or unit rule, for determining electors. Parties that dominated state politics understood that the unit rule could shut out the minority party and thus deliver *all* of the state's electors to their party's candidate. States also realized that when their electors were unified they were more decisive in determining the outcome of the Electoral College vote and were more important in the victor's political coalition.[13]

These developments have resulted in the electoral college system that operates today. Popular votes are aggregated in each state; the candidate with the most votes in each state gets all of the electors of that state (save in Maine and Nebraska), and the candidate with the majority of electors in the College becomes president.

REFORMING THE ELECTORAL COLLEGE

There have been numerous proposals to retain but reform the Electoral College.[14] Retaining the Electoral College means that each state still would have a role to play in presidential elections and would have electors equal to its total number of senators and representatives; small states would thus retain their disproportionate representation in the College. We will focus on three possible reforms.

The most frequently discussed Electoral College reforms propose altering the unit rule that gives all a state's electors to the candidate with the most popular votes within the state. One such reform would determine electors within each congressional district. Another reform would allocate a state's electors in proportion to the candidates' popular votes within the state. A third reform would address the problem that arises when the winner in the Electoral College is a candidate other than the winner of a national popular vote. This reform, "the national bonus plan," would retain the Electoral College, but would give an extra 102 electoral votes to the candidate with the most popular votes overall, practically ensuring that there would be no discrepancy between the outcome in the Electoral College and the popular vote.

Of course, there have been other proposed reforms of the Electoral College. For example, some people have called for "automatic" electors that would eliminate the possibility of a "rogue" or "faithless" elector casting a vote for a candidate other than the one to whom she is pledged. Some proposals have also called for eliminating or changing the House contingency procedure. In framing the issue of electoral reform, we deliberately excluded such reforms from our immediate agenda. To keep the project manageable, we examine only briefly in our concluding chapter the implications of having automatic electors or of abolishing the existing House contingency procedure.

The District Plan

One reform would have other states adopt the district plan used in Maine since 1972 and in Nebraska since 1992. If this plan were adopted nationally, each state would have popular elections resolved by plurality rule in each congressional district, as well as a statewide popular election decided by plurality rule. The winner of the popular vote in each district would get one electoral vote, and the winner of the statewide popular vote would receive two such votes (corresponding to the electoral votes provided to each state because of its senatorial representation). Advocates argue that this plan would increase representation by allowing minority interests that have little hope of winning at the statewide level but who are concentrated in certain geographical areas to have their preferences advanced in the Electoral College.

Analyses find that the nationwide implementation of the district plan would have resulted in Nixon defeating Kennedy in 1960 and in an Electoral College deadlock between Carter and Ford in 1976.[15] One estimate suggests that the district plan would have led to a Bush victory over Gore, 288 to 250, in the 2000 election.[16]

Proportional Allocation

A related reform would also eliminate the unit rule for states, but it would ignore congressional districts and allocate electors proportionate to the votes a candidate received in each state. In a state with 20 electoral votes, if three candidates split a state's popular vote, say, 50–40–10, the one with 50 percent would get 10 electoral votes, the one with 40 percent would receive 8 electoral votes, and the candidate with 10 percent would get 2 electoral votes. In practice, the proportions would not work out so neatly, and practical questions would emerge as to how to deal with fractions (and perhaps small percentages.)[17] Some proportional allocation schemes fractionalize automatic electors, meaning that proportionality would be calculated to, say, one-tenth of an elector. For example, a candidate getting 25.5 percent of the popular vote in a state with 30 electors, would, under strict proportionality, be entitled to 7.65 electors, which would be rounded to 7.6 (or 7.7) electors. As this example shows, fractionalizing electors may minimize rounding errors but it does not eliminate them, as rules for rounding off would still be required. In Europe, many allocation rules have been studied and utilized for dealing with this problem.[18] Rather than address the complexity of these rules, we can simply propose that electors be allocated in proportion to popular votes received throughout the state with rounding decisions favoring the candidate(s) with the largest number of votes.

Like the district plan, the proportional allocation plan wins backing from those who seek enhanced representation of minority interests. Indeed, proportional allocation may better represent minorities spread throughout a state. For example, Green Party voters may comprise 15 percent of a state's electorate but lack sufficient concentration in any one congressional district to win electors under the district plan. However, if the Green Party got 15 percent of the vote in a state with 7 electors, it would be entitled to one elector, and it would thus be represented in the Electoral College.

Because different proportional allocation rules can produce different outcomes, we cannot be sure who would have won the 2000 election under proportionality procedures. If we allocated votes by rounding to the whole elector in favor of the candidate with the most votes within each state, Bush would have defeated Gore, 271 to 264, with Nader getting 3 electoral votes. Rounding to the tenth of an elector, always favoring the candidate with the most votes in a state, the electoral vote tally would have been Bush 260.9, Gore 259.1, and Nader 13.8,[19] and the House would have named the president.[20]

The National Bonus Plan

Unlike the first two reforms, this recasting of the Electoral College would retain the winner-take-all provisions adopted by most states. There would still be 538 automatic electors casting ballots on the basis of popular elections in the fifty states and the District of Columbia, but there would also be a national popular contest. The winner of the national popular vote on Election Day would get all 102 bonus electors, which would be almost one-third of the 321 electoral votes needed to get a majority of the 640 electoral votes in the expanded College.[21] By winning the popular vote, Gore would have accumulated 368 electors, for a decisive victory in the 2000 election.

Like the district and proportional allocation plans, this scheme seeks to democratize the Electoral College, but its conception of democracy focuses less on representation of diverse interests and more on achieving popular sovereignty. In effect, the bonus plan is a barely disguised version of the popular plurality procedure. The bonus plan ensures that "the popular will," indicated in the national popular vote, will prevail. But by preserving the Electoral College, it arguably maintains some of the positive consequences of that system as well.

ABOLISHING THE ELECTORAL COLLEGE

A more direct approach to achieving popular sovereignty in the election of the president is simply to abolish the Electoral College and adopt a national popular vote. If the fundamental flaw of the Electoral College is the possible mismatch between the popular vote and the electoral vote, then the obvious solution is to abolish the electoral vote in favor of some scheme of counting popular votes. Three popular voting schemes for aggregating votes throughout the nation are considered here.

A National Popular Vote with Plurality Rule

Under this "popular-plurality" system, across the country citizens would cast their ballots for one candidate (and a running mate). The candidate with the most votes wins. Just as county borders are irrelevant when states choose their governors through elections with plurality rule, state borders would be irrelevant to our national presidential election. Proponents of this system claim that it works well in state gubernatorial races,[22] that it counts all votes equally, and that it provides popular sovereignty by reaching decisions based on the dominant views of citizens.

With a margin of about 540,000 in the popular vote, Gore would have won had this system been in place in 2000. Of course, this assumes that nothing but the outcome would have changed under the popular plurality system. But, as we shall see, many other changes — such as a much more extensive array of candidates on the ballot — would likely accompany adoption of this electoral rule, and outcomes cannot be easily predicted.

A National Popular Vote with a Majority Rule

One criticism of conducting popular votes with the plurality rule is that a prolif-eration of candidates could lead citizens to scatter their votes widely. The highest vote-getter could win despite receiving only a small percentage of the vote. Fears that a president could not govern effectively if supported by only, say, 25 or 30 percent of the voters has led some reformers to suggest that a runoff election be held between the top two vote-getters if neither receives a certain percentage of the vote. Typically, 40 or 45 percent is proposed as the necessary threshold.[23] A national popular vote with a majority rule — the "popular-majority system" — is a variant of such a reform proposal. Here voters would again cast a single vote for any candidate in a presidential election, but if no candidate received a ma-jority (50 percent plus one) in the initial balloting, a second election, limited to the top two vote-getters, would be held in about a month. We adopt the 50 per-cent threshold for an initial election because of the importance of "majority rule" in democratic theory and because, for analytical purposes, this threshold clearly differentiates this proposal from the plurality proposal. On seventeen occasions in American history, no candidate won a majority of the popular vote, so runoff elections would probably be common under this procedure. Indeed, the existence of these rules could encourage European-style elections. Many candidates and parties would contest the initial balloting, with parties forming broader political coalitions in advance of the runoff.

Since neither Gore nor Bush had a majority of the popular vote in 2000, they would have competed directly against each other in a runoff. Nader voters might have switched to Gore in the runoff, leading to his ultimate victory, but such a prediction is highly problematic. We cannot know which candidates and parties would have emerged if this system were in place, or what deals would have been cut between the leading and defeated candidates. Moreover, different sets of voters go to the polls in the first and second rounds of voting.

Despite such uncertainties, a national popular vote with a majority rule has real attractions. It would again ensure that all votes count equally and it would also enhance popular sovereignty. In addition, the ultimate winner could claim a majority mandate.

A National Popular Vote with Majority Rule in an Instant Runoff

This variant on the above popular majoritarian proposal — known as the "single-transferable vote" or "alternative vote" method in the comparative electoral systems literature — may have sufficiently distinct implications to merit consider-ation as a separate proposal.[24] Under this method, voters would be asked during a single election to rank-order their presidential preferences, rather than simply to indicate their first choice. Most instant-runoff proposals allow voters to indi-cate their first, second, and third choices. The top choices of all voters are initially counted, and if one candidate gets a majority, he or she wins. But if no one gets a majority, computer technology "instantly" recalculates the results in the following manner. The candidate getting the fewest first-place votes (probably a regional or fringe party candidate in the American context) would be dropped from consideration, and that candidate's votes would go to the second-ranked candidate. If this reassignment of votes did not result in one candidate receiving a majority, the process would be repeated. The candidate with the next lowest first-place votes would be eliminated, and the votes for that candidate would be transferred to the second (or third) ranked candidate on ballots cast for the eliminated candidate(s). This process would be repeated until one candidate achieved a majority.

Proponents of this method claim that it has benefits beyond saving the costs of conducting a second runoff election and avoiding "voter fatigue." They claim this method enables voters to express their genuine preferences for candidates who emphasize causes and issues that some voters strongly support but who have little chance of winning. Enabling voters to indicate their second choice, which will be counted if their first choice is eliminated, allows citizens to avoid the dilemma of being a "sincere" or "sophisticated" voter. A sophisticated voter would calculate that his sincere first choice (for example, Ralph Nader and the Green Party) has no chance of winning. Without the rank-order ballot and the single-transferable voting method, the voter might put aside his genuine preference for Nader and vote for his second choice (e.g., Gore). He would prefer Gore to Gore's strongest competitor (e.g., Bush) and fear that sincere voting would sufficiently reduce votes for his second choice that his least preferred candidate would be elected. With the rank-order ballot and single-transferable voting method, the voter would have his second (or third) choice counted in the event that his sincere preference is eliminated. Proponents argue that democracy is enhanced by procedures that encourage voters to express their genuine preferences.

The questions at the center of this book can now be stated more precisely. The question of whether the Electoral College should be reformed requires us to ask whether schemes involving the district plan, the proportional allocation of electors, or the national bonus plan are improvements on the existing Electoral College. Similarly, the question of whether the Electoral College should be abolished requires us to consider whether a national popular vote with a plurality, a national vote with majority rule and possible runoff, or a popular vote with an instant runoff are beneficial alternatives to the Electoral College.

SEARCHING FOR "THE BEST" VOTING SCHEME
A science of politics might aspire to know the one best political system. At least since the influence of Descartes in the early seventeenth century, modern political theory has sought to understand the one best system through a deductive mode of analysis. Certain underlying assumptions or axioms are said to be self-evident (or at least compelling), and the system consistent with these assumptions is deduced to be the best system. Perhaps the most impressive of such endeavors have

been the works of Hobbes and Rawls,[25] but neither of these deductive models achieved its objective: a political system so compelling in its deductive logic that all thoughtful people would agree that it was the one best system.

A science of politics might, nevertheless, know the one best electoral system, or even more modestly, establish the one best method of counting votes. The theory of public (or social) choice is the branch of political analysis that has focused on this question, and public choice theorists have employed the same deductive methods employed by grand theorists and philosophers seeking answers to larger questions about the best political system and the most just society. This work, which can be highly technical, leads to some powerful claims about how voting procedures ought to be designed.[26] For our purposes, one conclusion of public choice theory is especially important: no method of aggregating votes satisfies all reasonable assumptions of a fair voting process. This conclusion is clearly expressed by William Riker, perhaps the best-known public choice theorist in political science.

> If a voting system is to be really fair, more than two alternatives must be allowed to enter the decision process; a decision method must be able to operate on three or more alternatives, but no one method satisfies all the conditions of fairness that have been proposed as reasonable and just. Every method satisfies some and violates others. Unfortunately, there are, so far as I know, no deeper ethical systems or any deeper axioms for decision that would allow us to judge and choose among these conditions of fairness. Hence there is no generally convincing way to show that one decision method is truly better than another.[27]

Indeed, Riker concludes that election results are often "meaningless" because "often they are manipulated amalgamations rather than fair and true amalgamations of voters' judgments and because we can never know for certain whether an amalgamation has in fact been manipulated."[28] For example, Al Gore's lead in the popular vote may have been "manipulated" in the sense that the broader rules and practices governing American presidential elections screen out numerous candidates whom many voters prefer. Thus, voters have little choice but to cast ballots that do not allow them to express their true preferences. Had the rules governing primaries and party nominations not eliminated many candidates and had campaign practices not deterred other candidates, Gore probably would have received significantly fewer popular votes (as would have Bush). In short, electoral rules limited voter choices and ensured that someone "won" — in actuality the "winner" simply survived the rules and procedures; he was not a "true public choice."

Public choice analysis thus led Riker to conclude that populist voting methods are without foundation and can even be dangerous because the winners of popular elections erroneously believe that their programs reflect the true will of the people. He maintains that "populism reinforces the normal arrogance of rulers with a built-in justification for tyranny, the contemporary version of the divine right of rulers."[29]

In summary, while the question of "how should we add up votes?" seems like a mathematical question that can be resolved with mathematical certainty, public choice analysis shows that there is no such solution. Not only is there no one best, most fair method of adding up citizens' votes to determine what "the will of the people" is — *there is no "will of the people" independent of the methods used to represent it.*

We agree that Riker is correct to point out that a justification for popular elections cannot be found in deductive arguments that such elections enable us to select presidents who are "the will of the people." But we disagree that this settles the question of the desirability of direct popular election of the president. The justification for popular elections is not that such elections are the best method of knowing the "true will of the people." The justification for popular elections — to the extent that they can be justified — is that such elections lead to preferred outcomes about the broad functioning of the political system.

Choosing among Imperfect Systems

As political theorist Herbert Storing pointed out during earlier debates over the Electoral College, there are two ways of thinking about and choosing among alternative electoral systems.[30] First, we can begin with a priori principles (e.g., having votes count equally and having counting systems that meet logical criteria for fairness). The limitations of this approach should be apparent from our discussion of social choice theory. This leaves Storing's second approach, which asks us to inquire about the outcomes and likely implications of different systems. How does the Electoral College affect the working of the American political system? And how would various reforms and alternatives to the Electoral College alter its operation? From this analytical perspective, one or more systems of popular election may offer significant improvements to political life that commend them over the Electoral College, even though these systems cannot base their desirability on consistency with an a priori principle such as ensuring the election of presidents who reflect "the will of the people."

Utilitarianism is the name philosophers give to a mode of analysis that judges institutions — in this case, electoral systems — by their consequences. Early "philosophical radicals" such as James Mill believed that utilitarianism justified many expansions of democracy, with reforms like universal suffrage and frequent elections that prompted political leaders to be more responsive to the will of the people. Such reforms maximized the pleasure and minimized the pain of citizens in the political system.[31] Perhaps a utilitarian analysis here would show that the reform or abolition of the Electoral College is an important next step in our progression toward a more democratic political system. But Mill's son, John Stuart, understood that utilitarianism could never permit a precise calculation of whether the consequences of reform enhanced or reduced overall utility. For John Stuart Mill, utilitarianism was merely an analytical tool that directed attention to the consequences of change and whether these changes could be judged beneficial.[32] Because an (electoral) reform may have some consequences that seem desirable, other consequences that seem undesirable, and still other consequences that provoke different judgments among people holding different values, utilitarian analysis is not likely to produce a consensus that such a reform serves the public welfare. It is also unlikely to produce a consensus about which reform is best. Nevertheless, utilitarian analysis can allow for better judgments about these questions because it can establish that some feared consequences either have little basis in fact or theory or that they would be relatively inconsequential. Conversely, substantial consequences can be demonstrated. Judgments based on such deliberations about consequences may be the best sort of understanding that can be provided when assessing political matters in which the ultimate truth of their goodness remains unknown.[33]

Adequate utilitarian analysis must not omit consideration of potentially important consequences so adopting a broad analytical framework is important. Many arguments for retaining the Electoral College are narrow because they stress the importance of a particular beneficial consequence that the system is thought to produce. For example, the Electoral College is often defended because it requires candidates to "win states in more than one region of the country," thus forcing them to "build crossnational political coalitions" that enhance their ability to govern because of their broad crossnational support.[34] Many reform arguments are also narrow, stressing a particular change that the reform might lead to. For instance, electing the president by a popular national vote with an instant runoff is predicted to encourage third parties to prosper without giving them the role of spoilers.[35] Such single arguments are important but not decisive because they must be assessed along with other potentially important consequences of these electoral schemes.

Because the Electoral College and its alternatives have been widely discussed, broad categories of potential consequences can be developed and catalogued. This book is organized around eight types of consequences; the categories cover the major effects that reforms might produce.

One category of consequences addresses issues of federalism. The Electoral College provides a role and identity for the fifty states in the presidential election system. Are there important consequences for basing presidential selection on votes cast by state-designated electors rather than on popular votes cast throughout the nation? How would various Electoral College reforms and alternatives affect the role of the states? Would national popular vote schemes create a greater national focus and a lesser state and local focus to our political life? Federal considerations may weigh strongly in favor of retaining the Electoral College, but assertions about the effects on federalism may be overdrawn, and normative judgments about the relative importance of state authority versus national authority remain problematic. In chapter 4, Don Haider-Markel, Mel Dubnick, Richard Elling, David Niven, and Paul Schumaker assess the implications for federalism of the Electoral College and alternatives to it.

Another category of consequences deals with the working of our national governmental institutions. Having a president whose legitimacy is widely accepted may be essential to the effective operation of our government. Does the Electoral College do an adequate job of providing the president with legitimacy? Would alternatives to it enhance or threaten presidential legitimacy? American national government is structured on the principle of separation of powers. Is the Electoral College or some alternative most compatible with this institutional arrangement? Given the separation of powers, what electoral system encourages the effective operation of the U.S. government? Moreover, political parties and interest groups affect the functioning of our national institutions. Does the Electoral College help parties play a positive role in our political system, or would an alternative electoral scheme enable them to do better in connecting our political leaders to each other and to the public? Do particular electoral systems enable excessive interest-group influence over the president and Congress? In chapter 5, Burdett Loomis, Jeffrey Cohen, Bruce Oppenheimer, and James Pfiffner discuss such issues.

A third category of consequences involves the operations of parties and interest groups. Received wisdom holds the Electoral College at least partially responsible for our decentralized two-party system in which both Republicans and Democrats emphasize issues that appeal to broad arrays of citizens and groups.[36] Alternative electoral arrangements might lead to stronger national parties, with diminished autonomy at the state and local levels. Electoral reform could also encourage greater prominence for third parties in both elections and governance. If a multiparty system were to develop under some alternative electoral system, parties would likely become more narrow and ideological. Appealing to specific interests (e.g., the Christian Right) and sectional groupings, they might cease to be the pragmatic, nonideological bodies that have historically characterized our party system. Although these implications seem to weigh in favor of retaining the Electoral College, we must realize that these claims may be overstated; the characteristics of our party system may be determined by other factors, including the political culture and the rules that govern most other American elections. In addition, the Electoral College may weaken our parties. An example of this is a minority party's relative inactivity in states with histories of strong support for candidates of the other party. Furthermore, the Electoral College may have enabled entrenched interests to dominate both the Democratic and Republican parties: electoral reforms might allow new parties representing emerging popular concerns to compete more effectively in presidential elections. Electoral reforms might also change the nature of our interest group system, for example, by encouraging some interests to pursue their agenda through third parties rather than by their connections with a major party. Thus, reforming or abolishing the Electoral College could alter the role and power of various interest groups in our political life. Such matters are considered in chapter 6 by Allan Cigler, Joel Paddock, Gary Reich, and Eric Uslaner.

Other possible consequences of electoral reform concern campaign strategies and organizations. Presidential campaign organizations exist to obtain and expend resources in ways that persuade and mobilize voters to support their candidate. The Electoral College is responsible for encouraging campaigns to spend their resources in a highly unequal manner, focusing their resources on large, competitive swing states. Reforms that diminish the strategic importance of such states might encourage campaign organizations to distribute their resources more evenly, since voters everywhere would be equally important. But electoral reform could have even more profound implications for waging political campaigns in America. The Electoral College arguably encourages presidential candidates to develop increasingly broad coalitions of political support as the campaigns progress. Large numbers of presidential hopefuls contest the early primaries, and many of these candidates craft their appeals toward a loyal but fairly narrow segment of the electorate (e.g., pro-life Republicans). As the November general election approaches, however, the two major-party candidates widen their political coalitions to appeal to a much more extensive array of citizens and interests. Electoral reforms could alter this dynamic, providing incentives for campaigns to bypass the primaries and carry their more focused appeals into the general election. The implications of electoral reform for how electoral and even governing coalitions are built could be enormous. These concerns are addressed by William G. Mayer, Emmett H. Buell Jr., James E. Campbell, and Mark Joslyn in chapter 7.

Debates about the merits of electoral reform have seldom focused on how such reforms might influence media coverage of campaigns and how campaign messages are communicated to voters, but some potentially interesting questions arise. Many academic observers of the media decry the journalistic focus on "the horse race" (who is winning and the strategies adopted by campaigns to win) rather than on more substantive matters such as candidates' positions on major issues, their ideological orientations, and their prospective ability to govern. The question thus emerges as to whether the electoral college system encourages such horse-race coverage and whether reform would lead the media to do a better job. Television networks might become increasingly influential under national popular vote schemes, and the role of local newspapers could be diminished as statewide electoral-vote contests receded in importance. Media coverage of election night would seem one c. the more likely areas to be affected by electoral changes, as the network's practices of declaring state-by-state victories would be altered under national popular voting schemes. However, it is not clear that electoral reforms would change the desire of the networks to "call the election" as early as possible. Perhaps no Electoral College reform could eliminate the likelihood that the networks will repeat the botched declarations of who won, even before the polls have been closed. Such matters are discussed in chapter 8 by Matthew Kerbel, Michael Cornfield, Marjorie Randon Hershey, and Richard Merelman.

Advocates of popular election systems stress possible impacts on citizenship. Organizations such as the League of Women Voters see the Electoral College as contributing to low levels of citizen efficacy and participation, especially in noncompetitive states.[37] Even when national elections are closely contested, in noncompetitive states the results often seem preordained, which leads to less citizen participation in campaign activities and reduced voter turnout. Advocates of popular elections contend that such contests would give party leaders in noncompetitive states greater incentives to turn out their voters, who would contribute directly to national vote totals. If the Electoral College really has such impacts, remedies might be found in several of the proposed reforms to it, as well as in proposals for direct national votes. But the role of the Electoral College in dampening voter turnout remains questionable, as citizens' decisions about whether or not to vote may flow from myriad other factors unrelated to the electoral system. Moreover, serious questions exist as to whether increasing voter turnout is important or beneficial to democracy. Perhaps high levels of voter turnout is important to increasing citizen trust in government and encouraging governmental attentiveness to all citizens, not just the particular kinds of citizens that are most apt to vote. Still, the marginal voter mobilized by alternative electoral systems might well be relatively uninformed and susceptible to manipulation. Conversely, the nonvoter may be no different from the voter on most important political dimensions, meaning that there would be few appreciable consequences to increasing voter turnout. In chapter 9, Robert M. Stein, Paul Johnson, Daron Shaw, and Robert Weissberg address these issues.

Casual observations of voting history in the United States and in other countries suggest that transitions of authority, especially in societies without established democratic rules, frequently occur in times of social and political instability. One virtue of democracy is that counting ballots, rather than crushing skulls, is the most peaceful method of achieving political change yet discovered.[38] But not all democratic elections are conducted free of turmoil. Defenders of the Electoral College note that the United States has experienced the longest stable democracy in history. Alexander Hamilton anticipated this result when he defended the Electoral College as being designed "to afford as little opportunity as possible to tumult and disorder."[39] In American history, winners within the electoral process and the constitutional process itself have been accepted when close elections have produced presidents who did not win the popular vote. Whether such stability has occurred because of, or despite, the Electoral College is unclear.

Answering this question calls for a cross-national examination of the causes of instability associated with elections. For example, instability might be likely when there is evidence or suspicion that election fraud has occurred. Likewise, the election of extremist candidates or their inclusion in governing coalitions might breed instability. Different electoral systems may affect the probability that instability will materialize. For example, the Electoral College could diminish the prospects of an extremist candidate winning office, while a popular vote under plurality rules might enhance such a prospect. Likewise, various electoral systems may have different capacities for handling threats to stability such as fraud. Some scholars believe that the electoral college system is particularly effective at enabling the detection of fraud and localizing its effects, but other systems could be just as (or more) effective on this front. To address questions about the implications of electoral reform for stability, chapter 10 provides the views of three political scientists who have studied governmental and social instability throughout the world: Erik Herron, Ron Francisco, and O. Fiona Yap.

A final yet especially important implication of electoral reform concerns the "fairness" of the Electoral College and alternative systems. The broad question here is whether particular systems contain "built-in advantages" that favor one group over another.[40] For example, the Electoral College is said to confer a special advantage on citizens of small states by allocating two electors to each state regardless of their population. The presence of such a built-in advantage is not necessarily unfair if it is part of a broader agreement devised to produce a stable political system. Thus, defenders of the Electoral College can at least argue that there is nothing unfair about that system's built-in advantage for small states.[41]

Other built-in advantages may be more justifiable to the extent that they *should* be part of a broader social agreement for producing a well-ordered and just society. In one of the most important works of contemporary political philosophy, John Rawls presented a theory suggesting that an unequal distribution of voting power is fair if the inequality benefits those groups normally having little political power.[42] If the poor and racial minorities are otherwise underrepresented and relatively powerless in the political system, it may be fair if the method of electing the president provides them with some systematic advantage. Strangely enough, the Electoral College may do just that. Because the poor and racial minorities are concentrated in the larger competitive states that are most important to presidential candidates, they may be especially responsive to these voters.[43] But is this proposition correct? Would an alternative electoral system be more fair to minorities and the poor? In chapter 11, these questions are examined by Robert L. Lineberry, Darren Davis, Robert Erikson, Richard Herrera, and Priscilla Southwell.

When thinking about electoral reform in counting presidential votes, the merits and liabilities of the existing electoral college system must be given special attention. Before recommending that we reform or abolish the Electoral College, it is important that the institution be fully understood. Beyond knowing its formal features, we should know the intentions of those who created and refined these institutions. What were their ideals regarding an effective government? Was the Electoral College a central institutional device for achieving these ideals or was it merely a "jerry-rigged improvization"[44] to avoid deadlock over the broader constitutional framework? How has the Electoral College evolved, and what lessons can we learn from previous efforts to amend and change the system? Political theorists are especially concerned with understanding our institutions and ideals in historical context, and their judgments are especially important in assessing the success or failure of the Electoral College in providing smooth transitions of power, even in situations where the public is deeply and closely divided. Four political theorists—Donald Lutz, Philip Abbot, Barbara Allen, and Russell Hansen—address these issues in the next chapter.

NOTES

1. See, for example, Gary Rose, *Controversial Issues in Presidential Selection* (Albany: State University of New York Press, 1991), 203–26; and Judith A. Best, *The Choice of the People? Debating the Electoral College* (Lanham, Md,: Rowman & Littlefield, 1996).
2. Robert Hardaway, *The Electoral College and the Constitution: The Case for Preserving Federalism* (Westport, Conn.: Praeger, 1994), ix.
3. The participants are not a random sample of political scientists. We began by discussing the project with our colleagues at the University of Kansas and some of our acquaintances in the larger discipline. As they indicated interest in the project, they suggested and sometimes recruited others whom they thought especially knowledgeable and insightful about the issues raised. In such a process of selection, it turned out that eight of our participants have previously written on the Electoral College. For the most part, their writings can be described as descriptive and explanatory, rather than prescriptive and evaluative. Those who previously had written on the College were evenly divided in their attitudes about it.
4. Only six of our participants indicated that they were "firmly committed" to their position on the Electoral College prior to their involvement in the project.
5. Approval voting allows people to support more than one alternative. Thus, many participants said through their ballots that they could support either the existing system, some modification of it, or replacing it with some form of national popular vote. Maintaining the current system was initially approved by 63 percent of the participants, but an equal number approved at least one method of significantly modifying that system. And almost half the participants indicated that they could approve an electoral system that abolished the Electoral College.
6. In this preliminary ballot, we did not insist that participants rank-order alternatives of which they disapproved. Thus, retaining the Electoral College could be the last choice of some people who simply disapproved of it along with several other options.
7. The role of approval voting in arriving at accurate collective choices is most strongly indicated by the work of Steven Brams and Peter C. Fishburn, *Approval Voting* (Boston: Birkhause, 1983). The role of the Borda count in such choices is most strongly indicated by Donald Saari, *The Geometry of Voting* (Berlin: Springer, 1994). For a discussion of the work of Brams and Saari, see Dana Mackenzie, "May the Best Man Lose," *Discovery,* November 2000.
8. Maine abandoned the "winner-takes-all" allocation of electoral votes in 1972, while Nebraska abandoned this feature in 1992. Both states aggregate individual votes by congressional districts as well as for the state as a whole and award one elector to the candidate with the most popular votes in each district and two electors to the candidate with the most popular votes throughout the state. This method will be discussed below, but these provisions have thus far not affected the overall results in these states.

9. Some Republican representatives who serve in states that voted for Gore (e.g., Delaware's Mike Castle, the state's only House member) might have considered casting a Gore ballot, especially in light of popular vote count.

10. Among the key interests mollified by the Electoral College were southerners who understood that their voting power would be reduced by a popular voting scheme comprised of white males. Under the Electoral College, black slaves would be taken into account in the allocation of electors under the previous compromise that counted a slave as three-fifths of a citizen for purposes of determining representation in the House.

11. *Federalist Papers,* No. 68.

12. As is discussed in chapter 3, Thomas Jefferson and Aaron Burr received the same number of votes in 1800.

13. A fifth change occurred with the adoption of the Twelfth Amendment in 1804. The designers of the Electoral College originally assumed that the top vote-getter overall would be president and the second top vote-getter would be vice president. Thus, they gave electors two votes (under the constraint that no more than one of these votes could be for a candidate from an elector's home state), but they failed to provide electors with a way to differentiate (or discriminate) between the candidate they supported for president and the candidate they supported for vice president. The development of congressional parties and the election of 1800 brought about a need for change because the presidential nominee of the (Democratic) Republican party (Thomas Jefferson) and the vice presidential nominee of that party (Aaron Burr) each received the same number of votes, and Burr refused to step aside for Jefferson. Thereafter, electors were required to cast one vote for the president and a second separate vote for the vice president. The Twelfth Amendment is discussed in more detail in chapter 3.

14. Other listings of proposals to change our method of selecting the president are provided by Neal R. Peirce and Lawrence D. Longley, *The People's President: The Electoral College in American History and the Direct Vote Alternative* (New Haven: Yale University Press, 1981), 131–80; and Stephen J. Wayne, *The Road to the White House, 2000* (Boston: Bedford/St. Martin's, 2000), 310–16.

15. The results under the district plan for 1960 and 1976 are provided by Nelson Polsby and Aaron Wildavsky, *Presidential Elections: Strategies and Structures of American Politics,* 10th ed. (New York: Chatham House, 2000), 251.

16. Popular votes for the presidency were not reported by congressional districts and had to be calculated by a time-consuming process that continued into summer 2001. According to a preliminary estimate, Bush would have won in 228 congressional districts and Gore would have won in 207. Adding in the results of the statewide contests and in Washington, D.C., Bush would have captured 288 electoral votes compared to 250 votes for Gore. See Clark Bensen, "Presidential Election 2000 Congressional District Preliminary Study," at www.polidata.org.

17. In some proportional systems, candidates must attain some minimal threshold to qualify for any electors — even though a strict proportionality principle would dictate otherwise. The purpose of minimal thresholds — typically of 5 or 10 percent — is to minimize the capacities of fringe candidates or those representing merely regional interests from being "spoilers" who prevent the major candidates from getting an electoral majority. There may be good arguments for having such thresholds, but they undermine the logic of the proportionality principle, which is to ensure adequate representation for voters having minority views and interests. Thus, the proportional allocation reform that we consider here does not include minimal thresholds.

18. The most used such method, the d'Hondt system, is discussed in chapter 10.

19. Other candidates would have 4.2 electoral votes.

20. The authors of chapter 10 conclude that the d'Hondt system would have Gore receiving 268 electoral votes and Bush receiving 267 electoral votes. Here too the issue would have to be resolved in the House.

21. See William Keech, *Winner Take All: Report of the Twentieth Century Fund Task Force on Reform of the Presidential Election Process* (New York: Holmes and Meier, 1978). Setting the national bonus at 102 electors appears arbitrary, but may be based on having 2 additional electors

for each state and the District of Columbia. Presumably this number was selected because it was large enough to practically assure victory for the candidate with the most national popular votes. This number may be symbolically important, appearing to be based on federal principles recognizing the role of states while in fact enhancing national principles.

22. Defenders of the Electoral College might dispute this claim, believing that popular state elections have encouraged the selection of many state and local politicians having few qualifications other than their ability to appeal to popular impulses.

23. For example, in 1969 the House approved a constitutional amendment for a direct popular vote that called for a runoff between the top two vote-getters if no one secured 40 percent of the vote.

24. Perhaps the Center for Voting and Democracy has been the most vocal proponent of this method. Their proposal — which brings together a number of electoral reforms as a "Voters Bill of Rights" — is discussed at www.fairvote.org. They note that the method is used to elect members of the House of Representatives in Australia and the mayor of London.

25. Thomas Hobbes, *The Leviathan* (1651); John Rawls, *A Theory of Justice* (Cambridge, Mass.: Harvard University Press, 1971). These theories are discussed as deductive theories in Paul Schumaker, Dwight Kiel, and Thomas Heilke, *Great Ideas/Grand Schemes* (New York: McGraw-Hill, 1996), 43–78, 257–60.

26. One of the most important, decisive results is known as May's Theorem. Suppose we are choosing between two alternatives and all voters are either indifferent between them (so they abstain) or are prepared to cast a vote for one or the other. Kenneth May proved, formally, that majority rule is the only fair system, in the sense that it is anonymous (reaches the same result if the ballots are counted in any order) and responsive (if there is a tie vote, then a change of one voter's opinion in favor of an alternative should break the tie in that alternative's favor). If one is choosing between only two alternatives, and one wants to adhere to these minimal standards of fairness, then majority rule is the only acceptable procedure.

May's result is extremely powerful, but it leaves an important question: what procedure should be used if there are more than two alternatives? Political scientists have been debating this question for a long time. Generally, a voting system can have two kinds of appealing qualities. It can be fair, or it can be logical. The goal in this debate is to interpret the words *fair* and *logical* and then present a voting system that meets these conditions.

It seems easy, but it is not. Nobel prize winner Kenneth Arrow showed that, on a very general level, a system that is fair is generally going to generate illogical results in some elections. For example, a fair system might generate a "voting cycle," a peculiar sequence of decisions in which candidate A defeats B, B defeats C, but (illogically!) C defeats A. On the other hand, a system that always generates a logical ordering of the alternatives certainly violates one of the conditions of fairness, perhaps by excluding some voters from participation because their opinions are illogical or by letting one single logical person dictate the result.

27. William H. Riker, *Liberalism against Populism: A Confrontation between the Theory of Democracy and the Theory of Social Choice* (San Francisco: W. H. Freeman, 1982), 65.

28. Ibid., 238.

29. Ibid., 249.

30. Walter Berns attributes this idea to Herbert Storing in his testimony at hearing on "Proposals for Electoral College Reform," before the Subcommittee on the Constitution of the Committee of the Judiciary, House of Representatives, 4 September 1997. Serial No. 87, 37–40.

31. James Mill, *Essay on Government* (1820).

32. John Stuart Mill, *Utilitarianism* (1863). For a concise contemporary discussion of utilitarianism, see Will Kymlicka, *Contemporary Political Philosophy* (New York: Oxford Press, 1990), 9–49.

33. Benjamin Barber, *Strong Democracy* (Berkeley: University of California Press, 1983), 139.

34. Judith Best, testimony at hearing on "Proposals for Electoral College Reform," before the Subcommittee on the Constitution of the Committee of the Judiciary, House of Representatives, 4 September 1997. Serial No. 87, 24–29.

35. Center for Voting and Democracy. See their website at www.fairvote.org.

36. John Wildenthal, "Consensus after LBJ," *Southwest Review* 53 (Spring 1968): 1113–30.
37. Becky Cain, testimony at hearing on "Proposals for Electoral College Reform," before the Subcommittee on the Constitution of the Committee of the Judiciary, House of Representatives, 4 September 1997. Serial No. 87, 19–22.
38. Friedrich Hayek, *Constitution of Liberty* (Chicago: University of Chicago Press, 1969), 109.
39. Alexander Hamilton, *Federalist Papers,* No. 68.
40. Charles Beitz, *Political Equality: An Essay in Democratic Theory* (Princeton: Princeton University Press, 1989).
41. Of course, those who question the fairness of this inequality can argue that changing circumstances require a modification of an agreement that is more than two centuries old.
42. Rawls, *Theory of Justice.*
43. Polsby and Wildavsky, *Presidential Elections,* 245–53.
44. John Dickinson, quoted in John P. Roche, "The Founding Fathers: A Reform Caucus in Action," *American Political Science Review* 55 (December 1961): 811.

CHAPTER 3

The Electoral College in Historical and Philosophical Perspective

Donald Lutz, *University of Houston*
Philip Abbott, *Wayne State University*
Barbara Allen, *Carleton College*
Russell Hanson, *Indiana University*

IN THE WAKE of the presidential election of 2000, there have been numerous calls to reform or abolish the Electoral College. In our view, the merit of these proposals cannot be judged without understanding why the Electoral College was established in the first place and how it resolves important political questions that naturally arise in selecting a president within our federal system. How well these political questions are resolved is a matter for others to decide; here we are content to bring underlying questions to the forefront of debate by reconstructing the history of the Electoral College. We then suggest principles and important considerations that may be used to evaluate the adequacy of alternative methods of selection, including the Electoral College.

THE CREATION OF THE ELECTORAL COLLEGE

On Tuesday, 29 May 1787, the members of the Federal Convention meeting in Philadelphia adopted what has come to be known as the Virginia Plan. This plan, largely the work of James Madison, became the working document for the remaining debates that led to the adoption of the present Constitution of the United States. Article 5 of the Virginia Plan said, in its entirety,

> 7. Resolved that a National Executive be instituted; to be chosen by the National Legislature for the term of [unspecified] years, to receive punctually at stated times, a fixed compensation for the services rendered, in which no increase or diminution shall be made so as to affect the Magistracy, existing at the time of increase or diminution, and to be eligible a second time; and that besides a general authority to execute the National laws, it ought to enjoy the Executive rights vested in Congress by the Confederation.[1]

On Wednesday, 13 June, the Convention readopted the Virginia Plan with a number of modifications. In this version the executive was limited to a single person, which indicates that the original plan assumed a multiple executive, and the term of office was set at seven years with the executive ineligible for a second term.[2] The executive was still to be elected by the national legislature. On 6 August the Convention adopted what is basically now the United States Constitution. In it Congress continued to elect the executive branch to a single seven-year term.[3] Not until 4 September, less than two weeks before finally adjourning, did the Convention receive a committee proposal to alter the Constitution to elect a president and vice president using an electoral college.[4]

The Virginia Plan would have created a unitary national government that relegated the states to basically the status of administrative units. Less well appreciated is that the Virginia Plan would have created something very close to a parliamentary system with the executive and judicial branches becoming creatures of the legislature. Even the second branch of the legislature, later termed the Senate, was to be selected by the popularly elected first branch that came to be the House of Representatives. Implicit in the design of the executive was that it be roughly equivalent to a council of ministers in the original version, and then to a prime minister in the revised version. As the debates wore on during the summer of 1787, the unitary plan was rejected in favor of what we now know as a federal system. But the implications of this basic shift for the executive branch were only slowly recognized. If a general commitment to preserving state government led to considerable fear that the national government might become too strong overall, a general commitment to separation of powers in state governments led to the fear that Congress might be too strong even in a federal system. As a result, the executive and judicial branches were gradually pulled away from congressional control even as the Senate was moved to an independent status through election by state legislatures.

The first proposal for electors came from James Wilson on 2 June, but he proposed dividing each state into districts with each district electing one elector.[5] Hence, his proposal bypassed state governments and retained a unitary system. On 18 June Alexander Hamilton proposed his own comprehensive plan, which used Wilson's format for electing what Hamilton termed a "governor."[6] On 19 July Elbridge Gerry proposed having the national executive selected by the state governors.[7] Gerry's proposal, like Hamilton's, was ignored, and on 20 July Wilson's idea was taken up again in terms of how many districts each state should have.[8] The question, not settled on that day, was whether the number of districts, and thus the number of electors, should be equal to the number of representatives allotted to each state. Debate on the election of the executive was thus brought into the more general debate between large and small states. The large states preferred representation proportional to population, whereas small states preferred equal state representation. The Convention would resolve the general question eventually in the so-called Connecticut Compromise, whereby the states were given equal representation in the Senate, but the House was apportioned by population. The issue of selecting the executive was more difficult to resolve. The Federalists proposed on 24 July that the presidential electors be selected by lot from members of the House of Representatives. This proved problematic both because some thought popular election was a better method for identifying electors who were worthy men and because it still involved the House too much in the selection process.[9]

Members of the Convention did not invest much time and energy in the debate over executive selection, primarily because other matters were seen as more important, but also because they were in uncharted waters greatly complicated by crosscurrents of other issues. Still, by 24 July they had unknowingly made an important distinction between the identification of presidential candidates and the selection of the president from among these candidates. On one hand there was considerable concern that candidates selected through direct election would not be "worthy" because the people at large had no simple way to identify such candidates. On the other hand there were fears that making the nomination of candidates too dependent on Congress undercut the role of the states. At this point no one had come up with the idea of connecting the selection of electors to the states. Yet, by distinguishing the process of identifying worthy candidates from the process of selecting among those candidates, the Convention delegates opened up the possibility of what came to be the ultimate solution: state electors would identify the top five candidates, and Congress would select from among these five candidates with each state's delegation having one vote.

There was little further debate on the matter, and it is fair to say that the Convention delegates "backed into" the final solution. No coherent theory supported this solution, although it is also fair to say that as originally designed the Electoral College was commensurate in its details with the broader constitutional principles of federalism, separation of powers, and checks and balances. A review of the Electoral College's basic features will allow us to identify its internal logic, permit some discussion of the reasoning that connects the College to broader constitutional principles, and set the stage for explaining later changes.

The process of selecting candidates for the presidency was separated from the process of selecting the president from among those candidates. In the first process, each state legislature decided how the state's electors would be picked. There could be popular state elections, the legislature could pick the electors, or some other means might be devised. This was commensurate with the ability of the state legislatures to pick their respective senators and was a direct expression of federalism. Each state was allotted a number of electors equal to the number of representatives it had in Congress, plus its two senators. While on the one hand this tended to favor states with larger populations, by also giving electors for the

senators it tended to help protect the interests of the small states — much like the
Connecticut Compromise that mixed proportionality with equality in the overall
Congress. In the election of 1792 the largest state had three times the number of
electors that the smallest state had, which significantly overweighed the smaller
states. In the election of 2000 the ratio between the largest and smallest state was
more than seventeen to one, which means that the overweighing is now of greatly
reduced significance.[10]

Senators, representatives, and others holding "an office of trust or profit" in
the national government could not serve as electors, which reflected federalism
and the separation of powers. The electors met in their respective states, safe from
interference by Congress and national cabals, and each elector nominated two
persons, one of whom was not to be from their state. The intent was for the electors to deliberate free from interference in their search for "worthy" candidates.
That one of their votes must be for someone from another state required them to
stretch beyond parochial considerations and seek people of national reputation.
Deliberations were to be collective, but each elector cast his own vote in the end.
Eventually the vice president was to be selected from among these same nominees, which meant that the president and vice president might well have been
political opponents. This possibility led to results in the election of 1800 that required an alteration in the process and that produced the Twelfth Amendment.
The certified votes of the electors were then to be delivered to the U.S. Senate
where the second part of the overall process began.

In the framers' original formulation, the U.S. Senate opens and counts the
ballots, and the person with the greatest number of votes becomes president, as
long as that person wins a majority of the electors. If there is a tie, or if no one
has a majority, the House of Representatives' makes the selection. In the case of an
even split of electoral votes, House balloting is limited to the two candidates. If no
one has a majority, the House selects from among the five with the highest vote
totals. After choosing the president, the remaining person with the most electoral
votes becomes vice president. If there is a tie, or if no candidate has a majority, the
U.S. Senate selects between the two. When the House votes, each state has one
vote to cast, which it casts in accord with the majority of its House delegation.
The president must have the votes of a majority of the states.

There is no doubt that the process is complicated, but so is the process for
passing legislation. It is more accurate to say that the overall process of the Electoral College, as the framers envisioned, embodies a high level of deliberation and
consensus. The complications result from applying the principles of federalism,
separation of powers, and checks and balances. In this sense the Electoral College as originally designed reflects the underlying structure of the Constitution.
The U.S. government was designed in every respect to be complicated. Although
the Convention delegates backed into the design for the Electoral College, it was
not arbitrary or random in its design. Historically, simple and straightforward

proposals for replacing the Electoral College have confronted the very principles underlying the entire document.

The most frequent complaint lodged, aside from its complexity, is that the Electoral College is undemocratic. Three members of the Constitutional Convention did doubt the ability of the general electorate to identify appropriate, "worthy" presidential candidates on its own, in large part because of the size of the country and its considerable population.[11] James Madison, among others, worried about the possibility of majority tyranny, which some have chosen to interpret as less than a perfect commitment to majority rule.[12] But the U.S. Constitution was not designed to prevent majority rule, or else why worry about majority tyranny in the first place? Rather, it was designed to produce deliberative majorities that achieved consensus beyond one-half plus one. Anxiety about majority tyranny also rested on a concern for minority and individual rights. We should remember that Madison's original proposal, the Virginia Plan, would have put the House, elected directly by popular vote, at the center of national government. If the Electoral College is complicated, then so are bicameralism, the veto and veto override, and federalism in general. If it is undemocratic, then so are rights that prohibit majorities from restricting, for example, the speech of unpopular minorities. The point here is not to defend the original Electoral College, but to suggest that its replacement or modification, in order to be successful, will need to address concerns broader than mere complication or perceived antimajoritarianism. These are reasonable criticisms, but criticisms do not constitute arguments for replacement or modification. Each proposed replacement or modification must be addressed positively on its own terms. And, indeed, there have been major modifications in the original design.

ALTERING THE ELECTORAL COLLEGE: THE TWELFTH AMENDMENT

Once the founders' choice of the Electoral College is explained, the history of the Electoral College can be presented as the history of efforts to reform the Electoral College. All told, more than one thousand amendments to alter the process of presidential selection have been submitted to Congress, but only one has succeeded. The lone success was the Twelfth Amendment, which is usually described as merely a technical correction to the Constitution. But this amendment had major implications for the selection and functioning of the presidency. Why this is so can be demonstrated by rehearsing the strategic considerations encouraged by the Electoral College before the Twelfth Amendment.

The Twelfth Amendment replaced the procedure by which electors voted for two candidates for the office with one that required electors to vote for a president and "in distinct ballots" cast another vote for vice president. In addition to ending the "dual vote" system, the amendment reduced from five to three the number of candidates to be considered for president by the House of Representatives in the absence of electoral majority. If there was no majority for vice president, the

Senate would choose from the two persons with the highest numbers on the list. The amendment also included provisions for the vice president to act as president if the House has selected no president by 4 March (a provision further clarified by section 3 of the Twentieth Amendment).

The original dual voting system of Article II provided an arena for complex voting strategies as a party system rapidly developed in Washington's second term. *Federalist XX* described presidential selection as a reflection of the elector's judgments about individual talents, character, and qualification. But if votes were also cast in support of party agendas, decisions had to be made as to how to promote each party ticket: If one party's candidate for president had little prospect of success, should electors supporting that party cast both of their votes for their preferred vice-presidential candidate in the hopes of at least selecting him? Or should electors cast one of their votes for the opposition party's weakest candidate in hopes of denying the presidency to the opposition party's preferred candidate?

In 1801 Thomas Jefferson, the newly elected president, explored the risks of these strategies from a (Democratic) Republican standpoint, with an eye toward the upcoming election in 1804.[13] The party could again support Burr for vice president or scatter its second electoral votes among several candidates. But, he wondered, "If we do the first we run, on the one hand, the risk of the Federalist Party making Burr President." On the other hand, pursuit of the other strategy might not only give the vice presidency to the Federalists but also "pave the way for the Federalist's successful candidate to that office to become President." Adding to these uncertainties were the tactics of factional leaders within a political party. In 1796 the Republican electors discarded their second vote while Federalists used theirs to maximize their chances for capturing the presidency. Indeed, the Republican strategy worked to the extent that Jefferson came in second in the balloting and became vice president. But, after the election, Federalists wondered if the strategy of discarding their second vote, as developed by their leader Alexander Hamilton, had an ulterior purpose. Did Hamilton really want Pinckney, the Federalist candidate for vice president, to win the presidency?

The calculations engaged in by electors operating under the original Electoral College suggest two interesting considerations. First, such strategic voting is similar to the coalition building that precedes the formation of a government in a multiparty, parliamentary system. The installation of dual voting, and the appearance of strategic action, may indicate that "the founders" were still operating with some of the presumptions of the Virginia Plan in mind. That is, they might not yet have realized how much they had already departed from parliamentary government as a result of their various compromises. Second, the rule that electors cast at least one vote for a citizen of another state was meant to move beyond state parochialism and broaden their horizons so as to take national considerations into account. The emergence of parties injected a level of concern for party interests that does go beyond a state, but falls short of the nation as a whole. The broadening intended by the institutional design of the Electoral College is thus truncated through interaction with the political parties it encouraged.

In the election of 1800, the complicated strategic calculations encouraged by the original design of the Electoral College reached new levels of sophistication. As the party system moved from one of largely elite competition toward mass participation, a tie in the Electoral College resulted between Jefferson, the Republican Party candidate for president, and his vice president, Aaron Burr. Some Federalists preferred Burr to Jefferson; others thought a deadlock might induce Jefferson to make policy concessions in exchange for the presidency; still others were willing to engage in the high-risk route of adjourning without electing anyone in hopes that in the interregnum a Federalist could be installed in the office. It is difficult to determine accurately the Republican response since most of the available comments were made after the crisis. There were threats of armed resistance on the part of some states as well as plans to hold a new constitutional convention. Finally, after thirty-six ballots in the House of Representatives, Jefferson was elected president. Ironically, the Federalist Alexander Hamilton was instrumental in swinging the election to Jefferson, his Republican opponent, no doubt aided in his decision by an overriding dislike of Aaron Burr. It is possible that these intricate strategies might have continued for some time, and even become embedded as a traditional norm in the political culture of presidential selection, if the Twelfth Amendment had not altered the equation.

Despite the close call in the 1800 election, a "discrimination" amendment, so called because it discriminated between votes for president and vice president, failed to pass the Senate by a single vote in 1801. Legislation was again introduced in the next session but action was delayed by the Republicans, who feared they did not have enough votes. In 1803, the pressure of an upcoming presidential election made the issue of an amendment an urgent one. Federalists strongly opposed the amendment on two grounds. First, they argued that the amendment diminished the power of small states and thus violated the spirit of the compromise on this question that had been set at the Constitutional Convention. They were especially upset by the change from five to three candidates to be considered by the House under the contingency route to presidential selection. Second, they argued that the amendment violated the general principle of minority rights. Federalists were quite frank about the fact that under the conditions of the new amendment, they would no longer have a chance to elect a Federalist vice president. Even some Republicans, imagining themselves to be in a minority at some future date, questioned the wisdom of the change. Nevertheless, the Twelfth Amendment passed Congress and was ratified in time to take effect before 1804.

The Twelfth Amendment shows the adaptability of the Electoral College to changing political circumstances. The amendment accommodated party competition by ensuring the election of a president and vice president from the same party, and it ended the complex plotting by electors on how to cast their two votes. On the other hand, the amendment, true to Federalist protestations in Congress, accelerated the demise of the Federalist Party. The Federalists might have elected a vice president in one or both of the next two elections and thus kept the party alive as a force in national politics to provide alternatives to Republican policies. The amendment also diminished the office of the vice president. In the immediate succeeding elections, Republicans nominated men near the end of their political careers. The ambiguous status of a vice president today is due to many factors, but the Twelfth Amendment certainly altered the institution early and significantly. Would vice presidents from a party other than the president, as was Jefferson in the Adams administration, have proved a source of chaos and gridlock or would some variant of a parliamentary system with an opposition-in-waiting have evolved? Or, to consider another possibility, would the (abandoned) practice of dual voting have reduced party conflict over time? There are no clear answers to these hypothetical questions, but one can say that even the correction of minor "oversights" to the Electoral College can produce significant consequences.

THE TWELFTH AMENDMENT AND THE PARTY SYSTEM IT HELPED TO FORM

Aside from altering the status and functioning of the presidency and speeding the demise of the Federalist Party, the Twelfth Amendment also contributed directly to the development of a party system in the United States. It thus indirectly worked against subsequent reform proposals, which have generally been opposed by political parties that fear the electoral consequences of changing or abolishing the Electoral College. The party system that the Twelfth Amendment encouraged also led to popular election of the electors in every state — an institutional move permitted but not required by anything in the U.S. Constitution. This in turn made inevitable the unit rule whereby all the electoral votes of a state are awarded to the party that wins a plurality in that state. In following the interlocking institutional consequences of this seemingly inconsequential amendment, we can see how it helped make the Electoral College extremely difficult to modify or replace.

Prior to enactment of the Twelfth Amendment, the person with the majority of electoral votes became president, and the person with the next highest total became vice president, whether or not that person was from the same party. Thus, Jefferson became vice president in 1796 when John Adams was elected president, though the two ran against each other for the top office. After enactment of the Twelfth Amendment, presidential and vice presidential candidates ran as teams from the same party and were elected as such. This change eliminated any representation of the minority party within the executive office and gave the winning party full control of the executive branch. It also encouraged the formation of electoral coalitions, and hence the two-party system, in order to win the presidency/vice presidency.

Institutionally, the Twelfth Amendment relegated the vice presidency to secondary importance, and made the presidency both more unified and more partisan. Over time, there were few internal challenges to the growth of presidential powers, and the party that was shut out of the executive was forced to make its stand in the legislature, increasing the potential friction between branches, especially during periods of divided control. However, although the vice presidency was itself weakened by the Twelfth Amendment, its political status grew in one way: the new arrangement allowed for the grooming of "heirs." This was important because, since the vice president begins with a natural advantage in visibility and experience, he has a natural edge over any candidate from another party (or within his own) when he runs for election to the presidency. The possibility of lengthening a party's control of the executive through such an "heir" is thus enhanced, subsequent term limits for individual presidents notwithstanding.

The term Electoral College is a misnomer. For one thing, Congress was expected to select the president most or even all of the time. In this sense the electors were not really supposed to be electors originally, but nominators. In the absence of political parties, this may well have turned out to be the case. But the party system that the Twelfth Amendment helped to create greatly reduced the probable role of Congress. By identifying and campaigning for their strongest candidates, the parties became the nominators; it was increasingly probable that the electors in name would be the actual electors as parties grew better organized and more effective. Although not originally designed to do the electing, the Electoral College came to make the actual selection among nominees identified by the parties.

Also, the Electoral College is a misnomer insofar as the electors never meet as a single body but as members of fifty state "colleges." The intent of this aspect of its institutional design is reasonably clear — the president was to be, like the Senate, the creature of the states and not of Congress. The intent behind leaving the manner of selecting the electors up to the states is less clear. Some evidence suggests that some delegates at the Constitutional Convention expected the state legislators to do the selecting, as with U.S. senators. Others, including James Madison, may have expected popular elections to be used, although probably from districts within the state rather than statewide contests. Regardless, the fundamental principle of federalism running through the U.S. Constitution led to the emerging party system being based on the capture of state executives and legislatures, with the national party organized as an assemblage of state organizations. The strong popular basis of state politics virtually guaranteed that the people rather than the legislature would elect members of the Electoral College, and by 1832 all states but one (South Carolina) used such elections. Popular selection of the electors in the context of state-based parties placed enormous pressures on the parties to move to a "winner-take-all" system for a state's Electoral College votes. As early as 1800 Thomas Jefferson noted that once some states moved to what is now known as the unit rule, it would be "folly and worse than folly" for the other states not to follow, since any state that divided its electoral votes would have less impact on the outcome than one that cast all of its electoral votes for one candidate. Several states are currently debating whether to move back toward proportional allocation of their respective electoral votes. Two hundred years after Jefferson's statement it is still the case that any state not using the winner-take-all system reduces its impact in the Electoral College. Since this reduction in impact grows more pronounced the more electoral votes a state has, beyond the possibility of a few of the smallest states dropping the winner-take-all system the move back toward proportional allocation does not have a good prognosis for success.

As the presidency became the focal point of electoral competition at the national level, the winner-take-all rule became politically irresistible. Until the 1830s several states awarded electoral votes on a proportional basis, but the practice died in all but two states as each state sought to maximize its influence in presidential elections, and parties sought to maintain their electoral advantage in an increasingly regionalized party system. Reform proposals foundered on these shoals in the twentieth century, when divisions among reformers made it impossible to navigate the process of amendment. Some reformers tried to revive proportional allocation of electoral votes as a way of limiting the president's powers by shrinking the winner's apparent mandate. Others wanted to expand the president's power by connecting it to a popular mandate based on direct election. The prominent alternatives that have been repeatedly proposed through the years, most of which are discussed in this book, were so numerous as to divide proponents of change into warring camps pressing different political principles. In the face of this division, state-based party systems have rather easily fended off proposals to change the process of presidential selection.

Note that none of the later changes in the Electoral College discussed here resulted explicitly from a constitutional amendment and therefore do not require a constitutional amendment to undo. However, the post-Twelfth Amendment party system generated few incentives to initiate bills in multiple state legislatures or in Congress to undo these changes.

THE HISTORY OF THE ELECTORAL COLLEGE:
THINKING ABOUT PERFORMANCE

There have been fifty-four presidential elections in the history of the United States, and the mechanics of selection have been an issue in eight of them:

- 1800: the House of Representatives chose Jefferson, who was tied with Burr in the Electoral College;

- 1824: the House of Representatives chose John Quincy Adams, although Jackson had a plurality in the Electoral College;

- 1876: a few disputed popular votes determined the outcome in several states, and hence in the Electoral College; this resulted in Hayes defeating Tilden by one electoral vote, although Tilden had a 3 percent margin in the popular vote;

- 1888: Benjamin Harrison won a majority of the Electoral College, although Cleveland had more popular votes;

- 1912: Wilson won a majority of the Electoral College, but only a plurality of popular votes;

- 1948: Truman won a majority of the Electoral College, but only a plurality of popular votes;

- 1960: amid charges of voting irregularities, Kennedy barely carried the popular vote in Illinois, and won a majority in the Electoral College;

- 2000: amid charges of voting irregularities, George W. Bush barely carried the popular vote in Florida, and won a bare majority in the Electoral College, while losing the national popular vote.

After each of these elections, calls for reform temporarily increased, as did scholarly attention. Ours is but the latest in a series of "white papers" on reform of the Electoral College. Debates on changing the Electoral College tend to be highly partisan. Those arguing for change treat some of the elections cited above as examples of Electoral College "failure," whereas those preferring to keep the Electoral College do not regard these elections as "failures." We are less concerned here with labeling than with understanding the consequences of rules that define a political institution. One of the fundamental premises underlying this book is that while electoral rules have consequences, there is no optimal set of rules for resolving differences. It depends upon what type of outcome is preferred and which principles are seen as more important.

Perhaps the only American national election that clearly "failed" was that of 1860, which resulted in a Civil War. This electoral failure was not a direct result of the Electoral College. Although the Electoral College produced a clear winner and was in this sense a technical "success," it failed to deal with the deep controversies dividing the nation. Probably no electoral method would have been successful under the circumstances. Those who worry about the "failure" of the Electoral College do not cite the election of 1860. Instead, they invariably argue that in one election or another the Electoral College failed to produce an outcome that was preferred by most voters. Let us examine the eight elections cited above in the light of how the Electoral College fared with respect to the popular vote.

Prior to 1828 there were no national vote totals, since as late as 1824 a third of the states still used their state legislatures to select their respective members of the Electoral College. This means that as contentious as the elections of 1800 and 1824 were, we cannot make a comparison with the popular vote. The elections of 1912 and 1948 awarded a majority of electoral votes to the candidate who had only a plurality of the popular vote. Since any popular vote system would essentially rest on a plurality rule and since the Electoral College did not award victory to the candidate with the second highest total and thus did not violate the plurality rule, these are not problems using the popular vote criteria. This leaves for consideration the elections of 1876, 1888, 1960, and 2000.

In the election of 1876, the clear winner of the popular vote, Tilden, lost the election by one vote in the Electoral College. This is the one election out of fifty-four in which the Electoral College clearly "failed" to produce the winner by the popular vote criterion. In 1960, charges of vote fraud dogged the party that barely won the popular vote, although the Electoral College awarded the presidency to the apparent popular vote winner. By the popular vote criteria, then, the 1960 election was not a "failure," although as we shall argue later we probably do not know who actually won the popular vote and use of a popular vote system would have made this outcome even more problematic than use of the Electoral College. This leaves the elections of 1888 and 2000. In 1888 the Electoral College apparently reversed the popular vote outcome, although again the difference in popular vote totals was close enough to leave us wondering who actually won. Did this apparent outcome create a crisis of legitimacy? There were no riots, and the electorate calmly elected Grover Cleveland president in the 1892 election after his defeat four years earlier. His 1888 loss was by 65 electoral votes (a 16 percent difference) even though he had .8 percent more popular votes, and his victory of 1892 was by a 3 percent popular vote margin and a 29 percent margin in the Electoral College. The election of 2000 with a .5 percent difference in the popular vote is apparently the third time in American history that the Electoral College has provided a winner other than what the popular vote would have provided. The .5 percent margin, however, is within the range of *possible* counting error across the nation. If nothing else, the experience with recounting Florida votes in the 2000 election illustrates how difficult it is to get an accurate popular vote total.

This leaves the 1876 election as the only clear "failure" using the popular vote criterion. Still, despite the majoritarian impulse that runs deep in the psyche of Americans, if the constitutional electoral rules specify that electoral votes are what matter, why is the popular vote criterion useful for determining the winner when the existing rules have failed? As Brian J. Gaines recently put it; "To borrow an analogy, arguing that a candidate 'deserves' the presidency because he won a popular vote plurality is akin to arguing that a team 'really won' a football game in which it out-gained its opponents in total yards but somehow failed to score."[14]

Put most simply, the failure of a set of decision rules needs to be determined on the basis of those rules failing to produce what is supposed to be produced. The popular vote criterion is one way of suggesting a preferred alternative set of rules, but the suggestion is not self-justifying when one can think of others, such as a set of rules based on a majority of eligible voters where voting is mandatory. The real problem in 1876 was the possibility of fraud or miscount where a few hundred votes in one state reversed what the rules called for — a winner based on who actually won the electoral vote in an honest, accurate count. It is important to note as well that election fraud was the direct outcome of severe sectional animosities, mirrored in party alignment, from the Civil War and Reconstruction. The 1876 presidential election was the first post-Civil War contest in which Democratic and Republican parties were at parity, when both confronted the issues of Southern "home rule," "reconciliation," and "unredeemed" states. Hence the failure was due less to the Electoral College than to the aftershocks of the systemic breakdown of 1860.

If this sounds as if the "failures" of the Electoral College have been explained away, the intent is otherwise. Instead, the point is that close elections will be a problem for any electoral system, including the Electoral College. Since 1824 six elections have had less than a one-percent popular vote difference between the two major candidates: 1880, 1884, 1888, 1960, 1968, and 2000. If one accepts the possibility of counting error as well as vote fraud, all six elections must be considered possible "failures," using the standard of the popular vote. That is, we cannot be absolutely certain who actually won the popular vote in any of these elections. At the same time, none of the alternatives to the current Electoral College promises to be any less controversial or less of a threat to legitimacy when the national difference is less than one percent. Is the assistance given to legitimacy by the tendency of the Electoral College to add an average 20 percent to the election outcome differential worth the possible damage to legitimacy if the electorate is otherwise conditioned to view a popular vote total as the normal standard?

We know of no good systematic study that examines the prevalence of voting fraud, although we know it has occurred regularly in the history of American elections in all parts of the country. Perhaps we should assume that attempts at fraud cancel each other out. Nor do we know of any good study of counting error, although social scientists know it exists. One of the authors of this chapter took part in an exercise at the University of Michigan's Survey Research Center about a third of a century ago. Eighteen teams of three doctoral students each were handed a large stack of punch cards and told to carefully count them by hand. By machine count there were 1,807 punch cards, which is about the size of the national sample used by political scientists in survey research. Instead, the counts ranged from more than .5 percent above that number to more than .5 percent below. One team came up with the number 1,807, although this was consistent with a random occurrence since for 1,807 a +.5 to -.5 percent spread is a total of eighteen, and there were eighteen teams. There was a second hand-count with a similar spread of results. This exercise showed that simple mechanical recounting, even without looking for such things as dimpled chads, will not necessarily produce a more accurate total, but it will almost always produce a new total. Additional recounts will just generate new totals. Nor is counting by machines the answer. Those who make voting machines admit that error rates, which vary by machine, tend to be at least one percent. When counting 100,000,000 votes from several thousand counties using a variety of voting methods, the assumption of a one-percent counting error is undoubtedly quite conservative. In national elections human error enters in another way. A certain small, but inevitable number of voters make mistakes marking their ballots unless there is some mechanical means to prevent such a ballot from being cast until corrected. In the 2000 election more than 1,500,000 ballots were thrown out nationwide as a result of voter errors — three times the 500,000-vote difference reported between the two major candidates.

One irony of the 2000 election is that although the Electoral College may well have produced a winner contrary to the one with the highest popular vote total, it also allowed us to identify Florida as the place to focus our recount efforts. If we had been using a nationwide popular vote system, we would have had to recount the entire nation if there had been a challenge. While an apparent 500,000 popular vote difference in 2000 would probably have been viewed as substantial enough to preclude the need for any recount if we had been using a popular vote electoral system, the 1960 outcome was close enough that a national recount might well have been called — indeed, should have been called. A number of states have a provision for an automatic recount if the difference is less than a certain percentage, and the 1960 (.2 percent) difference was less than, for example, the .3 percent automatic recount trigger used by New Mexico.

These considerations raise a number of questions that must be settled for any electoral system. Should the various approximations of the popular vote system include an automatic recount trigger? For that matter, shouldn't the popular vote in the states for their respective electors under the current Electoral College include a proviso for recounting? If automatic recounts using the same rules and mechanisms are no more accurate than the original count even though a different number is produced, shouldn't we determine what kinds of rules and mechanisms will enhance the relative accuracy of a recount? Indeed, shouldn't we develop rules and counting mechanisms that reduce the probability of serious counting error to begin with? What is "serious" counting error? Should we develop a uniform process for counting votes? Should we not work harder to educate the public not only about how to cast a usable ballot, but also about the process and mechanisms for detecting and correcting errors, intentional or otherwise? These are questions that need to be addressed regardless of our preferred electoral system. There will be close elections in the future no matter which electoral system we use. There will be counting errors no matter the electoral system. If we keep the current Electoral College, we still need to think hard about the inevitable future close elections, counting error, voter error, and fraud. If we move to some other electoral system, we are not excused from that same hard thinking.

THE HISTORY OF THE ELECTORAL COLLEGE: BROAD LESSONS
Although any number of "lessons" might be gleaned from the history of the Electoral College, we would like to highlight the following half dozen as possibly illuminating the operation of any presidential electoral system in the future.

1. The Electoral College may have had a certain accidental quality at its birth, but it nonetheless reflects and embodies fundamental principles of the U.S.

Constitution. We have seen how the Electoral College emerged as a natural extension of the principles of federalism, separation of powers, and a deliberative process that informed the design of all the institutions of the U.S. Constitution. The Constitutional Convention's move from a parliamentary design to an independent executive selected by a national constituency conditioned the very existence of the Electoral College. The previously approved bicameral Congress retained a role, but one that had to involve both houses in some way if it involved either of them. With the separation of powers already in place, it made sense to separate the process of selecting presidential candidates (through the Electoral College) from the process of selecting among those candidates (in the House). The Electoral College then operated historically to reinforce the independent executive, bicameralism, and thus the separation of powers.

2. Incremental changes in an electoral system can lead to more substantial consequences in other political institutions. The supposedly "technical" correction of the Twelfth Amendment is a case in point, as is the nonconstitutional move in all but two states to a winner-take-all rule. Institutions do not function in isolation, but in a network with each other. A constitution identifies and describes a basic institutional network and provides the essential rules defining the interrelationships among these institutions. Moreover, institutions also have inevitable interlocking effects on each other that are either too complicated to lay out or are unforeseen and unintended. Analyzing a political institution in isolation from the rest of a constitutional system is ordinarily difficult, and the history of the Electoral College reaffirms this basic lesson in constitutional design.

3. An essential aspect of the history of the Electoral College is its interconnection with the extraconstitutional institution of political parties. We have seen how the inception of party politics complicated the operation of the Electoral College, leading to the Twelfth Amendment, which in turn hastened the development of a party system. Later alterations served to strengthen the two-party system, which subsequently helped preserve the Electoral College. This relationship has been bolstered by an amendment process that makes it easy for the two major parties to protect the Electoral College and thus makes replacing this institution very difficult — indeed, highly unlikely. If the Electoral College is altered or replaced, the change will need to make sense in terms of the rational interests of the major political parties at that time. Likewise, the party system will itself be altered by any change in the current electoral system. For instance, movement toward proportional allocation of electoral votes will encourage the development of a multiparty system, which might work well in a parliamentary regime, but under our constitution it increases the likelihood that presidents will be chosen by the House of Representatives under a state unit rule that is highly inegalitarian.

4. If the history of the Electoral College consists of many attempts to alter or replace it, that history underscores how difficult it is to amend the U.S. Consti-

tution. Except for Australia, the United States has the most difficult amendment process in the world. As a result, of the approximately eleven thousand amendments that have been proposed, only twenty-seven have been adopted. More than one thousand of these would-be amendments have proposed altering or eliminating the Electoral College. The amendment process is so difficult because of a historical "accident," when a temporary political situation became embodied in American constitutional law. It has always been understood that to change an agreement, one must return to the same process that produced it. The amendment process thus returns to the same level of consent as was used for its adoption. At the Constitutional Convention, it was understood that the unanimity rule could not be used because Rhode Island was going to reject whatever emerged from their deliberations. On the one hand, the Convention delegates wanted and needed a ratified Constitution. On the other hand, those who ratified it had to include the large states and produce a nation unbroken by geographical gaps. Experience in the Continental Congress had shown that there was a critical threshold at nine states. If a proposal had the approval of nine states, it almost always included Massachusetts, Pennsylvania, and Virginia. If Massachusetts was on board, so was the rest of New England (except Rhode Island). That is, Massachusetts led the New England coalition. The same was true of Pennsylvania for the middle states, and Virginia for the South. As a result, when at least nine states supported a proposal, there were almost automatically eleven or twelve, whereas if fewer than nine states supported a proposal it was usually not eight or seven states but fewer than seven. This prudential calculation led to the nine-state ratification rule, although New York threatened not to play its subordinate role to Pennsylvania, having rapidly become its near economic equal over the previous two decades. For this reason, the *Federalist Papers* were thus thrown together and aimed directly at New York. The calculation worked, as the nine-state requirement yielded ratification by twelve states (Rhode Island held out until after the first national election.)

Amending the constitution thus requires a two-thirds majority in Congress plus ratification in three-fourths of the states. Nine out of thirteen states is 70 percent, which is close to half way between a two-thirds (67 percent) and three-fourths (75 percent) majority. The two steps to the amendment process thus bracket, and together recapitulate, the ratification percentage. What makes legal sense, however, does not always make good political sense. The resulting amendment process has been so difficult that we have turned to the Supreme Court to effectively amend the Constitution through interpretation. If this has been one consequence of the amendment process, another has been the inability to alter or abolish the Electoral College. In the absence of compelling reasons for change or elimination, debate about the Electoral College has been surprisingly thin and desultory through the years. Whatever two parties were most entrenched had no trouble keeping these more than 1,000 proposed amendments bottled up in committees. Contemporary congressional Democrats and Republicans will almost certainly maintain this record.

5. A broader look at comparative constitutional history suggests that while other democracies reject the Electoral College for their own use, they also reject most of the rest of American constitutional design. The Electoral College used by the United States is sui generis. Historically, however, outside of some Latin American countries, few democracies have adopted direct popular election of their respective executives. Instead, the chief executive is usually elected by a legislature/parliament based on proportional representation within a multiparty system. Put another way, the political system of the United States is just as unusual for its relentless separation of powers, for its popularly elected executive, and for its two-party system as it is for its Electoral College. Other democracies have not so much rejected the Electoral College, as they have rejected an executive separate from the legislature. Thus, whether to use a direct popular vote or an electoral college never became an issue in most other democracies. There is no compelling lesson from constitutional history outside the United States that supports keeping, altering, or replacing the Electoral College, unless we feel compelled to move to a parliamentary, proportional representation, multiparty system. We are "free" to do as we wish for our own prudential reasons, but deciding what to do is not simply a "game." Competing principles and values are at stake and should be the focus of debate over keeping, altering, or replacing the Electoral College.

6. Finally, just as there are no compelling technical reasons why we should keep the present Electoral College, there are likewise no compelling technical reasons why we should change it. Most elections that produced controversy for the Electoral College would have produced substantial controversy for any of the proposed alternatives suggested in this volume. A direct popular vote scheme, in particular, may well have resulted in even more frequent controversies because any close election would have been open to the charge of possible miscounts, if not fraud. Indeed, a popular vote system not only invites a multiparty system, which tends to produce more close elections, but also invites systematic fraud to be buried in dispersed areas across the nation by those multiple parties. In sum, no electoral system can prevent controversy in a very close election. If there is no magic in the electoral system itself, then we are left to choose among the options for reasons other than the technical efficacy of the system. That is, if different electoral systems flow from or reflect one set of values or another, selection will inevitably be made on those grounds rather than on technical ones.

ELECTORAL COLLEGE: THE PRINCIPLES AT STAKE

Above all, debate over the Electoral College reduces to two basic positions — keep the Electoral College or move the method for selecting the president closer to an unfiltered popular will that is based on majority rule. With few exceptions those who debate the matter do not address the important distinction in decision theory between what is "most preferred" versus "preferred by most," although the problem facing us raises what political theorists term the "intensity problem."

The notion of minority rights assumes that the important interests of an intense minority are seriously threatened and need protecting. A minority that has no strong feelings on a given issue does not need protecting. Problems arise with a system based on "preferred by most" in the following circumstances: when an intense minority faces either an apathetic or intense numerical majority; or when there are two opposed and intense minorities facing an apathetic majority that holds the key to the decision. The latter instance is more common in American politics. Think of abortion, where two-thirds of the electorate is against abortion on demand, and two-thirds are opposed to complete prohibition of abortion. The muddled middle ends up satisfying neither minority in the policies it is willing to support, while both minorities attempt to raise the intensity of the middle in their direction. Historically, racial discrimination in the United States since the end of slavery has been of this nature, although it has also been at one time or another considered an example of an intense minority facing an intense or apathetic majority. Often, but not always, those supporting the present Electoral College have tended to emphasize the importance of the intensity problem, while those preferring change have tended to minimize its significance. Rather, they have focused on the importance of legitimacy and fairness.

The theory is that the current Electoral College somehow allows a combination of states with less than a majority of the potential popular vote to protect their interests. This argument makes sense if the potential minority has a geographical basis, or one predicated on small state interests versus large state interests. In late eighteenth-century politics in the United States this argument had some force, but the greatly reduced impact of giving two senatorial votes to each state regardless of size mitigates this argument. Nor is it clear how small states or states with small populations scattered across a continent are likely to have similar interests. The recent gloss on this argument is that a popular vote system would lead to campaigns that largely ignore states with small populations, but this is already a tendency in elections using the Electoral College. Even large states are sometimes ignored in current elections, as were California and Texas in the 2000 campaign. The outcome in those states was a foregone conclusion because of partisan distributions, and neither party wasted much time, effort, or money to contest them. Still, the intensity problem remains a consideration, only now it is not state-based. What the intensity problem does is call into question a simple plurality popular vote system as morally superior to the Electoral College. Neither seems to address the intensities of minorities scattered across a number of states large and small. The moral basis of a popular vote system rests entirely on an appeal to equality.

Arguments from equality get us back to what is meant by majority rule. Decision theory has long considered the ideal form of majority rule for purposes of legitimacy to be unanimity. The theoretical grounding for a one-half-plus-one majority is that it is the minimal acceptable form of majority rule, which makes it both acceptable and the easiest to achieve. However, in consent theory anything larger than one-half-plus-one is always preferable to this minimal standard, just as unanimity is always preferable to any smaller majority. In other words, although we have come to accept one-half-plus-one for practical reasons, there is nothing admirable about this minimal majority rule per se in moral terms other than it always is preferable to minority rule. Ironically, the use of a simple majority in a system where voting is optional, and where about half of the electorate does not vote, is formally equivalent to minority rule. The use of a plurality rule with more than two candidates simply compounds the theoretical problem. The argument from majority rule would then seem to require, at a minimum, support for a runoff election and probably mandatory voting. Put another way, the current argument from majority rule is not seriously based on a majority rule principle but upon grounds of practicality under a norm of satisficing. Even though the Electoral College creates the appearance of a larger majority and sometimes produces majorities as high as 95 percent of the electoral votes, it is subject to a similar criticism. It is an appearance, not the reality, of majority rule. Strictly speaking, majority rule as envisioned by Locke, Algernon Sidney, and the other early liberals who first codified the concept requires at least one-half-plus-one of all citizens, or something approaching this.

The appeal to minority rights also cuts in more than one direction. At the founding there were real and important differences in the political cultures of states, and between clusters of states. An appeal to minority rights then was more an appeal to regional minorities — something that does not resonate as strongly today. If one looks at the outcome of recent elections on a map of the United States, however, persistent regional differences would remain. Whether this is a potential minority rights problem is open to question. One might argue that with the direct popular election of the president these regional differences would finally be put to rest, although it may actually come down to ignoring regional differences.

The concept of minority rights today refers most obviously to Americans of African, Hispanic, Asian, and Native American heritage. Certainly a direct popular vote system would minimize the perception that, as was charged by some in Florida after the 2000 election, minority votes were excluded unfairly. Of course, this might be so because any such tampering would be buried in a nationwide result that minimized the perception of such abuses and made them difficult to find.

A direct popular election of the president might also result in at least a minimal reduction in the effect minorities have on the outcome. Under the current system there are ten or twelve states in which African Americans have a good chance to determine the direction in which the entire state's electoral votes are cast. Hispanics too are on the verge of becoming the swing vote in five of the six largest states, as well as several smaller states. A direct popular electoral system would flatten out minority votes toward perfect equality so that a white vote in North Dakota could cancel out an African American vote in New York. In contrast, today an African American vote can be part of a bloc vote that shifts New York's outcome in a way that may magnify that African American's vote. This is no reason not to move to a direct popular vote system, but we need to be analytic about the principles that actually animate a choice as well as be honest about probable consequences of keeping, altering, or replacing the Electoral College. Discussion in a later chapter will address the possible effects of Electoral College changes on minority voter impact, although the effects do not appear to be important.

Those opposing the present Electoral College invariably cite equality as a reason for opposition. The problem usually cited is that the Electoral College, by giving two electoral votes to each state for its senators, gives voters in the smaller states more weight relative to those in larger ones. This has led to calls for altering the electoral vote distribution so that the number of electoral votes is proportional to the population of a given state — that is, by eliminating the two senatorial-based electoral votes per state. Is there an argument from equality that points toward more than this adjustment and implies the need to replace the Electoral College entirely? Put another way, does an argument from equality automatically imply a national majority as opposed to a state majority? The continued use of state majorities would, in the absence of the two senatorial-based electoral votes, produce an outcome different from that of a national majority only if we retain the unit rule where the state majority determines the allocation of all state electoral votes. The winner-take-all rule, as the unit rule is commonly termed, does not require a constitutional amendment to change, whereas eliminating the two senatorial-based electoral votes does require a constitutional amendment.

Given the difficulty of amending the U.S. Constitution, a rational actor pursuing greater equality might well seek to alter the unit rule and move to a requirement for proportional allocation of state electoral votes based on the popular vote in a given state. Seeking a nationwide popular majority system, which is unlikely ever to be approved because it requires a formal amendment, would seem to promise no payoff in terms of equality because of likely failure. On the other hand, pursuing the nonamendment route to require assigning a state's congressional district electoral votes in proportion to the state's popular vote, a much easier prospect than pursuing a constitutional amendment, leaves only the slight inequality of the two senatorial-based electoral votes per state. This brief discussion illustrates the extent to which apparent pragmatic arguments are still conducted within the framework of deeper principles. The trade-off one is willing to accept is largely tied to the principle one prefers. This example also shows how difficult it is to be a rational actor in this controversy, since anyone pursuing greater egalitarianism by moving to proportional allocation of state electoral votes also increases the likelihood that presidents will be chosen by the House of Representatives using a state unit rule that is not egalitarian. In short, pursuit of greater equality through change may result in equal or less equality because of interaction effects.

Equality as a principle may also cut more than one way. Even with the current system that gives proportionally more weight to the smaller states in the Electoral College, presidential election campaigns pay more attention to the concerns of citizens in larger states; such a strategy should reap many more votes per dollar invested. Any move away from the Electoral College might increase this inequality of attention to the concerns of citizens in small states. Put another way, the concerns of voters from smaller states already seem to be less than equally addressed, so equality-based arguments may be disingenuous — more a matter of appearance than political reality.

This gets us back to the deeper concern for legitimacy. Regardless of how any change actually works with respect to political equality, legitimacy may be best served by the formal equality of a nationwide popular majority. Still, as noted, no electoral system has an advantage with respect to legitimacy when the popular vote is evenly divided. There seems to be no advantage, for example, in giving the popular vote winner an additional hundred electoral votes, since in a very close election the legitimacy for assigning those hundred votes is as open to question as it is with any electoral system.

Where does this leave us? No one is happy with the outcome of close elections, but they will occur occasionally no matter which electoral system we use. We should spend at least as much time improving the administration of elections as we do on debates over the relative merits of electoral systems. The success or failure of any selection system depends on efficient, accurate, uniform, and fair procedures for casting and counting ballots. The current systems fall woefully short when evaluated on these criteria. Improved administration might obviate the need for constitutional reform, which is unlikely in any case. And even if reform is warranted, its success will hinge on effective administration — especially if the change is to a direct election format.

NOTES

1. This text is taken from James Madison, *Notes of Debates in the Federal Convention of 1787* (New York: Norton, 1987), 31.
2. Ibid., 116.
3. Ibid., 392.
4. Ibid., 574.
5. Ibid., 50.
6. Ibid., 138.
7. Ibid., 327.

8. Ibid., 331–36.

9. Ibid., 356–62.

10. In the aggregate, however, the overweighing of small states is still potentially important in very close elections if the electoral votes of the smaller states tend to go to one candidate, who is thereby advantaged when even a marginal advantage could be decisive. Given the geographic distribution and diverse interests of the smallest states, a small state "stampede" toward one candidate is very unlikely. The very close 2000 election was typical. Gore and Bush split the sixteen smallest states, which together are about one-third of all the states and comprise most of the small state statistical advantage. Bush carried the next six largest states in the Great Plains, but their combined advantage deriving from the two senatorial-based electoral votes was eliminated when Gore carried any one of the largest twenty-five states. One does not win the presidency by attempting to combine the small state advantage in the Electoral College.

11. Elbridge Gerry, Roger Sherman, and George Mason in comments on pp. 51, 306, and 308, respectively, in *Notes of Debates in the Federal Convention of 1787.*

12. Madison made this argument most famously in *Federalist,* No. 10. See *The Federalist,* ed. George Carey and James McClellan (Dubuque, Iowa: Kendall/Hunt, 1990), 43–48.

13. The party of Jefferson is sometimes called the Democratic Republican Party, to distinguish it from the modern Republican Party.

14. Brian J. Gaines, "Popular Myths About Popular Vote–Electoral College Splits," *PS: Political Science and Politics* 34, no. 1 (March 2001): 71–75. The quote is taken from p. 75.

CHAPTER 4

The Role of Federalism
in Presidential Elections

Donald Haider-Markel, *University of Kansas*
Melvin Dubnick, *Rutgers University-Newark*
Richard Elling, *Wayne State University*
David Niven, *Florida Atlantic University*
Paul Schumaker, *University of Kansas*

ACCORDING TO MANY SCHOLARS, a prominent rationale for the creation and maintenance of the electoral college system was the effect such a system has on preserving federalism in the American system. Although some have argued that the system was intended to be antidemocratic, most scholars agree that the electoral college system, along with other components of the original design, helped ensure a federalist system. Most important, the electoral college system was partly designed to guarantee that the interests of all states would be fairly represented. By having state-selected electors nominate a president and by having state delegations in the House settle the question when no contender had captured a majority in the Electoral College, it seemed likely that presidential aspirants would be attentive to state-level interests and concerns. However, given the informal modifications that have occurred in the operations of the electoral college system, is this the way the system actually works today? Does the system still make sense in an era where every official besides the president is elected by popular vote? In this chapter we discuss these questions and evaluate the merits of the existing Electoral College and various alternatives to it. We recognize from the start that any discussion of the Electoral College and its effects on federalism will be peppered with normative evaluations of state versus national power.[1] We begin with reflections on the original design and the evolution of the Electoral College. Then we provide a broader discussion of the positive and negative impacts of Electoral College reform or the abolition of the system.

FEDERALISM IN THE ORIGINAL DESIGN
OF THE ELECTORAL COLLEGE

The original design for selecting a president solved two problems that faced the framers.[2] First, having the president selected by national popular election would permit the uninformed masses to choose a president based on demagogic appeal rather than on qualifications.[3] Establishing an electoral college ensured that the final arbitrators of a state's preferences would be knowledgeable, upstanding citizens who would choose, through careful deliberation, a person qualified for the position. Second, in a popular vote system, states with large populations would clearly be "kingmakers"; although citizens of small states would play some role, their preferences would likely be overwhelmed. Establishing the Electoral College enabled the framers to ensure that all states played a role in the process. Clearly, they were less concerned with the equality of individual voters than with the relative influence of states as a whole.[4]

The framers of the Electoral College were concerned about three federalist goals: (1) distributing power fairly among large and small states; (2) distributing power appropriately between state governments and the national government; and (3) basing presidential legitimacy on federalist (rather than populist) principles. Each of these points is discussed below.

First, as with the establishment of a national legislative body, there was concern over how any electoral system would distribute power fairly, given the conflicting interests of small and large states. From the beginning the republic was viewed as a "nation of equal states" and this conception led to the notion that each state should have relatively equal weight in selecting our one national leader, the president. As originally conceived, the Electoral College went a long way toward achieving this goal. The framers believed that the electoral college system would most often serve as a nominating device and that the "eventual election" of a president would usually occur in the House of Representatives.[5] In the House, each state delegation was given one vote, making each state equal regardless of state population, but this system was unfair to large states. So in the Electoral College each state would be assigned electors based on its population in the same way each state was allocated seats in Congress (two Senate seats plus House seats distributed by population). This compromise gave small states equal power if the election was decided in the House. But in the Electoral College (which would always nominate candidates and also select the president if a majority was reached) large states would have the greatest influence while small states would still have a disproportionate influence compared to a system that allocated electoral votes based solely on population.

Second, given their considerable distrust of national government, the framers wanted to develop a system that helped clarify the distribution of power between the national government and the governments of the states. The founders understood that the president would be the most powerful *national* leader; thus, parochial considerations should weigh less strongly in his selection than in the selection of members of Congress. At the same time, the founders wanted to ensure that presidents would remain attentive to the states.

Under a popular election system, presidents might be less likely to view states as distinct and thus likely to emphasize the nation's interests as a whole, for better or worse. Clearly, those concerned about preserving the power of state governments would be dissatisfied with an arrangement that encouraged presidents to place national interests above the interests of particular states, and perhaps the national government above state governments. One method of presidential selection that might have solved this problem was to have the president chosen by state legislatures, but this proposal was rejected as making the president too much a creature of the states.

Between the extremes of national popular elections that emphasized a national orientation and elections by state legislatures that emphasized more local orientations, the Electoral College offered a compromise solution. It gave states a large role in the selection process, but still prevented excess parochialism. The states were empowered to decide how electors would be chosen, and electors were expected to represent all parts of a state. Additionally, electors would cast their votes in each state capital, preventing "national cabals" from taking over the process if the votes were cast in the nation's capitol. The Electoral College was thus viewed as a device that encouraged presidents to support and uphold rights of the states, perhaps even to the extent of viewing states as mini laboratories for effective government. But electors were also supposed to be enlightened citizens who would deliberate on the qualifications of nationally-prominent figures who would serve interests that transcend state borders.

Thus, the Electoral College was created by the framers *primarily* as part of a series of institutional devices to solve the politically sensitive issue of state-national relations in the proposed system, and only secondarily to deal with the issue of selecting the president. Put another way, the creation of the Electoral College provided the framers with one more opportunity to enhance the political viability and legitimacy of constitutional changes. By the time they considered the issue of presidential selection, they had already fallen into a pattern of creating various institutional arrangements (involving the principles of separation of powers and federalism) to appease the expected opposition to any constitution that strengthened central government authority. Seen in this light, the Electoral College was part of a package of institutional compromises emerging from the convention that addressed the most critical concerns of potential critics and opponents.[6] The Electoral College was developed as a method for selecting a president who would have a national perspective that was inclusive of state interests, by giving the states a significant but not overwhelming role in his selection.

Third, the framers faced the issue regarding the source of the president's power and legitimacy. Contemporary democratic theory and cultural norms emphasize that power and legitimacy are derived from popular "majority rule" (as Andrew Jackson was to claim as the basis of his presidential power beginning in 1832).[7] However, when forming our Constitution, the founders instead sought to base the president's power and legitimacy on "the federal principle." Because the founders placed emphasis on the federal basis of presidential power, a myth has developed that portrays the framers as "antidemocratic," fixated on minimizing the potential for liberty-threatening "mobocracy." In fact, the framers seemed more preoccupied with showing some deference to the states than with the evils of popular votes. Popular election of electors was neither advocated nor in any way restricted. Were they more opposed to popular rule, they would have put some relevant restrictions on how state legislatures chose the College electors, but the means for selecting electors was intentionally left up to the individual legislatures, where populist sentiments were often strong. Two states opted for direct election in 1788, five in 1792 (with two using district-based elections), and six in 1800 (with only one determining electors using a statewide approach). By 1824, all but two states were using some form of popular election process to select electors. In the elections of 1832 and 1836, only South Carolina avoided popular election of electors, and that state would continue to hold out until after the Civil War.[8]

The founders did not intend to prevent popular participation and majority rule. Rather, they sought an electoral process that would achieve fairly broad consensus, or supramajorities, rather than bare-minimum majorities. The original design was intended to foster collaboration among electors from different states in an effort to promote regional or even national aims and attain widespread support for the chosen candidate. As indicated by James Madison, the founders adopted the Electoral College as "a very compound source" of power that would produce presidents who derived legitimacy from both national and state sources and who would have broad support among the public and across the states.[9] To win the presidency through electoral college procedures, the founders thought that candidates would have to appeal to most citizens in most states, regardless of region.

Judith Best has presented perhaps the most forceful meaning and import of the federal principle. Best points out that while the majoritarian principle is simply concerned with "who gets the most votes," the federal principle is concerned with the distribution of votes. Under the federal principle, the president eventually selected would be that candidate who had the most widespread support across all the states in the nation.[10] Indeed, a good deal of our debate about Electoral College reform is based on historical myths that divert attention from, and even distort, the efforts of the framers to create a core "federalist" institution. There is a major historical distinction between presidential "selection" and "election" that is often ignored. The College was designed as a means to engage states in the "selection" of a president, and his subsequent "election" if necessary. The framers believed that — after the Electoral College initially "selected" George Washington — no one was likely to get the majority votes required to be selected by the Electoral College. More often than not, the "election" would be thrown to the House, where state delegations would seek to form coalitions with other state delegations to choose a person who best represented regional or national concerns. From this perspective, the Electoral College's value as a core "federalist" institution comes not only from its deference to state legislatures in determining how electors would be chosen, but also from its potential capacity to foster multiregional and national alliances. In sum, the system was designed to be a more deliberative and accommodating process than it has become. Today, the Electoral College is largely an aggregative process in which the electoral votes attained in the various states are simply summed up to achieve a result.

FEDERALISM AND THE EVOLUTION OF THE ELECTORAL COLLEGE
Although the original conception of the electoral college system did a good job of addressing federalist concerns, its evolution may no longer serve these concerns and may in fact thwart some of them. The system has clearly been transformed by the development of a competitive two-party system and by having electors pledged to party slates, by using statewide popular elections (rather than state legislatures) to determine electors and by the winner-take-all feature most states use to award their Electoral College votes. Any discussion of reform must address how these changes have altered the way the Electoral College now works in terms of achieving federal goals.

The Distribution of Power across States
The framers' compromises involving the distribution of power among the states has been undone by a variety of changes. First, a House election of the president has not occurred since 1824, so the equality among states at that stage is more formal than real. Given the development of democratic norms emphasizing the voting equality of all citizens, this change is positive as it would be unfair to voters in large states to have presidential elections resolved by a process that gave all states equal weight in the selection of the president.

Second, the advantage that the "Connecticut compromise" (for Senate seat allocation) gives to small states within the Electoral College is now fairly minimal. Giving all states two electors regardless of size gives small states more influence than they would have if the allocation of electors were based only on size of population. But the enhanced power that the Electoral College gives to small states (e.g., North and South Dakota, Vermont, Wyoming, Montana) is not very large.

So one might ask (as students often do) what the actual difference would be between a state's influence in the electoral college and a state's influence in the popular vote. To address this question, we have calculated the influence in presidential elections of each state (and the District of Columbia) in three ways.

First, to show each state's influence in the electoral college system, we divided each state's Electoral College votes by the total number of Electoral College votes. Second, to show each state's influence if we had a national popular vote, we divided the number of persons who cast ballots in each state in 1996 by the total number of voters in the 1996 presidential contest. Third, to show each state's potential influence if we had a national popular vote and if all eligible voters in fact voted, we divided the number of 1996 eligible voters in each state by the total number of eligible voters in 1996.[11] The data are displayed in table 4.1.

As the table shows, most small states have more influence on the outcome of the Electoral College than they would if the outcome were based on the popular vote. Conversely, most large states have less influence in the Electoral College than they would had we employed popular vote. Small states (and the District of Columbia) are advantaged because the minimum percentage score in the Electoral College is .56 while the minimal percentage score in the popular vote system is .19. Large states are disadvantaged, as the maximum influence a state has in the Electoral College is lower, at 10.04 percentage points compared to 10.41 percentage points in the popular vote system. A simple T-test demonstrates that the differences between the influence of states in the Electoral College and their influence in a popular election given their 1996 levels of voter turnout are statistically significant (P > .000). However, even though the differences between systems are clear, the potentially different influence of various states in each system is not tremendously large.

Nevertheless, it is important to point out that these small differences can be decisive, as they were in the 2000 election. Suppose that electoral votes were allocated solely on the basis of population and that each state thus had the same number of electors as it has members in the House of Representatives. If we gave the District of Columbia one electoral vote, an Electoral College majority would be 219 electoral votes. Had that been the case, Al Gore would have had 225 electoral votes, ensuring his election and making the drawn-out affair in Florida irrelevant.[12] Thus, the inequalities favoring small states can enable them to dictate an outcome opposed by most voters throughout the nation.

But there are still further considerations. First, the current informal (or extra-constitutional) dynamics of the Electoral College may actually operate to enhance the power of large states. Voters in large states with extensive party competition have greater "voting power" than citizens in smaller states with little partisan balance.[13] This is because voters in competitive states have greater odds of altering the way that their state's electoral votes are cast and because large states are more likely to cast a bloc of electoral votes that are decisive to the outcome. Furthermore, candidates tend to focus on these large, contested states, spending more resources in them to win votes and perhaps making more promises of policy benefits to their voters (witness President Clinton's promises of military spending to key competitive states such as California during the 1996 campaign).

Table 4.1   State Influence in the Electoral College and under Popular Elections
(percentage of national votes cast)

State	Electoral College	Popular Election: Actual Voters	Popular Election: Eligible Voters
Alabama	1.67	1.59	1.65
Alaska	0.56	0.25	0.21
Arizona	1.49	1.46	1.66
Arkansas	1.12	0.92	0.96
California	10.04	10.41	10.03
Colorado	1.49	1.57	1.46
Connecticut	1.49	1.45	1.18
Delaware	0.56	0.28	0.28
Florida	4.65	5.51	5.68
Georgia	2.42	2.39	2.77
Hawaii	0.74	0.37	0.46
Idaho	0.74	0.51	0.44
Illinois	4.09	4.48	5.87
Indiana	2.23	2.22	2.13
Iowa	1.30	1.28	1.10
Kansas	1.12	1.12	0.98
Kentucky	1.49	1.44	1.50
Louisiana	1.67	1.85	1.61
Maine	0.74	0.63	0.48
Maryland	1.86	1.85	1.96
Massachusetts	2.23	2.66	2.38
Michigan	3.35	4.00	3.63
Minnesota	1.86	2.28	1.75
Mississippi	1.30	0.93	1.01
Missouri	2.04	2.24	2.01
Montana	0.56	0.42	0.33
Nebraska	0.93	0.70	0.62
Nevada	0.74	0.48	0.61
New Hampshire	0.74	0.52	0.44
New Jersey	2.79	3.19	3.09
New Mexico	0.93	0.58	0.62
New York	6.13	6.56	6.97
North Carolina	2.60	2.61	2.98
North Dakota	0.56	0.28	0.22
Ohio	3.90	4.71	4.27
Oklahoma	1.49	1.25	1.24
Oregon	1.30	1.43	1.20
Pennsylvania	4.28	4.68	4.73
Rhode Island	0.74	0.41	0.39
South Carolina	1.49	1.20	1.41
South Dakota	0.56	0.34	0.27
Tennessee	2.04	1.97	1.88
Texas	5.95	5.83	7.04
Utah	0.93	0.69	0.68
Vermont	0.56	0.27	0.22
Virginia	2.42	2.51	2.62
Washington	2.04	2.34	2.12
West Virginia	0.93	0.66	0.73
Wisconsin	2.04	2.28	1.95
Wyoming	0.56	0.22	0.18
Washington, D.C.	0.56	0.19	0.26

Additionally, we would point out that a system of fifty-one minielections, in which the winner of the state takes all its electoral votes, effectively eliminates three-quarters of the states from the election process. By the end of the summer of 2000, pollsters and campaign analysts judged no more than sixteen states were actively being contested. By October, that number was twelve. Indeed, eleven states and the District of Columbia have voted for the same party's candidate in each of the last eight presidential elections.[14] When Representative Stephanie Tubbs Jones (D-Cleveland) publicly worried that Al Gore was ignoring Ohio and her district, State Democratic Party chair David Leland defended the Gore campaign by saying that the decision was a matter of strategy, "It's a question of whether Ohio is in play."[15] Typical of laments aired across the country were the words of a newspaper columnist in California who wrote, "The Electoral College today makes California, the nation's largest state, practically irrelevant in presidential politics. . . . No wonder at least one of the major party candidates has ignored this state in the last three elections — it doesn't make good strategic sense to campaign here, or to run strongly on issues of importance to Californians."[16] Such was the nature of the California contest that Green Party candidate Ralph Nader ran a commercial stating "Al Gore is going to win California," therefore, why waste your vote on him. Hundreds of newspaper stories across the country noted that one or both presidential candidates had ignored, skipped, or surrendered their state, holding no campaign events, showing no commercials, not even posting any yard signs. Instead of reflecting the political character of each state, the current system reflects intense campaigning in limited areas and little more than indifference from the campaigns toward most of the nation.

In short, the winner-take-all nature of the current system encourages candidates to ignore states that are apparently safe for one side or the other and to focus on competitive states. The argument that this practical feature of the Electoral College enhances the power of large states, offsetting the advantage to small states in the actual allocation of electoral votes, is problematic. It depends on the assumption that less populous states are less likely to feature closely matched competition among presidential candidates than is the case in more populous states. Perhaps smaller states are generally less likely to be competitive because they are socially and economically more homogeneous than large states. But in particular elections, large states such as California and Texas can be noncompetitive and their voters too can be effectively disenfranchised by the electoral college system.

The data in table 4.1 also enable us to consider the issue of turnout. One argument against the Electoral College is that it rewards states with the lowest levels of voter turnout.[17] Consider the case of Alabama in the first row of the table. Its relative influence in the Electoral College (1.67 percent) is slightly greater than it would be if we had popular elections and all eligible voters cast ballots (1.65 percent), but its influence in the College is considerably greater than it would be given the number of its citizens who actually voted (1.59 percent). In other words, under popular voting systems, states are penalized in terms of their voting power if their citizens vote at lower rates than citizens of other states, but they are not so penalized under the Electoral College. Thus, some states could increase their influence under a popular vote system by increasing their turnout. As shown in table 4.1, Texas, for example, could increase its influence relative to other states under a popular voting scheme simply by achieving a greater voter turnout. But other states, such as Minnesota, which already has a relatively high voter turnout, would lose influence if other states were able to increase their voter turnout to similar or higher levels. To be sure, this has a regional bias. A popular vote would reduce the influence of most southern states because they tend to have relatively low voter turnout. Still, one of the advantages of a popular vote–based system is that the relative influence of higher turnout states is magnified.[18]

Taking these formal and informal biases into account, it appears that the current operation of the Electoral College allocates unequal influence to citizens of different states in a curvilinear manner. Small states have disproportionate influence due to their overrepresentation in the Electoral College. Large, competitive states have more influence simply due to the winner-take-all provision. Thus, citizens in middle-sized states are relatively disadvantaged. Finally, the Electoral College provides a system — unlike popular vote schemes — in which states have no incentive to increase their voter turnout.

The Balance of National and State Power

The current operation of the Electoral College may give states a smaller role in the selection of a president than originally envisioned. If this is true, the states may have a lower capacity to constrain a president who seeks to nationalize power at the expense of the states. Along with other factors, the current system may indeed help presidents expand and consolidate power at the national level. Presidents Roosevelt and Johnson are only the most visible examples of presidents who have expanded considerably the power of our national government, perhaps at the expense of state governments.

When the Florida legislature took steps to ensure that Republican electors would have their votes counted in Congress in the aftermath of the November 2000 election, Americans learned that state legislatures are still formally responsible for the selection of electors. But the role of the states and state legislatures in nominating and electing presidents is now far less than the founders envisioned. Simply put, electors are now faithful agents of national parties rather than independent actors who consider "local information" and deliberate about state interests, casting their ballots devoid of national pressures. For the most part, state legislatures appoint electors from lists provided by the party with the most votes in the statewide popular election, and electors are bound to cast their vote for the candidate of the winning national party. Electors have little or no choice or independence as to how they cast their ballots, making the notion of deliberation moot. The initially honored "independent elector" — so crucial to deliberation and protecting state interests — has become the despised "rogue elector" who has abandoned (or lost faith with) his/her national party in order to act on the basis of state and local concerns.

To illustrate how much our expectations have changed regarding the national versus state dominance of the electoral process, consider the following incident. In January 1969, Senator Edmund Muskie, the unsuccessful Democratic vice-presidential candidate, held up congressional counting of Electoral College votes of the 1968 presidential election to challenge the electoral ballot of Lloyd Bailey of North Carolina. In 1968 Richard Nixon won the popular vote in North Carolina, and thus the thirteen electors selected by the North Carolina Republican Party were expected to cast their ballots for Nixon. Although twelve electors cast their ballots for Nixon, Bailey cast his electoral ballot for George Wallace, pointing out that Wallace had won Bailey's congressional district. Senator Muskie was not able to overturn Bailey's vote. But the fact that 33 members of the Senate and 169 members of the House voted to strike Bailey's ballot suggests the extent to which we now expect presidential elections to be determined by popular support for national parties rather than by electors who act on the basis of state and local concerns.[19]

Although the Electoral College surely prompts candidates to be attentive to state electorates in their campaigns, it is difficult to see how the current operation of the Electoral College helps produce presidents who are sensitive to preserving state power and curtailing national power. But it is equally difficult to be critical of a more nationalized presidential selection system if the kind of federal system envisioned by the founders is not the sort of federal system that most Americans today actually desire. Two trends from the mid-1970s to the mid-1990s suggest our vision of federalism has changed. First, Congress has becoming increasingly oriented to aiding people and not places. For example, general revenue sharing to both state and local governments has been eliminated. Even with Republicans in control of Congress, the notion of providing assistance to states or localities per se is a fairly alien concept to most members of Congress. Second, the Supreme Court in its *Garcia v. San Antonio* (1986) decision, and several subsequent decisions in the late 1980s [*South Dakota v. Dole* (1987), *South Carolina v. Baker* (1988)], has expressed the view that the states should not look to the courts to protect their interests. To be sure, Supreme Court Justice Sandra Day O'Connor has expressed the view that states should not be viewed as "mere field-hands" of the federal government and since the early 1990s the Supreme Court has been articulating what appears to be a view that is much more solicitous of the power and authority of subnational governments. However, we are not convinced that this more recent trend will continue in the face of powerful economic, demographic, and technological forces that are increasingly creating a "national consciousness."

In summary, the Electoral College originally had features that valued the "states qua states," but these features have become less relevant as the system has evolved. Perhaps the mere presence of state boundaries in the Electoral College makes presidential aspirants more attentive to preserving the powers of the states than would alternative national popular elections. But whether or not the Electoral College is more effective than other electoral systems in preserving states' rights may be of little concern to most Americans. Even in the American South, which has always been our most "state-conscious" region, most citizens now have an identity that is grounded in being an "American" as opposed to being an Alabaman, a Texan, or a Floridian. If indeed we increasingly view ourselves as Americans and see issues as national rather than statewide in scope, the Electoral College is likely to be seen as an anachronism whose time to depart the scene of American government has come.

Reinterpreting the Federal Principle

Finally, the realization of the federal principle — at least as that principle was originally conceptualized — may be less central to the successful operation of our electoral system now than it was when the Electoral College was created. In this section, we argue that the Electoral College is less able to produce a broad political consensus behind our president than it was in the past. We further argue that the most desirable consensus in America today would focus less on agreement among state interests than agreement across the social cleavages that presently divide our country.

The present operation of the Electoral College is not as geared to the production of supramajorities as was the initial conception. As discussed previously, the initial Electoral College was a system "composed of the most enlightened and respectable citizens,"[20] bearing no obligation or excess fealty to any political leader who could thus "enter upon the task free from any sinister bias."[21] The task of electors was to find persons most qualified for the position so that Congress could, in the subsequent election, focus on forming broad alliances of states seeking their common interests. In short, the initial system was geared to produce presidents who were widely supported. Today the Electoral College may give the impression of producing supramajorities because it often turns narrow popular majorities or even pluralities into wider Electoral College majorities. However, such victories cannot mask the reality that the present electoral system does little to discourage a polarized public, at least if the measure of such polarization is the closeness of the popular vote. The present system encourages two highly competitive national parties, and the "thin majorities" attained by the winning candidate are both frequent and often applauded as illustrating the vitality of the two-party system that is sustained by the Electoral College.[22]

While the electoral college system may be less capable of producing supramajorities today than in the past, the desirability of electing presidents who have broader support may be as urgent today as ever. However, our conception of what comprises a broader consensus than a "thin majority" has probably changed. According to Judith Best, the federal principle seeks "broadly inclusive alliances of political minorities that can compromise. The states are such political minorities, and they are the building blocks of the political majorities in the United States."[23] But perhaps the states are not the building blocks they once were. At our founding, citizens might have had stronger state-defined identities and their interests might have been well organized by the states. But in contemporary America, states may be less relevant "minorities" than are various racial, ethnic, religious, gender, and other identities and interests (such as progun, prolife, or profamily) that comprise our heterogeneous country. The ease of transportation and interstate migration in the modern era has clearly helped to decrease state identities. In addition, intrastate homogeneity has increasingly succumbed to intrastate diversity, as evidenced politically by the increasing number of occurrences of having one U.S. senator from a state who is very liberal and another who is very conservative. Such differences would not be possible in the more homogenous states that were the concern of the founders.[24]

The Electoral College may well be suited to ensuring that winning candidates get fairly widespread support across most states, but perhaps contemporary America needs another electoral system that produces presidents who have widespread support across these other divisions that define minority status in our country today. Although campaign strategists still put together a victory map based on linking enough states together to obtain 270 Electoral College votes, they also build electoral coalitions composed of many minority groups within those states, including Evangelicals, African Americans, and women, among many others. Perhaps devising an electoral system that encourages candidates to create the broadest electoral alliances of such minority groups by finding common ground among as many minorities as possible is the most urgent need for our political system.

POTENTIAL REFORMS AND THEIR IMPACTS

We believe that there is nothing inherently or necessarily antidemocratic about the Electoral College. Our problems with the College are not really with the institution per se, but with how it has evolved. In fact, we might find reforms of our two-party system or reforms in campaign financing to be the keys to enhancing democracy. However, we agree that it is useful to consider some major changes in the way states choose their electors. Modifying or eliminating winner-take-all laws or selecting electors on a district-by-district basis are reforms that are possible under the current Constitution. Such reforms might also be feasible politically because they would not engender the immediate opposition of small states. Both the district plan and the proportional allocation plan would continue the formal but small overrepresentation of smaller states in the presidential selection process. Because smaller states would not lose the boost in their influence provided by adding two electors regardless of their population size, they would have no self-interest to serve by opposing these reforms. Indeed, small states that are currently not competitive may have even more to gain under these plans because the votes of their citizens could be more valued and thus more sought after by the parties and candidates.[25] We believe that one key benefit of reforming the Electoral College by eliminating the unit rule is its positive effects on the party system.

The District Plan

Some of us support reforms that would allow states to select electors by popular vote within congressional districts. This change brings us closer to two of the framers' priorities. First, it would create another federalist layer in the presidential selection process. Second, it would further spread out the election contest, increasing competition in more states and in more districts within states. Madison argued that the president should be "indirectly derived from the choice of the people," a feature of presidential selection that rapidly melted away to become 51 minielections, many of which are insufficiently competitive to give the people meaningful choices.[26] By adding congressional districts to the equation, this situation can be significantly changed.

Having 435 district elections — plus 50 state elections (to allocate the electors provided to states for their senators) and 1 election in Washington, D.C. — may be preferable to the present 51 elections. This is because the candidates and their campaign organizations would have more difficulty determining "safe states" that can be ignored in the campaign. Candidates now have the resources to conduct polls in every state and can take advantage of vast quantities of media polls regularly conducted in most states. This is not the case in 435 congressional districts. This means there will be greater uncertainty about the outcome of presidential races in the districts, which will discourage candidates from concentrating their efforts in the few key states that are seen as toss-ups. Indeed, uncertainty of outcome in congressional districts is demonstrated by the fact that during the presidential elections that have occurred since 1992, an average of one hundred districts have split their vote between the congressional candidate of one party and the presidential candidate of the other.[27]

We also think that that the autonomy of American subnational governments is substantially enhanced by the existence of decentralized political parties. The primary reason why American parties are decentralized is that they are "electorally preoccupied" — what they care about is winning elective offices, and most electoral offices are found in local and state governments. The present electoral college arrangements may reinforce the decentralized nature of the parties by giving state parties incentives to carry their states for their party's candidate. If this is true, it may be the case that a district-based allocation of Electoral College votes may similarly reinforce party activity at the district level, enhancing the autonomy of subnational politics and governments.[28]

In general, the district plan may energize politics at the substate level, as parties and other organizations devote more attention to districts or pockets within particular states. However, depending on such factors as the competitiveness of specific districts and the distribution of media markets, some districts or parts of a state may see more campaign attention than they did previously, but other districts may see little change. For example, under the current system candidates have no incentive to campaign in Kansas because the state has voted Republican in the last eight presidential elections. Under a district plan at least one district — the third congressional district in northeast Kansas — might gain attention because the district is currently competitive for the congressional seat. Furthermore, the third district overlaps with the media market of Kansas City, Missouri, meaning money spent in that market reaches parts of Kansas as well as parts of Missouri. However, other districts in Kansas are not competitive and do not overlap with significant media markets. As such, those districts would still likely be ignored in a district system.

Further, given the geography involved, residents of noncompetitive districts may benefit from the "spillover campaigning" that would occur when a candidate campaigned in a nearby competitive district. For example, in 1996 Bill Clinton won New York by 28 points and both New Jersey and Connecticut by 18 points. Under the winner-take-all electoral college scheme, he simply had no reason to concern himself with these states, and both he and Republican nominee Bob Dole limited their advertising and public appearances in those states during the final months of the campaign (as did Gore and Bush in 2000). However, if candidate Clinton had an interest in winning congressional districts he would have needed to contest New Jersey District 5 and New York District 1, which were very much up for grabs. To do so, he would have entered a media market that would carry his message into not just those two districts, but thirty-eight other districts in the tristate area that receive New York City television broadcasts.

The implications of Electoral College reform for the distribution of power between state and national government are less clear. The district plan (like the proportional allocation plan) would still involve aggregating votes at the subnational levels and presumably leave unchanged the incentives that candidates have to balance national interests and orientations with state and local ones. Still, the district plan might bind the president and state governments closer together because presidential candidates would acquire an active interest in the redistricting process. Since congressional districts would comprise the primary unit of the president's electoral future, presidential candidates would take a greater interest in the composition of state legislatures who carve up the maps defining these districts and who provide partisan advantages and disadvantages in the process.

In summary, congressional districts as a base of the Electoral College would award electors to supporters of those candidates who dominate particular areas of a state but are outnumbered throughout the state. For example, in the Eighteenth District of Texas, the Democratic nominee receives about three times as many votes as the Republican; the district plan would meaningfully reward Democratic voters rather than having their preferences being completely overridden by state sentiment that favors Republicans. Since congressional districts are by definition entities that exist within states, this change is by no means a threat to federalism. Hamilton hoped the electoral college system would produce a president with a "diffusive sympathy with the whole society."[29] Surely this is better produced when presidential candidates must concern themselves not just with the limited number of competitive states but also with districts in virtually every state of the union. Rather than being a radical attack on the Electoral College, the district plan is really a step toward the original design and intent of the constitutional framers.

Proportional Allocation

The proportional allocation plan could also improve the functioning of the Electoral College without abolishing it. Unlike the district plan, this system would not create an extra federal layer for purposes of presidential elections, but it would further the federal principle of encouraging candidates to seek support in all states and throughout each state. Candidates could never assume a safe state (or district) and would have incentives to respond to the interests of various minorities throughout the states whose support could win them extra electors.

One possible advantage of proportional allocation over district allocation is that the presidential election process would not be affected by how state politicians carved up districts. While this would reduce the concern of presidential candidates with the composition of state legislatures, it might be desirable to avoid increasing the partisan stakes in the redistricting process.

Proportional allocation might be less effective than the district plan at energizing the national parties to become more active within congressional districts. But this reform might improve the party system by enhancing the role of the weaker (or minority) party within one-party-dominant states and by enhancing the role of third parties in all states. Such parties currently have few incentives to be very active in states where they have little opportunity to win under the unit rule, but closing the gap in their vote totals and those of the dominant party (or parties) would be rewarded under proportional allocation. Whether or not such outcomes would be consistent or inconsistent with a revised federalist principle depends on the interpretation of that principle. At first glance, the present unit rule would seem to enhance the attainment of a broad consensus because it discourages opposition to the dominant party, producing supramajorities for the dominant party. But it is questionable whether this is the sort of consensus that is sought by the federalist principle. Proportional allocation could energize minority parties and represent minority interests in a manner that forces dominant parties within states to be more accommodating of such interests. Dominant parties within states could no longer remain content knowing that they could capture all of the state's electors simply by defeating the minority parties. To attain as many electors as possible, they would have incentives to capture as many votes as possible and thus they would have incentives to become more inclusive of the diverse interests within the states.

If the federalist principle is interpreted to mean enhancing the inclusiveness of the electoral process, then reforms that enhance voter turnout — bringing into the electorate those citizens who feel inefficacious given the lack of party competition and the unit rule — would also seem consistent with that principle. Proportional allocation should make minority and third parties more active and influential within states, and this could well enhance voter participation, particularly among voters who feel underrepresented by the dominant party.[30]

National Popular Vote Schemes

The various popular vote schemes would, of course, require the abolition of the Electoral College and eliminate most geographical considerations from the selection process — as votes would no longer be aggregated at the state level. The participants in this chapter agree that a significant virtue of popular vote systems is that they would have the greatest potential for placing "full and equal value" on voters in every state.

If popular elections were used, small states would lose their formal over-representation currently provided in the electoral college system. Since the voting power of citizens would be equal regardless of where one resided, the greater voting power of citizens in large competitive states would also be lost. However, the structure of media markets would still likely make populous states more important simply because voters in those states would be easier to reach. It is also unclear whether candidates would deemphasize large competitive states under popular vote systems because these would remain the places where most votes reside. But under popular voting methods, campaigns may increasingly focus on noncompetitive populous states because large winning margins in these states could be decisive in the national aggregate vote totals.

One potential effect of a popular vote election (under both plurality or majority rules) as well as the national bonus plan (which could well be a de facto national popular vote system) might be that presidents would be more likely to pursue a truly "national" interest, without focusing on the particularized concerns of states. Under this system, presidents, regardless of their ideological orientations, might also be likely to pursue policies that enhance or enlarge the scope and power of the federal government. Whether this would be good or bad depends on one's perspective on states' rights. National popular elections that lead to diminished state autonomy may be bad if it leads to more national policies and regulations that are insensitive to local needs and values and that deny states the opportunity to be laboratories of innovation and experimentation. But national popular elections that enhance national power may be desirable for solving national problems and for establishing laws and regulations that states often avoid for fear of losing out in competition with other states for wealth and capital.[31]

Because some research suggests that the votes of U.S. senators are closely linked to presidential performance rather than to state economic conditions, a popular vote system may serve to further distance senators from state-specific interests.[32] Thus, abolition of the Electoral College could lead to a lesser concern for the interests of particular states throughout national government.

In addition, any type of popular vote system would likely require national rather than state and local control over who votes and how people vote. Without national standards, there would be a race among the states to expand their electorates to have a greater influence on the national election results. National popular elections would also likely require standardized vote-casting and counting systems to ensure that all votes count the same throughout the country.[33]

The implications for the federalist principle of adopting a national popular voting scheme are not as clear as claimed by defenders of the Electoral College. Direct popular elections are indifferent to where votes come from and campaigns would only be concerned with maximizing vote totals. Therefore, these particular changes might hamper the realization of federalist principles and make governance little more than a matter of simple "majority rule" principles — clearly not what the framers intended. But, we have already pointed out that federalist principles have previously been diluted through the creation of a two-party system, among other factors. It is not clear that the current electoral college system does much to promote a broader political consensus than a thin majority or that campaigns are very much concerned with ensuring that their governing coalitions reach out and accommodate the interests of citizens in all states. Some research suggests that some minority groups do very poorly under the current arrangement.[34] Certainly, presidential campaigns of the past have written off large sections of the country because they thought their best strategy was to focus on particular states having the requisite votes to win the election.

However, it is not clear that national popular voting schemes would lead campaigns and presidents to be more accommodating of other (racial, ethnic, etc.) minorities than does the current system. Perhaps the most promising reform in this respect is the instant runoff. Advocates of this electoral system claim that it would facilitate the mobilization of various minority interests around third party candidates, increasing their involvement and importance in the political process.[35] And the "transferable vote" aspect of this system would encourage the candidates of each major party to accommodate the interests of third-party voters in hopes that these voters would list them as their second choice and thus contribute to their ultimate victory as the votes are retabulated after the elimination of third-party candidates.

It might well be good for democracy if the instant runoff produced such accommodation of minority interests, but this effect is only loosely linked to furthering the federalist principle, and may even go against state-centered interests. However, it would involve reconceptualizing the federalist principle to mean maximizing political support across various minority interests rather than across the various states.

FINAL THOUGHTS

The discussion above outlines some of the key issues involved in maintaining or reforming the current presidential election system. We have engaged in this discussion with minimal regard to what options might be politically feasible, but the reader should be aware that total abolition of the Electoral College seems highly unlikely. Given this constraint, what reforms are likely to be adopted?

Most likely any reforms will occur through changes in state rules regarding the allocation of electoral votes. However, because such reforms would benefit minority or third parties, and because such parties have little influence in state legislatures, most states are unlikely to pursue reform. Although some members of our group marginally support Electoral College reforms that could be initiated by states — particularly district level selection of electors in the Electoral College votes — we expect there is little support in most states for such reform.

It seems likely that any changes to the current system will change how federalism operates in American politics. Preferences for various reforms seem to depend, to some extent, on normative support or opposition for federalist principles, and as such, there is no clear direction for reform. And although we have noted that evolution of the electoral college system has already warped some of the framer's federalist intentions, modern reforms should be aware of the antifederalist impacts of the reforms we have outlined here.

Finally, this discussion raises many broader questions concerning representation and bias in a democracy. Many of the problems associated with the 2000 presidential election — and with American politics generally — are due to factors other than the Electoral College and would not be overcome by adopting alternative electoral systems. Some of the bias in our system of government, including the Electoral College, results from a desire to balance diffuse interests. If we truly want to reconsider the structure of our system to ensure fairness in elections and the policymaking process, we should also explore reforms of our legislative system, especially the heavily biased nature of the U.S. Senate (toward small states) and the rigidity of a bicameral legislature that is elected separately from the executive. Furthermore, we have alluded to the problematic nature of individual votes having more weight in some states versus others. It seems to us that this problem is compounded by the fact that voters in some states may have less certainty that they can reasonably reach a polling station and that their votes will be accurately counted. Reformers might find it more fruitful to pursue policies that would truly ensure the "one person one vote" principle that should be protected under the equal protection clause of the Fourteenth Amendment to the Constitution. Such reforms might include national vote-counting standards and conditions for recounts, among others. However, as with any reform of the Electoral College, these types of reforms would have significant implications for federalism and especially for the distribution of power between national and subnational governments.

NOTES

1. Forrest McDonald, *States' Rights and the Union* (Lawrence: University Press of Kansas, 2000).
2. Interestingly, the idea for using an electoral college approach was not well received when first proposed by Alexander Hamilton early in the convention proceedings. On 18 June 1787 he proposed a strong executive to be elected for life by electors selected by voters in election districts. The proposal was neither discussed nor voted upon. At that point, more attention was paid to proposals that would have the president elected by the legislature. Presidential selection did not come up again for another month as delegates turned to matters related to Congress. In mid-July, questions were raised about congressional selection of the president and there was heated discussion of a popular election proposal that was voted down. At that point, an electoral college process (with electors selected by state legislators) was proposed and debated. While nothing definite resulted from that extended discussion, the principle of having the president elected through some form of electoral college mechanism seemed to gain some acceptance. Nevertheless, selection by the legislature remained the accepted motion to that point. It wasn't until the final days of deliberations in early September that Pierce Butler of South Carolina put forward an elaborate electoral college scheme that provided the basis for the institution that eventually emerged in the proposed Constitution. For an interesting overview of discussions among the framers about electing the president, see Forrest McDonald, *The American Presidency: An Intellectual History* (Lawrence: University of Kansas Press, 1994), chapter 7.
3. The framers mentioned a few interesting points in this regard. In *Federalist Papers,* No. 50, James Madison suggested that if popular elections were used to choose the president, "The executive power might be in the hands of a peculiar favorite of the people." In *Federalist Papers,* No. 64, John Jay suggests that average voters would be "liable to be deceived by those brilliant appearances of genius and patriotism which, like transient meteors, sometimes mislead as well as dazzle."
4. Thus the studies showing the inequality of voting power among individuals across the states are irrelevant from the perspective of the founders. For a review of studies on the relative influence of voters see Lawrence D. Longley and Neal R. Peirce, *The Electoral College Primer, 2000* (New Haven: Yale University Press, 1999).
5. *Federalist Papers,* No. 39.
6. Created relatively late at the Constitutional Convention, the Electoral College reflected previous federalist compromises (e.g., the representation schemes of the Great Compromise, a constitutional role for state legislatures). If the Electoral College is part and parcel of the overall constitutional design, this has important implications for reforms — especially those direct election proposals that would eliminate the state-centered features of the College. The key issue in Electoral College reform may be whether reforms effect the very foundation of our constitutional design, not whether they further democracy.
7. Sidney Milkis and Michael Nelson, *The American Presidency: Origins and Development, 1776–1998,* 3d ed. (Washington, D.C.: CQ Press, 1999), 119.
8. Ibid., 119.
9. *Federalist Papers,* No. 39.

10. Testimony of Judith A. Best before the House of Representatives Committee on the Judiciary, Subcommittee on the Constitution hearings on "Proposals for Electoral College Reform: H. J. Res. 28 and H. J. Res. 43," 4 September 1997.

11. In the figure and table, the values attained from these procedures here have been multiplied by 100 to yield a percentage.

12. John Mark Hansen, "How Federalism Put W. in the White House," unpublished paper, Department of Political Science, University of Chicago.

13. See Longley and Peirce, *Electoral College Primer 2000*, 150–53. Also see James C. Garand and T. Wayne Parent, "Representation, Swing, and Bias in U.S. Presidential Elections, 1872–1988," *American Journal of Political Science* 35 (October 1991): 1011–31; George Rabinowitz and Stuart Elaine MacDonald. "The Power of the States in U.S. Presidential Elections," *American Political Science Review* 80 (March 1986): 65–87; Seymour Spilerman and David Dickens, "Who Will Gain and Who Will Lose Influence under Different Electoral Rules," *American Journal of Sociology* 80 (June 1974): 443–77.

14. Marc Sandalow, "Now the Hard Part: Candidates Hit Swing States for Key Votes," *San Francisco Chronicle*, 19 October 2000, A1.

15. Robert Vickers, "Feeling Taken for Granted by Gore: Some Blacks Object to Suburban Focus," *Cleveland Plain Dealer*, 3 November 2000, 1B.

16. Timm Herdt, "Casting Less than Half a Vote: In the Electoral College it takes 2.7 of us to Equal 1 in Wyoming," *Ventura County Star*, 29 November 2000, A16.

17. After all, candidates win the same number of electoral votes in a state regardless of how many of its citizens actually vote, whereas candidates that turn out more supporters in a state would be rewarded under a popular vote system.

18. To be sure, the levels of voter turnout across states — like the competitiveness of elections within states — vary from election to election. Thus, generalizations about which particular states are advantaged by how the Electoral College rewards competition- and low-voter-turnout states are less convincing than the general assertion that the power of states is influenced by such factors.

19. Metrick, Gene, "North Carolina Man was in the National Spotlight as an Elector in 1968," *Rocky Mountain Telegram*, 13 December 2000, A1.

20. John Jay, *Federalist Papers*, No. 64.

21. Hamilton, *Federalist Papers*, No. 68.

22. The original Electoral College design was also intended to reduce corruption and produce stability. But as state elections became the means by which electors were chosen, a national election day was eventually needed to prevent states from attempting to manipulate the process by voting late and holding the nation's highest office hostage to their peculiar schedule. Of course, through the vehicle of contests and recounts, we saw that exact nightmare return in 2000. The nation, the vote counters of Florida, and the electors of Florida knew that its votes were enough to decide the election. Indeed, far from being free from tumult and disorder, the 2000 election in Florida was defined by tumult and disorder. Moreover, Florida's electors were subject to media and political pressures to consider their actions and reveal their intentions regarding their Electoral College vote. Hamilton boasted that even opponents of the proposed Constitution will "admit that the election of President is pretty well guarded." Surely he did not intend those guards to be replaced by the whims of voters in a few competitive states.

23. Judith A. Best, *The Choice of the People* ? (Lanham, Md.: Rowman & Littlefield, 1996), 36.

24. However, there is still evidence that states remain different from one another along multiple dimensions, including their views of the role of government and the issues government ought to address. See, for example, Robert Putnam, *Bowling Alone* (Cambridge, Mass.: Harvard University Press, 2000).

25. However, large states may be disadvantaged by these plans because abolishing the winner-take-all feature of the current system would decrease the voting power of citizens in these states and reduce the importance of these states in the campaign. One exception to this change might be the structure of local media markets. If media markets still tend to favor large states, with significant overlap across districts, the power of individual voters might not be diluted.

26. *Federalist Papers*, No. 39.
27. "2000 National Election Report," issued by Polidata Demographic and Political Guides (available at www.polidata.org/prcd/default.htm).
28. William Riker, *Federalism: Origin, Operation, Significance* (Boston: Little, Brown, 1964).
29. *The Federalist Papers*, No. 59.
30. Another way that the Electoral College could be reformed to encourage voter turnout is to allocate electors to states on the basis of the number of voters in the previous two or three elections, rather than on the basis of census counts of the population. This would reward states with more vibrant civil societies and create strong incentives for both political parties in a given state to support policies and practices likely to increase voter participation.
31. See McDonald, *States' Rights and the Union,* for a full discussion of these issues.
32. Lonna Rae Atkeson and Randall W. Partin, "Economic and Referendum Voting: A Comparison of Gubernatorial and Senatorial Elections," *American Political Science Review* 89 (March 1995): 99–107.
33. One could also make an argument for federalizing all elections now to ensure that all votes count the same.
34. See Spilerman and Dickens. "Who Will Gain and Who Will Lose Influence," 443–77.
35. One might see the negative consequences of such a system if it had been in place in the 1950s and 1960s as the South put forth relatively strong regional candidates.

CHAPTER 5

Electoral College Reform, the Presidency, and Congress

Burdett A. Loomis, *University of Kansas*
Jeffrey Cohen, *Fordham University*
Bruce I. Oppenheimer, *Vanderbilt University*
James P. Pfiffner, *George Mason University*

> *At its best, the Electoral College operates in an inherently distorted manner in transforming popular votes into electoral votes [and] has enormous potential to be a dangerous institution threatening... the legitimacy of our presidents.*
>
> —*Lawrence Longley and Neal Peirce,*
> The Electoral College Primer 2000

IN THE END, winning an election, especially a presidential election, means that one can engage in the legitimate use of power. As this project unfolded, we kept returning to the idea that, for governing institutions, the most important goal of the electoral system is to produce a clear and legitimate winner. In examining the range of alternatives, we kept asking the basic question: What would this system do to affect the legitimacy of the president? And the issues surrounding legitimacy led us directly to consider, first, the president's capacity to govern effectively and, second, how a range of electoral systems would shape the impacts of parties and interest groups on governing institutions. From these perspectives, the status quo of the Electoral College remains acceptable, though it has its flaws both in terms of procedural clarity and legitimacy of outcomes. Overall, however, we come to the conclusion that a popular-plurality vote system without any runoff would offer the best possibility of offering up a clear and legitimate winner.

Although much of our analysis must be speculative, our conclusions are based on what we know about the president and Congress. Moreover, we have the modest advantage of observing the first few months of the George W. Bush administration. In many ways, Bush's actions provide real-life tests for generaliza-

Table 5.1   Confidence in National Institutions, 1998–2001

"As far as people in charge of running _____ are concerned, would you say you have a great deal of confidence, only some confidence, or hardly any confidence at all in them?"

	A Great Deal of Confidence (in percentages)			
	January 2001	January 2000	January 1999	January 1998
U.S. Supreme Court	35	34	37	37
The White House	21	21	22	20
Congress	18	15	12	12

Source: Harris poll, various dates, from PollingReport.com

tions about legitimacy in the wake of an election that tested our electoral system more than any contest in almost 125 years. We find it instructive that President Bush has placed a number of major issues on the governmental agenda, even as he faces an evenly divided Congress. Tax cuts, missile defense, energy policy, education, and Social Security reform, among other issues, have received serious congressional consideration in the months following his inauguration.

This chapter will first examine how the Electoral College and its alternatives might maintain or even strengthen the legitimacy of national institutions in an era when they have been seriously questioned. The analysis will then turn to further implications for how the president and Congress would most likely operate under different electoral systems.

LEGITIMACY AND THE PRESIDENT

Although the electorate has rated individual presidents relatively highly in recent decades, the presidency — like most other governmental institutions — receives less popular support than do the presidents themselves. For example, Bill Clinton's job approval ratings remained in the 60 percent range during the 1998–2000 period that followed his impeachment episode. And despite his narrow, contested victory, George W. Bush raised his job approval ratings to about 60 percent in April 2001. Still, as shown in table 5.1, support for the presidency and Congress as governing institutions has been much weaker in the recent past. Although these polling data collected over the past four years demonstrate that only about one American in five has much confidence in the presidency, they also show that the 2000 election has not further reduced public support for the presidency or for the Supreme Court or for Congress. As the 2000 election recedes into history, its contested nature does not appear to have further reduced public support for national institutions.

More important, perhaps, is the overall trend toward increasing cynicism within the public. In assessing their overall relationship with government, "trusting" citizens in 1965 outnumbered their "cynical" counterparts by a 52 percent margin. Ten years later, the "cynical" outnumbered the "trusting" by 30 percent, and this margin had grown to 40 percent by the mid-1990s.[1]

Moreover, the two most recent presidents have faced serious, specific challenges to their legitimacy. Both Bill Clinton and George W. Bush have been confronted with substantial numbers of citizens who have viewed their presidencies as illegitimate, based either on personal conduct (Clinton) or electoral circumstances (Bush). Such assessments have followed partisan lines, but their depth and negativity have far surpassed normal partisanship.

Taken together, these findings suggest a troubling decline in the legitimacy of the presidency. In that most other national institutions have also lost support among the public at large, this trend may reflect a deeper, more profound loss of social capital and distrust of national institutions. Nevertheless, the loss of generalized support for the president and Congress remains our major basis for concern in evaluating the Electoral College and alternative electoral systems.

LEGITIMACY AND ELECTIONS

All reasonably fair electoral systems *can* convey legitimacy. In a sense, that is their main function: to confer legitimacy upon the candidate or party that wins by the rules of the game. Looking at other nations in the post–World War II era, we can see a wide range of systems that accomplish precisely such a result; the number of such democratic nations and the variety of systems are growing, albeit unevenly. At the same time, no system is immune from challenges to legitimacy, especially when elections are close. At one level, such challenges may be literally academic, as scholars demonstrate how different systems would produce different results from the same set of preferences held by the public.[2] More profound challenges come when elites question election results within an institutional context, as when many Republican representatives began to label the Democrats' continuing control of the U.S. House as "corrupt."

Indeed, one benchmark in Republicans' questioning of the House Democrats' legitimacy came in 1984–85, when the Democratic majority voted to seat incumbent Representative Frank McCloskey (D-Ind.), whose race in Indiana's Eighth District was decided by a handful of votes and whose opponent's victory had been certified by the Indiana board of elections.[3] In the wake of this partisan episode and subsequent majority rulings on procedures, House Republicans led by Representative Newt Gingrich (R-Ga.) increasingly came to label the House under Democratic rule as "corrupt" and to question the legitimacy of the institution. In a sense, this constituted a tactical move, but such an expression of illegitimacy both undercut the elected majority's capacity to govern and changed the nature of subsequent elections, when partisan attacks were combined with those on the institution as a whole. In 1994, of course, this set of tactics worked to propel Gingrich and his fellow House Republicans into majority status.

Likewise, the Supreme Court faced questions of its own legitimacy when it ruled, in effect, to stop the Florida recount in *Bush v. Gore*. The four dissenting justices argued strongly that the Court's interjection into the controversy risked its generally high level of public support, which depends almost completely on maintaining an unchallenged sense of legitimacy. As Alexander Hamilton observed in the *Federalist Papers,* the Supreme Court's only power derives from its judgment.[4] To the extent that this judgment is questioned, as in *Bush v. Gore,* the Court's legitimacy is bound to suffer.

Although presidents such as Andrew Johnson, Richard Nixon, and Bill Clinton have placed their own legitimacy at risk through their actions in the White House, the greatest risk to presidential legitimacy comes at the ballot box. Members of Congress win their seats in 535 separate races, with only the occasional challenged result. Supreme Court justices go through the confirmation process, which assures them of legitimacy, even when the proceedings are contentious. But presidents must rely on a single (if compound) electoral process to win legitimacy. Any ambiguity or perceived unfairness will diminish both the office and its incumbent.

In our judgment, presidential legitimacy is best protected by electing the chief executive in a national popular election using a popular-plurality system (our first choice) or by the Electoral College as it currently stands. The former system offers the advantages of directly connecting the individual citizen to the nation's highest office. Indeed, the legitimacy of the popular election of the president is buttressed by the probability that many, if not most, citizens who now go to the polls think that they are voting for president, not a slate of electors. Some state ballots specify that the presidential vote is for a slate of electors, but many do not.[5] The election of 2000 may have provided a national civics lesson on the Electoral College, but any number of voters remain convinced that they do cast their ballots directly for a presidential candidate.

More important is the real challenge to legitimacy presented by the 2000 elections. Although all surveys taken in the wake of the Supreme Court decision found that substantial majorities of the public considered George W. Bush the legitimate president, in at least one poll a majority of Democratic voters (56 percent) refused to make such a concession, albeit in the immediate aftermath of *Bush v. Gore.*[6] African Americans have proven especially unwilling to regard George W. Bush as the legitimate winner. In addition, by mid-December 2000, when the Court announced its decision, a majority of the voting public had concluded that a structural problem existed in our election system. Fifty-five percent of the public concluded that "this situation reveals serious problems in the country's system of electing the president," up from 32 percent a month earlier.[7] In addition, we strongly suspect that many Republicans would have seriously questioned the legitimacy of a Gore presidency that was decided by a Florida recount.

Not only does the public harbor suspicions about the electoral system, but minority-party voters in such one-party states as Kansas, Mississippi, or Massachusetts are also systematically rendered irrelevant in the current state-by-state winner-take-all rules. Citizens in many states thus get little sense of how the presidential campaign is being conducted. A voter in Wichita or Hattiesburg or Worcester, to the extent that she relied on local coverage and local advertisements, would have been simply unaware that a presidential election was underway during most of the 2000 campaign. More broadly, as former Representative (and former Clinton White House Counsel) Abner Mikva put it, "There is only one system that treats all Americans equally. That system is direct election."[8]

The plurality direct election option might have one further salutary effect on legitimacy. Such a system would likely have a positive impact on turnout, especially in those states that are not currently competitive. Utah Democrats, for example, would have more motivation to go to the polls, secure in the knowledge that their votes would contribute to a national total, even if they were sure to be outnumbered by Utah Republicans. Moreover, in presidential years this could affect congressional elections as well, given that overall turnout would be greater. There might be a bit more of a national component in determining legislative election outcomes, which would offer the possibility of stronger presidential coattails. Such reasoning also applies to Senate elections.

On the whole, we preferred the plurality system to the majoritarian models with their runoff provisions. Although these systems have worked adequately in other nations, our preference was for procedures that buttressed the two-party system, which would be weakened by requiring that the winner receive a majority, most likely in a runoff election. In addition, the possibility that different procedures might produce different outcomes could become a serious problem. For example, suppose the system provided for a runoff (either delayed or instant). How would the public react if, in a three-candidate field, A received 47 percent of the vote, B received 40 percent, and C 13 percent, while in the runoff contest, B defeated A by a 51–49 percent margin? Candidate A's supporters could certainly raise legitimacy concerns.

At the same time, we did see some real merit in the president receiving a majority of the votes; this in itself might well enhance legitimacy. And runoff elections are frequently used to select governors and senators, especially in the South. In such instances, the final-round winners who come from behind generally have little trouble with being viewed as legitimate.

Thus, there was some sentiment for an instant-runoff system, in that it would not require an extended campaign that might well end up with a smaller turnout for the runoff than for the initial balloting. Getting a winner early in the process was seen as having some advantages. Nevertheless, the instant-runoff system would encourage third parties to contest presidential elections more vigorously. Although the existence of single-member districts with a plurality rule would still promote the two-party system in congressional elections, we worry that a runoff procedure would encourage party fragmentation. In the end, adopting a system that would encourage a third-party candidate to exercise disproportionate power over the election of the president runs against the tide of most American practices.

The district and proportional allocation systems both generate serious issues of legitimacy. Apportioning electors by congressional districts within each state appears to increase the chance that the winner of the electoral vote will not receive the most popular votes; in 2000, for example, Bush's electoral vote total would have increased, in that many Gore votes were packed into highly Democratic districts. Preliminary estimates place the outcome of a district plan at a 288–250 victory for Bush in the Electoral College — further stretching the legitimacy problems for a "winner" who lost the popular contest by more than a half-million votes. In addition, the 1960 and 1976 elections would have produced different results.[9] In 1960, Kennedy's 303–219 margin would have become a 280–252 Nixon advantage.[10] In 1976, Carter and Ford would have tied, based on a congressional district apportionment of electoral votes. Overall, veteran political analyst Rhodes Cook concludes that Republicans currently are somewhat advantaged in close elections, and the average difference between the current system and congressional district system reflects a net change of forty-three electors — clearly enough to shift the results of a competitive election.[11]

As for proportional allocation, we found many of the same problems that plague the runoff system. That is, with relative frequency no majority winner would emerge from the Electoral College. This is especially true if fractional electoral votes are awarded. But even when a third-party candidate must win enough popular votes to capture a full elector in a given state, the elections of 1960, 1968, 1992, 1996, and 2000 would have produced no clear Electoral College winner. Although candidates would certainly campaign differently, with different strategies and tactics, under a proportional representation or runoff format, it remains true that these systems appear more inclined to encourage deadlock than the Electoral College or popular vote schemes.

In the end, we emphasize legitimacy for two distinct, if related, reasons. First, legitimacy is important in and of itself. That is, a legitimate presidential election is part and parcel of a stable political community; such a community enjoys a generous supply of political and social capital that comes from its perceived inclusion within a "prosperous political system."[12] This is especially important for the American president, who must act in the symbolically crucial role of head of state as well as being the chief executive of the government. Second, legitimacy has an instrumental purpose, whether in a fledgling democracy or in the well-established but unwieldy checks-and-balances system of the United States. Legitimacy helps presidents to govern, especially as they work with other institutions to solve collective problems.

American institutions, by design, have never been models of efficiency in addressing and solving national problems. Quite the reverse. Both the internal workings of institutions and the relationships between them create obstacles to effective and efficient political action. The governmental system thus needs to have as much support as it can muster. Political scientists John Hibbing and Elizabeth Theiss-Morse argue that the public holds Congress in low esteem in large part because of its complex rules and arcane traditions.[13] Likewise, the advantages of the Electoral College's past performance are offset by its complexity and potential for producing a winner who has received a smaller number of votes than his opponent. Given the checks and balances that all presidents face, a system that erodes legitimacy adds one more formidable obstacle to the exercise of effective executive leadership within the governing process.

LEGITIMACY AND GOVERNING

No matter how important it is for both presidents and political theorists that the chief executive's election be regarded as legitimate, the main value of legitimacy does not derive from merely possessing it. For legitimacy to have much worth beyond keeping rioting crowds off the streets, presidents must build upon this form of political capital in order to govern as effectively as possible.

The public's reaction to the 2000 election and the Court's *Bush v. Gore* ruling demonstrates how legitimacy relates both to a popular vote option and the current electoral college system. In the wake of the most convoluted electoral process in 125 years, the public expressed both its frustration with the Electoral College and its ultimate support. In one survey more than 60 percent of those sampled supported "changing to a system in which the president is elected by direct popular vote, instead of by the Electoral College."[14] Only one respondent in three backed the Electoral College. Nevertheless, despite their qualms about the Electoral College, citizens generally thought that George W. Bush would be able to govern effectively (62 percent) and to "accomplish most of the goals he laid out in his campaign."[15]

The public concluded that the Electoral College did not represent the best way to elect a president, which raises some questions about Bush's legitimacy. At the same time, the electorate thought that Bush, a minority president emerging from a close, flawed election, could govern effectively on the agenda he had set during the campaign. Thus, the current electoral system, even in the worst of circumstances, retains enough legitimacy to allow a president a reasonable chance to govern.

Still, elections can grant presidents only so much authority. None of the electoral systems seem capable of regularly producing an actual mandate that would assist a president in passing an extensive policy agenda. The realities of governing are anchored within the separation-of-powers system that includes, besides the presidency, one institution (the House) selected on a one-person, one-vote basis, one extremely malapportioned institution (the Senate), and one branch (Supreme Court) consisting of nine lifetime appointees. Only the most sweeping of electoral triumphs (e.g., 1964) can move a complete presidential agenda, and for just a limited period of time.[16]

We rejected the idea that any of the electoral systems would offer presidents a meaningful mandate. More important was the idea that a chief executive be regarded as legitimate by the electorate. Indeed, enjoying a partisan or ideologically compatible working majority in Congress accounts for most of a president's legislative success. For the most part, the extent to which an electoral system helps or hinders the president from coming to office with a working majority in Congress will have the greatest impact on presidential-legislative relations. In this sense, the popular-plurality and electoral college schemes may offer the most hope (however modest) for producing a broad partisan coalition that could assist in governing. Majority popular vote systems would seem to do much the same, but second-round elections may well create implicit coalitions among parties that would reduce a president's own leeway in pursuing an agenda.

ELECTIONS, PARTIES, AND GOVERNING

Underlying much of our thinking on legitimacy and its implications for governing lies a mostly unstated but clear preference for a two-party system in the United States. Although political parties have never been "strong" here (in the centralized, disciplined mode), they have provided the means to address, if not overcome, the built-in fragmentation of the institutional checks and balances of the American political system. To the extent this is so, the Electoral College and its alternatives need to be examined in terms of how they affect political parties as linking mechanisms.

In part, we find the direct election by a plurality the best alternative and the current Electoral College an acceptable choice because these procedures both tend to lead to two dominant parties, given their winner-take-all characteristics. Despite a recent history of divided government, the two-party system increases the likelihood that a single party will control both the presidency and Congress. Indeed, electing the president by a popular vote with a plurality rule might well create additional presidential "coattails" in some legislative races. This could help address the fragmentation that defines the American political system. Overall, we find the preelection coalition-building characteristics of American parties to be important elements in linking voters to elected officials as well as connecting elected officials, one to another. In particular, we see the runoff alternatives as allowing voters to make a cost-free initial vote that may (or may not) reflect a sincere preference but which will increase party fragmentation. In addition, a third (and a fourth) party has a great incentive in a runoff system to hold the margin below 50 percent; it can lay claim to delivering the winning margin to the ultimate victor and thus exercise influence disproportionate to its size within the electorate.

The impact of the proportional allocation schemes on parties likewise weighs against their adoption, in that such procedures would likely lead to an increased likelihood of deadlock in the Electoral College (see above). Given the narrow margin in 2000, even a few proportionally allocated Nader votes would have created an Electoral College stalemate. Moreover, the proportional allocation framework might well encourage third parties to engage in bargaining that placed their electors up for grabs; state laws on faithless electors notwithstanding, third parties could negotiate with one or both of the major parties to form a de facto coalition government. Conversely, requiring electors to follow through on their pledges would mean that presidential elections would regularly be thrown into the House of Representatives. Given our successful track record over the past 200 years, even James Madison, who feared parties but was a pragmatic politician, would be less than pleased with such a result.

Finally, the results of presidential elections under proportional (or runoff) procedures would place increased strain on relations between the executive and legislative branches. Given the winner-take-all rules for congressional elections, the likelihood of a third party gaining many (even any) legislative seats would remain slim. But such parties might well have played major roles in determining who was chosen to be president. As instruments for governing, the major parties would almost certainly be weakened.

ELECTIONS, ORGANIZED INTERESTS, AND GOVERNING: AN "INTEREST-GROUP PRESIDENCY?"

In contrast to members of Congress (especially the House), whose relatively homogeneous districts lead them to be highly dependent on a few major local interests, presidents have more room to maneuver in balancing the appeals of many large organized interests. To a considerable extent an "interest-group Congress" already exists, given its highly permeable, highly representative nature.[17] Likewise, the presidency has become increasingly attentive to specific interests and population groupings.[18] We see any further evolution of the executive branch into an "interest-group presidency" as working against policymaking that addresses some overall sense of national well-being.

Currently, the race for the presidency intersects with organized interests in two crucial ways. First, presidential campaigns have grown more and more dependent on large "soft money" contributions from interest groups. Although reform legislation could change this by 2004, the soft money connection is presently a major feature of presidential election politics. Second, the strategies of running presidential campaigns require that major organized interests in a relatively small number of swing states become disproportionately significant. For example, labor unions in Michigan (and other industrialized Midwest states) and Cuban Americans in Florida exercise influence far beyond their numbers because they represent pivotal groups in large, highly competitive states. The Electoral College places great emphasis on such groups, while downplaying the importance of organizations that ally with weaker parties in noncompetitive states (e.g., the Chamber of Commerce in Massachusetts or farmers in upstate New York).

Changing the format of presidential elections would alter, perhaps dramatically, the ways in which organized interests participate in these contests. Given a plurality system, candidates would still campaign disproportionately in given regions, but they would need to mount far more serious national efforts. Organized interests might well react in a couple ways. First, large membership groups would likely increase their efforts to get their members to the polls. National Rifle Association members in safe Republican states such as Montana and Mississippi would be just as valuable to turn out as those in Michigan or Pennsylvania. Indeed, such "get out the vote" (GOTV) initiatives are extremely well suited to large membership groups, from the Sierra Club to the Christian Coalition. At the same time, these national tactics would generally complement the work done by parties and might lead toward less fragmentation than recent independent advocacy efforts of groups in a limited number of states.[19]

Second, organized interests that lack large memberships might well adopt a national advertising strategy, much as the pharmaceutical industry did in the 2000 election.[20] Such national campaigns are very expensive, and even well-heeled interests might decide to "invest" their funds in key House and (especially) Senate races. This is one area in which the proposed banning of soft money might make substantial differences in both conducting campaigns and attempting to govern. If parties cannot solicit such funds to pay for television advertising, they may, with a wink and a nod, encourage organized interests to purchase national ads on their own. While complying with the parties' desires, these groups could easily frame issues in ways that differ from the emphases of either the parties or their candidates. In such a situation, they might well move campaign rhetoric in directions to which the candidates would object. Likewise, groups could act to further their own interests and to enhance their own influence with a would-be president, even if that were not in the president's interest, once he had won the election. For example, Bill Clinton's support from (and promises to) gay rights groups may not have enhanced his capacity to govern, especially early in his term of office.

As for the other electoral options, the behavior of organized interests would probably change least if the district allocation plan were adopted. That is, interest groups already concentrate their resources in highly competitive statewide races (whether in backing Senate candidates or seeking electoral votes) and close House seats. Under a district plan, calculating how to distribute their resources might be difficult, but it would be a familiar problem to party leaders who already coordinate the spending of hundreds of millions of dollars in dozens of media markets. In this sense, the district plan would differ little from elements of our current electoral system that encourage the development of an "interest group presidency."

The runoff options would present organized interests with new puzzles to solve. A two-stage procedure might well lead groups to husband their resources until the second round, especially if it were clear that no candidate would likely win a first-round majority. Moreover, much spending in a second round might be directed at increasing turnout, in that voting participation generally declines at the runoff stage. Whether groups' tactics would make presidents more or less beholden to interests we have no way of knowing. What would change the balance among interests would be for a third party, such as the Green Party, to identify thoroughly with a single interest (environmentalists). Such a situation might well allow the interest to make a reasonable claim that it was responsible for the president's ultimate victory — or defeat, for that matter. This stands in contrast to the Perot phenomenon in 1992, when a strong third-party candidate drew support from across the entire political spectrum.

The instant runoff presents interests with a more complex situation, in that they must appeal to those with both strong and weak preferences. Large membership groups would probably opt for internal communication strategies, but other organizations (business, groups with few members) would need to adopt sophisticated ways to get their message across. Groups would certainly attempt to claim credit for putting the winning candidate over the top, but the immediacy of the results might well blunt those claims, even those that could be effectively documented. In addition, both runoff systems produce a majority winner, which may work against interests' claims of impact on the outcome.

ELECTING A LEGITIMATE, EFFECTIVE PRESIDENT

Although American presidents do hold "the most powerful office" in the entire world, they cannot always get what they want — or even what they need. The framers understood the potential power of the office, and placed it within a context of competing national institutions and relatively powerful states. At the same time, they knew that a chief executive must be perceived as legitimate; without that, the system of separation-of-powers could not succeed. Their desire for legitimacy was incorporated in their working assumption that George Washington would be chosen the first president and that Washington would lend his personal legitimacy to this new office. In a sense, the first run-through of the Electoral College was close to a rigged game. With Washington's ascension agreed upon, the founders gave their institutional design a little breathing room.

The Electoral College did operate as the founders had expected (see chapter 3), but it weathered some early storms (1800, 1824) as American elites struggled to invent a political party system that ordered our electoral politics. Over time, the Electoral College has consistently produced legitimate presidents; most presidential elections have added to our overall store of legitimacy. Thus, when a difficult election (such as those of 1824 or 1876 or 1888) comes along, we can draw upon our built-up account of legitimacy to help smooth the political waters. Placing Lincoln aside as a unique case, even the most vulnerable elected presidents, such as John Quincy Adams or Rutherford B. Hayes, have enjoyed adequate legitimacy. Only the unelected (as president) Andrew Johnson may have lacked enough legitimacy to govern even marginally effectively.

Despite the solid track record of the Electoral College, we still see some serious problems — actual and potential — in this system. Above all, it can and does (on occasion) name a winner who has received fewer votes than his opponent. If this were to occur more than occasionally, the public would express even more dissatisfaction with the system that it does at present. Legitimacy itself would be questioned, to say nothing of the problems encountered by such presidents when they attempt to govern.

Although we acknowledge the potential difficulties with the popular plurality election system, we are confident that American political parties, as effective adapters for more than 150 years, would continue building broad electoral coalitions in seeking to win an outright majority of the vote. Such a majority ensures victory in this system; even with third parties contesting the election, the incentives remain great to build an inclusive coalition. Moreover, that coalition would bring together many individuals who currently view their votes as wasted (i.e., Democratic voters in states that are dominated by Republicans or vice versa). Incentives for parties and groups to bring these voters to the polls might further increase support for the system — and legitimacy for the winning candidate.

As institutionalists, we are mindful of the unanticipated consequences that so-called reform might produce. Allocating electors by congressional districts would probably increase the likelihood of electing presidents who receive a minority of the two-party vote. Proportional allocation schemes would encourage third parties and allow the unrepresentative "one state, one vote" mechanism of the House to determine the winning candidate. Legitimacy would surely suffer under such circumstances.

The runoff procedures requiring a majority seem almost certain to encourage more parties, the weaker ones often holding the key to ultimate electoral victory in the second round. Instant runoffs would face the same problem, as well as leading to unforeseen consequences for both political parties and organized interests.

With legitimacy and the capacity to govern as central to the functioning of the presidency, we are willing to take the modest risk of calling for a popular plurality system. Under such a scheme, both legitimacy and governing capacity might be enhanced. Still, we acknowledge the risks of such a change and generally feel satisfied with the 210-year record of the Electoral College in our checks-and-balances system. Presidents are viewed as legitimate, and they can govern, albeit not as easily or effectively as we might desire.

NOTES

1. Harold W. Stanley and Richard G. Niemi, *Vital Statistics in American Politics, 1999–2000* (Washington, D.C.: CQ Press, 2000), 136.
2. See William Riker's *The Art of Political Manipulation* (New Haven: Yale University Press, 1986), a persuasive and charming introduction to the field.
3. For an extended discussion, see William F. Connelly Jr. and John J. Pitney Jr., *Congress Permanent Minority? Republicans in the U.S. House* (Lanham, Md.: Rowman & Littlefield, 1994), 79ff.
4. David R. Dow, "Biggest Loser Is Supreme Court's Legitimacy," *Houston Chronicle,* 14 December 2000, 47.
5. This passage is drawn from James P. Pfiffner, "Reevaluating the Electoral College," unpublished manuscript (1 January 2001), 7.
6. *Newsweek* poll, conducted by Princeton Survey Associates (14–15 December 2000). Accessed at www.pollingreport.com (11 April 2001).
7. ABC/*Washington Post* poll, 14 December 2000, accessed from www.pollingreport.com (11 April 2001).
8. Quoted in Judith Best, *The Case against the Direct Election of the President* (Ithaca, N.Y.: Cornell University Press, 1971), 125.
9. Rhodes Cook, *The Rhodes Cook Newsletter,* March 2001, 5.
10. Brian Gaines makes a strong argument that Nixon did win the popular vote, not on the basis of Illinois and Texas ballots, but on a reexamination of Alabama's results, where many votes credited to Kennedy certainly were cast for electors who would not have voted for him. See "Popular Myths About Popular Vote–Electoral College Splits," *PS* 34 (March 2001): 71–75.
11. Cook, 5; see also Nelson Polsby and Aaron Wildavsky, *Presidential Elections,* 10th ed. (New York: Chatham House, 2000), 245ff.
12. Robert Putnam, "The Prosperous Community: Social Capital and Public Life," *American Prospect* 72 (Spring 1993): 35–42
13. John Hibbing and Elizabeth Theiss-Morse, *Congress as Public Enemy* (New York: Cambridge University Press, 1995).
14. ABC/*Washington Post* poll, 14–15 December 2000 (No. 807), from *The Polling Report* (31 December 2000), 7.
15. Harris poll, 14–21 December 2001 (No. 1025), from *The Polling Report* (31 December 2000), 2.
16. See James Sundquist, *Politics and Policy* (Washington, D.C.: Brookings Institution, 1968) for the conversion of the joint congressional-presidential agenda into law in the mid-1960s.
17. Among others, see John Wright, *Interest Groups and Congress* (Boston: Allyn and Bacon, 1996), and William Browne, *Cultivating Congress* (Lawrence: University Press of Kansas, 1995)
18. James Pfiffner, *The Modern Presidency* (New York: St. Martin's, 1994), 44–45.
19. David Magleby, ed., *Election Advocacy: Soft Money and Issue Advocacy in the 2000 Congressional Elections* (Provo, Utah: Center for the Study of Elections and Democracy, Brigham Young University, www.byu.edu/outsidemoney/2000general/contents.htm).
20. Elizabeth Shogren, "Drug Firms Dig Even Deeper to Aid Campaigns," *Los Angeles Times* (27 October 2000), 26.

CHAPTER 6

Changing the Electoral College: The Impact on Parties and Organized Interests

Allan Cigler, *University of Kansas*
Joel Paddock, *Southwest Missouri State University*
Gary Reich, *University of Kansas*
Eric Uslaner, *University of Maryland*

POLITICAL PARTIES ARE at the heart of the scholarly controversy over the Electoral College. One major argument put forth by Electoral College proponents is that its rules and incentives are responsible for the maintenance of our two-party system, which is, in turn, a key factor in contributing to the long-term political stability of American democracy.[1] In this chapter we first explore the supposed linkage between Electoral College rules and the characteristics of the American party system and the normative assumptions that underlie the connection. We then consider some of the leading alternatives to the Electoral College, speculating about their potential impact on the nature of partisan politics. Finally, we explore the possible effects on the influence of various organized interests if the Electoral College were to be changed.

While we disagreed among ourselves on a variety of matters, overall we believe that there is no reliable, convincing evidence to suggest that changing the presidential election system, in and of itself, would alter significantly the party system in a predictable manner. There are simply too many other factors that reinforce our system of two-party dominance besides Electoral College rules. Although there may be good and desirable reasons to either retain or change our presidential selection process, anxiety over "destroying the two-party system" should not dominate the debate over possible reform of the Electoral College.

THE ELECTORAL COLLEGE AND THE PARTY SYSTEM —
THE CONVENTIONAL WISDOM

In the search for causal factors underlying the character of a nation's party system, electoral laws have traditionally been portrayed as playing a critical role affecting the number of parties, their organizational structure, and the intensity of partisan political conflict.[2] In the American case, both the single-member-plurality district system of selecting legislators and the Electoral College rules for selecting presidents have been credited with encouraging and maintaining a party system that is dominated by two decentralized and pragmatic parties. Some believe that the Electoral College rules, ironically designed by the founders to nominate and select a president before political parties were established, are paramount.[3] The necessity of constructing a national majority in the Electoral College vote dooms even regionally strong third parties, which at times are able to win pluralities in several states in their quest of the ultimate prize of the presidency.

The two-party bias of the Electoral College is certainly evident historically. Since the Civil War electoral votes have been won by only five third-party candidates, typically representing parties with regional strength. Ross Perot's independent candidacy in 1992 is the most recent example of the extreme difficulty candidates not representing one of the two dominant parties face in trying to accumulate any electoral votes. Despite receiving nearly 19 percent of the nationwide presidential vote, a percentage surpassed among third parties only by the Bull Moose Party in 1912, Perot did not win a plurality in any state and received no electoral votes.

We agreed that the Electoral College clearly reinforces the two-party system in fundamental ways. There is little doubt that the requirement that a candidate must win a plurality of votes cast in order to win an individual state, coupled with the requirement for a majority in the Electoral College to win the presidency, makes the task of third parties formidable. Historically, with the exception of the intraparty factionalism that led to the rise of the Bull Moose Party, only regionally strong third parties have been able to capture at least some electoral votes by winning a number of state pluralities. But even when such parties have the possibility of capturing some electoral votes, at best they can only play a "spoiler" role by preventing either of the two major parties from winning an Electoral College majority (something that has never happened). If a third party were to be successful in preventing either major party from achieving an Electoral College majority, the decision on who would become president would revert to the House of Representatives, with each state having one vote. It is highly unlikely that the House, made up of members of the two dominant parties, would ever select a third party candidate as president. Perhaps third-party electors could induce some representatives from their state to abandon their party's candidate, but such third-party influence in a House contingency election is highly problematic.

The incentives implicit in Electoral College rules have created a climate in presidential elections that encourages voters to think strategically in order not to "waste" their vote on third-party candidates. Although polls show regularly that many citizens are willing at least to entertain the possibility of considering a presidential candidate not from one of the two major parties,[4] in most cases voters are reluctant to support third-party candidates even if they prefer them on an issue basis. To vote for their most preferred choice opens up the possibility that voters may unwittingly be helping to elect their least preferred alternative.

Presidential candidates of the two major parties are well aware of strategic-voting thinking among the electorate and often design their campaign messages to remind voters who may prefer a third party candidate of the unpleasant possibilities in the likely event that their choice loses. For example, during the 1968 three-way contest among Democrat Hubert Humphrey, Republican Richard Nixon, and American Independent candidate George Wallace, Nixon operatives worried that support in the South for the segregationist Wallace had the potential of costing their candidate the election. Recognizing that their candidate was the second choice of many Southerners, the Nixon campaign throughout the South used the slogan, "A Vote for Wallace is a Vote for Humphrey." On Election Day Wallace's proportion of the vote was far less than one would have predicted based on preelection polls, with Nixon picking up the bulk of those who preferred Wallace but who decided to vote for one of the two major party candidates. In the 2000 election, Ralph Nader's Green Party candidacy was rewarded with far fewer votes on Election Day than had been predicted in the preelection polls, especially in important swing states such as Oregon and Michigan, as the Gore campaign reminded liberal voters that supporting Nader was self-defeating. One wonders how many of the over 97,000 Nader voters in Florida in the 2000 election are now having second thoughts, given the very close victory in that state of their probable least-preferred alternative!

The Electoral College contributes to the reinforcement of other party system characteristics as well. Party organizational structure parallels government structure, as parties organize around units of the federal system in order to contest elections. The need to aggregate state party electorates in the quest for the presidency elevates the importance of state parties, a factor that historically has contributed to the decentralized nature of American party organization. Such a decentralized party system helps promote the importance of state government in our federal system.

The Electoral College also reinforces the relatively low conflict, pragmatic nature of our party system, in contrast to more highly conflictual ideological systems. Along with other electoral laws, particularly the single-member-plurality district system, Electoral College incentives strongly encourage political movements to attempt to influence the dominant parties rather than form third parties that hope to capture the presidency on their own. Social movements and third parties quickly learn that they must tone down their extremist views if they are to be influential at all in pursuing their objectives within the dominant parties. Both Republicans and Democrats typically find it in their self-interest over time to attempt to incorporate popular issue positions of third parties and social movements to maximize their vote-getting potential. As a consequence, the two dominant parties tend to be rather centrist in issue orientation as they try to aggregate as many interests as possible.[5]

It should also be noted that our party system characteristics are mutually reinforcing. For example, a decentralized party organization would find it very difficult to support highly ideological parties, which typically involve top-down organizational discipline. Compared to our system where both major parties are essentially centrist in orientation, a highly ideological two-party system likely would be very unstable, as the losing party in elections would be much less likely to accept electoral decisions.

RETHINKING THE CONVENTIONAL WISDOM

While we agree that the Electoral College clearly contributes to perpetuating our party-system characteristics, we have a number of important reservations about the conventional wisdom. First, we are skeptical about assigning overwhelming importance to the Electoral College as a factor in party system maintenance. Parties do many things other than just contest presidential elections, and changing the process of presidential selection would not necessarily alter our party system characteristics. A variety of other institutional factors are also impediments to third-party creation and permanence, some perhaps even more influential than the Electoral College.[6] The single-member-plurality district system creates incentives for voters to cast their ballots for those with a chance for winning, thus hurting candidates with little support and essentially eliminating small, fringe parties. The open and permeable nature of American parties itself mitigates against the growth of third parties. For example, the use of the direct primary system of nominating congressional candidates and state officials has the effect of "channeling dissent into the two major parties."[7] Insurgent interests come to the realization that they can have a better chance working within the parties than going through the costly and barrier-filled route of trying to form a third party. The contemporary presidential nomination process, characterized by direct primaries and caucuses, has the same impact. Dissident interests, by and large, find it far more reasonable to work through the two dominant parties in an attempt to accomplish their goals.

Finally, many other electoral laws create overwhelming obstacles to third parties. Perhaps most noteworthy are the campaign funding statutes at the federal level for presidential elections, which make it difficult for third parties to acquire the resources needed to run serious campaigns. For example, in order to be eligible for even some public funding a party must have received at least 5 percent of the vote in the *previous* presidential election. Full funding goes only to those parties that received at least 25 percent of the vote. The state legal environment is crucial as well. State statutes ranging from provisions restricting ballot access to laws preventing primary losers from running in the general election under another party label handicap third parties, as does the prohibition of "fusion" candidacies.[8] According to party scholar Leon Epstein, state laws restricting third parties have created an "institutionalized electoral duopoly."[9] As long as Democrats and Republicans make the rules in Washington and in the state houses, and the judiciary is supportive, third parties will be legally disadvantaged.

None of this should be taken to mean that the characteristics of the party system are unchangeable, but electoral rule changes may play a smaller role than is sometimes believed, at least in consistently predictable ways. Our party system has changed a great deal since the New Deal encouraged party realignment during the 1930s. Still, as Eric Uslaner put it in our deliberations, "the ebb and flow of American parties seems to have little to do with structural change." For example, the reforms in the party nominating conventions put in place in the early 1970s by the Democratic Party were designed to give more power to primary election voters. Such voters were supposed to be more responsive to social forces and more ideological than the party professionals that had previously dominated the system. While the reforms did give us the very liberal George McGovern in 1972, sparking criticism among some political scientists that the changes had moved the parties in an ideological direction, the same system later produced moderate Democrats like Jimmy Carter, Michael Dukakis, Bill Clinton, and Al Gore.[10] Indeed, observers may have been too quick to assume that the structural reforms had any impact at all. Many of the "consequences" of reform, such as a more open nominating system and a greater role for public opinion, predated the party reforms of the 1970s.[11]

Although Democrats seemed to veer to the left in presidential politics during the early 1970s, the party's coalition base in Congress was in the process of disintegration. Ironically, just as the presidential wing of the party found its way back to the center (nominating Dukakis, Clinton, and Gore), congressional politics became both intensely partisan and highly ideological. All of this occurred with little alteration in the institutional rules of our system. The changes had more to do with broader changes in the political climate such as the enforcement of voting rights starting in 1965 (African Americans being allowed to vote in the South, leading to white flight into the Republican Party) and the reorganization of American political life around social issues (sparked by the growth of Christian fundamentalism, especially in the South).

The parties have also become more nationalized in recent decades, with national party organizations gaining strength vis-à-vis the state parties. While presidential delegate selection reforms contributed to this, national party organizations have been strengthened by the need for an enhanced role in raising large sums of money and funneling substantial portions to state and local parties and candidates. There is even evidence of nationalization of the party programs along more ideological grounds, suggested by the Republicans' "Contract with America" agenda in the early 1990s and the Democrats' "Families First Agenda" party program later in the decade.

However, despite such trends as party polarization and the increase in national party organization influence, the basic characteristics of our party system remain. Our two dominant parties are still decentralized organizations that can accommodate a wide variety of interests, and the Electoral College is only one of many factors that encourage our type of system.

The conventional defense of the current electoral college system based on its contribution to maintaining the two-party system ultimately rests upon normative assumptions concerning the value of such a system for the stability of American democracy. As Joel Paddock noted in our deliberations, "It is hard to imagine attempting to govern under the American constitutional system with more than two viable parties." As a practical matter, our system of separation of powers, in which the legislature and executive branches are elected separately, appears incompatible with a multiparty system. Multiparty systems work best with parliamentary forms of government, where there is the possibility of "cross-party coalitions forming to select the chief executive."[12] It is considered almost heresy among party scholars not to be supportive of the two-party system in the American context.

While none of us are anxious to embrace electoral rules that excessively fragment and polarize our political system, we were in some disagreement over whether or not the two-party system, as currently constituted, serves American democratic goals as well as its defenders would have us believe. The existing scholarship on the matter is open to interpretation. A case can be made that the major parties have reversed the decline that appeared so imminent a decade and a half ago and have reemerged as major actors in American politics. Today's nationalized parties are organizationally active, especially in campaigns.[13] Further, party identification is up, partisanship increasingly guides individual voting behavior, and the choice offered is between two parties reflecting distinct public policy visions and acting in a unified manner.[14] Indeed, some party scholars have made a powerful argument that fundamental changes in recent years have moved the American system closer to the responsible party model, with relatively unified parties offering the electorate meaningful programs and acting upon their programs once in office.[15] Political accountability seems more possible under such conditions.

But there is consternation in some quarters over the role that parties perform in contemporary American politics and who is represented in the process. In large measure, today's parties are conduits for raising and channeling money in political campaigns. Rather than mobilizers of the electorate, today's major parties act more as service vendors to party incumbents and other ambitious politicians rather than as constituent, rank-in-file oriented entities.[16] The low level of voter participation has suggested to some that many citizens feel unrepresented by the two existing parties comprising what political scientist Walter Dean Burnham has labeled the "party of the nonvoter."[17] Despite their shrill debates over social issues and the outright nastiness that has characterized the contemporary legislative climate in Washington, both parties are tied to big-moneyed interests and are hostile to any challenge to the system, such as major campaign finance reform.[18]

Whatever the case, the sanctity of the two-party system is being challenged in some quarters. One advocate for additional parties is prominent political scientist Theodore Lowi,[19] who believes third parties would energize both the citizenry and the policy process by bringing new ideas and policy innovation to the forefront. From Lowi's perspective, "both parties have been, in effect, majority parties," with little "incentive to use the electoral process to settle major issues of policy."[20]

IMPLICATIONS FOR PARTIES OF ELECTORAL COLLEGE CHANGE

Any discussion of the implications for political parties of modifying or replacing the electoral college system must be highly speculative. As we have argued, the Electoral College is only one among many factors that reinforce our party system characteristics, and it is difficult to access how a change in one factor would affect the system. The two major parties have historically proved to be very adaptable in coping with threats to their dominance and would be expected to remain so. And comparing various presidential selection alternatives to elections in our past is not very instructive, since the nature of campaigning and party appeals would have been altered to accommodate whatever rules were in place. At best we can make highly tenuous guesses as to how party politics would be different under new sets of electoral rules.

Direct Election of the President

Speculating about the impact of the direct election of the president is illustrative. While the various direct election alternatives are attractive for a variety of reasons — the most important, perhaps, being that they are more consistent with democratic norms as they are widely understood here and around the world — the potential impact of such a presidential selection system on political parties is far less clear. The traditional view is that a direct-election plan would "fundamentally alter the nature of the American party system. Its impact would be greatest on the number and internal power structure of the party."[21] As a group, we were far less sure that the effect would be so strong.

For example, a shift to a direct election system with a national plurality winner might have rather minimal effects upon the existing party system, particularly if other electoral rules, such as the single-member-plurality district system, did not change as well. Plurality systems exist for statewide offices such as that of governor, and they have not diminished two-party dominance within states. While more third parties would probably contest the presidential election under such a system, the incentives for third-party voters wouldn't be all that different. Voters leaning toward third parties would still have to calculate whether voting for a sincere preference as their first choice would damage the more mainstream candidate who is closer to their policy goals. It is not clear to us that two-party dominance would be seriously threatened.

Much would depend on the decision rule and the nature of the runoff provisions. For example, any popular election system requiring a majority of the popular vote would, in practice, be a two-ballot system similar to that used in France to select the president. A plurality winner system with a high cutoff (e.g., 40 percent) would create a somewhat similar situation. Such systems provide extra incentive for third parties to run in order to enhance their bargaining position, making party splintering possible and giving a much more ideological tone to the electoral process.[22] The parties would most typically represent more homogeneous interests, making bargaining and compromise more difficult. But even here potential supporters of third-party candidates would still be confronted with the possibility that other small parties might unify behind a more mainstream candidate, leaving them outside of an emerging governing coalition. The "wasted vote" notion is firmly ingrained in the mind of the American voter and would not change quickly.

Nor do we believe that other party-system characteristics would be altered much by using direct election alternatives. For example, such reforms would not likely alter the federal nature of the party system much beyond the changes that have already enhanced party nationalization. State and local parties would still have to elect candidates for other offices, but the trend toward party centralization might be accelerated. A direct election system would put even more of a premium on the ability of national parties to raise large sums of money, especially soft money, which could be transferred creatively to state and local party organizations throughout the country. It would remain difficult for third parties to build a nationwide permanent party organization, given all the other barriers facing third parties that we have discussed. The problems of such groups acquiring financial resources to seriously contest the presidential election would remain.

One member of our deliberative group, Joel Paddock, was somewhat attracted to the hybrid, national bonus plan (keep the Electoral College, but add 102 electors for the nationwide popular vote winner). He believed that such a plan would achieve the democratically attractive goal of direct elections, virtually ensuring that the person with the most votes would be elected, while avoiding the potential consequences of the direct popular vote, especially the proliferation of ideologically oriented splinter parties. Other members of the panel disagreed, feeling that, in practice, the national bonus plan would eliminate the Electoral

College and any of its benefits. To some it appeared to be a convoluted way of declaring the victor to be the popular vote winner. Because the national bonus plan would be a de facto national popular election with plurality rules, political actors would soon orient themselves as if it were a popular election. For party systems, the implications of adopting the bonus plan would thus be similar to those of adopting a popular vote with plurality rules.

Overall, we believed that a carefully constructed popular vote alternative to the Electoral College would not damage our two-party system in any predictable way. While there might be more third-party activity in presidential elections, crucial barriers to an extreme proliferation of parties would remain. Perhaps the biggest danger would be an elevation in intense partisan bickering and charges of fraud that might accompany a very close popular vote. The controversy over Florida in 2000 might seem mild in contrast.

Proportional Allocation

American party scholars are a notoriously conservative group, uneasy with any type of electoral system that would seem to create incentives for group splintering that may potentially endanger political stability. They are especially uneasy with proportional vote systems. The comparative politics scholar in our group did not have these inhibitions. Gary Reich was a strong proponent of a presidential selection process that retained the Electoral College, but allocated electoral votes within states proportionately to the popular votes candidates received in each state, rather than according to the current winner-take-all system. From Reich's perspective such a system would have several advantages: (a) it would reduce the likelihood of having a popular vote loser become president by making the popular vote and the Electoral College vote be more closely in accord with each other;[23] (b) it would represent the least drastic departure from the present system, and therefore would be more likely to garner political support; and (c) most importantly for our purposes, it has the greatest potential to strengthen the political parties without leading to a highly fragmented national party system (as tends to occur in countries that adopt majority runoff elections).

A case can be made that the most important impact of using proportional allocation to award electors is that it is likely to increase voter turnout in presidential elections. At the legislative level, there is some crossnational evidence that proportional representation elections result in higher turnout than plurality elections. Various reasons have been posited for this effect, including the fact that proportional representation makes elections more competitive than winner-take-all elections and makes voters feel less alienated than elections based on pluralities, where many votes are "wasted" on losing candidates.

To the extent that proportional allocation would make more states competitive in presidential elections, the parties would have a greater incentive to campaign widely; we might see less of the current phenomenon whereby presidential campaigns essentially write off certain states judged to be safely in their candidate's column. An increased mobilization effort by parties would have the effect of increasing turnout and strengthen ties between parties and allied groups. Stronger parties would be the result.

Reich acknowledges that one drawback to proportional allocation, at least at the legislative election level, is that it could encourage fragmentation of the party system. However, because winning the presidency requires candidates to have broad or nationwide support, he believes this would not be likely to happen in the United States if such a reform were adopted. The proportional distribution of state electors would not change the fact that presidential elections would still be winner-take-all, one individual being awarded the final prize. Some of the same pragmatic incentives that entice Nader and Buchanan sympathizers to vote for one of the major party candidates would still exist. From Reich's perspective, the adoption of this reform might actually give us the party-strengthening, turnout-increasing benefits of proportional allocation without splintering the party system.

While acknowledging that Reich had made a strong case for his viewpoint, the American party scholars in the group remained unconvinced. From their perspective, requiring proportional allocation within states might have the largest consequences for the party system of all the suggested reforms. On the positive side it would likely encourage the development of more competitive parties in noncompetitive states, energizing even weak parties at the state and local level to mobilize now that there would be a good possibility of garnering at least a few electoral votes. But the proportional plan would certainly encourage third-party candidates to make a greater effort, and the fragmentation of the party system would be the biggest danger of any proportional system. The relationship between proportional representation (PR) and the fragmentation of the party system at the legislative election level makes the potential use of proportional representation at the presidential level very risky; PR systems generally encourage multiple, ideological parties — a condition that does not suit the election of a single, powerful executive.

The likelihood of increased voter turnout due to proportional allocation was doubted as well. Voter turnout that appears higher in proportional representation systems may be due more to the fact that elections are less frequent and more focused in such systems. Perhaps even more important, the parties in PR systems are more ideologically distinct. People may feel that stakes are higher and may be more likely to come to the polls.[24] Finally, allocating electoral votes in a proportional manner would increase the likelihood of a very undesirable consequence; it would greatly increase the probability of presidential elections being settled in the House of Representatives, where the final outcome might be at great variance with any popular pluralities. Such results would damage the legitimacy of the presidential winner.

The District Plan

At first glance, the so-called district plan, now used in both Maine and Nebraska, would appear to be an attractive option for reforming our presidential selection system. Citizens of those states seem to be satisfied with their system. In such a plan, the plurality winner of a statewide presidential vote would get two electoral votes, while the winner of the popular vote in each congressional district in the state would get one electoral vote. The process certainly looks more democratic than the existing system, remains respectful of the federalist goals inherent in the Electoral College, and it could be implemented without amending the Constitution.

From the perspective of political parties, however, the consequences of the district system could be profound yet unpredictable. A case could be made, for example, that the district system could potentially energize local and state parties in areas of current weakness, with the added bonus of increased voter participation. Allan Cigler, who lives in the Third District of Kansas, where Democrats are competitive in congressional elections yet noncompetitive at the statewide level in presidential contests, believes a district plan would energize both Democrats and Republicans in his area during presidential election years. Presidential candidates might actually come to the state, a boost to both political parties. Elsewhere, we might see Republicans campaigning for the presidency in certain districts in the states of Massachusetts, California, and New York, while Democrats might no longer overlook competitive districts in Colorado, Georgia, and Virginia.

Ironically, however, in some areas party mobilization activities might actually decline. Paddock, for example, pointed out how a district plan might actually depress party involvement in his southwestern Missouri district. Democrats there are demoralized by typically losing by large margins within the district, but they take solace in the fact that their votes really matter in statewide elections (including the vote for president under the existing system) where Democrats are competitive. And with party and campaign resources spread thin, the currently competitive states might actually see less party activity.

Third-party effects would no doubt increase under a district system, where such parties could concentrate their resources and efforts to win a few electoral votes. The main danger here is not party proliferation in a manner that threatens two-party dominance, but that the electoral votes garnered by such parties could have a spoiler effect, throwing the final decision into the House of Representatives. The group felt this would be a very undesirable outcome given state equality in voting at that stage.

But perhaps the biggest negative of the district plan is even more fundamental. Congressional district boundaries are drawn every decade by state legislatures in response to a new federal census. The process is already highly partisan and conflictual, from deciding how the census is conducted to getting the legislature and governor in each state to come to some agreement about the configuration of districts. Having presidential election outcomes possibly determined by the partisan bias that is inevitable in redistricting decisions could undermine democratic legitimacy.

IMPLICATIONS FOR PARTISAN AND GROUP INFLUENCE OF ELECTORAL CHANGE

Assessing the impact of various presidential selection systems upon partisan bias is fraught with difficulty. Part of the problem is that while election laws tend to be static, societal changes may have an impact on who is advantaged or disadvantaged by the rules. One can recall the 1960s when Democrats believed that they were advantaged by the Electoral College because of the party's strength in metropolitan areas in large states, which were considered crucial in the electoral vote count, or recall the 1980s when Republicans believed they had a "lock" on the Electoral College due to their strength in the South and West. Neither party claims such advantage or disadvantage any more.

It strikes us as remarkable that neither political party nor any of their allied groups vigorously complained about the Electoral College after the 2000 election. The concerns were more about vote fraud in Florida than about the undemocratic nature of the Electoral College or who was advantaged or disadvantaged. In the wake of this election, changing the Electoral College does not seem to be a high priority of either Republicans or Democrats. With the exception of some minor complaints registered by broad-based public interest groups such as Common Cause, the League of Women Voters, and a host of smaller organizations operating largely through websites, organized interests seem largely uninvolved in the controversy, leaving the debate largely to journalists and academics.

We suspect two fundamental reasons for the lack of concern. First, established institutions are risk-averse, especially institutions that believe themselves to be players in the current process. But perhaps more important, the impact of rule changes in our fast-changing political culture is simply difficult to gauge.

Conventional wisdom suggests two kinds of interests are advantaged by the current electoral college system. First, minority racial interests in large competitive states are thought to be pivotal and are thus seen as receiving disproportional attention from presidential candidates seeking to capture the huge blocs of electors in such swing states. Organized labor would be similarly advantaged. Second, population categories concentrated in small states (such as agriculture interests) may dominate outcomes in those states that are overrepresented, on a population basis, in the Electoral College, thus making these categories of voters more salient than they would be under various popular vote or proportional allocation alternatives.

We have little confidence in such generalizations. One could argue that urban blacks, for example, are advantaged in key eastern swing states such as Pennsylvania by the current electoral college system. Massive voter turnout efforts in the urban areas of such states by groups like the National Association for the Advancement of Colored People (NAACP) no doubt were crucial in Gore's 2000 victory in that state. But African Americans in the nation as a whole may not be so advantaged. Black voters are no longer concentrated only in the nation's cities. In many southern states, where African American voters compose a large part of the electorate, they are relatively ignored under the current presidential selection system in which Democrats have difficulty seriously contending for statewide pluralities. Groups like the NAACP focus almost all their resources on what they believe are swing states. Adopting either direct elections or proportional allocation might mean that black voters would receive more attention from *both* political parties than they do now. Still, it should be remembered that in any electoral system, candidates tend to focus on the median voter rather than on particular narrow interests.

There is little doubt that population groupings concentrated in swing states are advantaged under the Electoral College, at least in terms of the difference they may make in elections (this may not translate into policy influence within the parties however). The problem is that designating which states fall into this category varies by individual election, making it difficult to discern which categorical groups and their organized representatives are *consistently* advantaged or disadvantaged. Both Michigan and Florida were key swing states in 2000, thus elevating the importance of organized labor in Michigan and blacks in Florida. Yet Michigan was not up for grabs during the Clinton years and Florida was considered a sure Republican state before 1996 (and even in the summer of 2000!). Ohio, long considered a quintessential swing state, was not really in play in 2000.

While it is hard to say which groups are consistently advantaged or disadvantaged under various presidential selection systems, we suspect group relations to the two dominant parties might undergo change if the Electoral College were eliminated. For example, would the direct election system strengthen or weaken the ties of allied groups to the parties (e.g., black interests to the Democrats, the Christian Right to the Republican Party)? Would such groups be less interested in coalition-building and accommodation and tempted to create their own party if they became disgruntled with the party with which they have been traditionally aligned? Would the district or proportional systems tempt concentrated minorities to offer their own candidates in order to develop even more bargaining power either with the party with which they are traditionally aligned or with the usual opposition? Whatever the case, there could well be unforeseen and unintended consequences in party/group relations as a result of changes in our presidential selection process.

CONCLUSION

The American two-party system is firmly entrenched in both the nation's multitude of legal structures at all levels of government and in the minds of its citizens.

We believe that either eliminating or modifying the Electoral College rules for presidential selection, by itself, would not significantly alter the nature of partisan politics in any predictable manner. Two parties would continue to dominate the system and grand coalitions would still have to be built pragmatically in order to achieve electoral success. Excessive concern about how changing our method of presidential selection would impact the contemporary party system should not dominate the debate over changing the Electoral College. Issues of democratic representation and legitimacy strike us as far more central to the controversy.

As both academics and political realists, we believe changing the Electoral College will remain a low-profile issue on the policy agenda. As would be expected from entrenched interests, neither of the two dominant parties has made the issue a policy priority, nor has any major interest group. The media have been uncharacteristically quiet, preferring to concentrate on the issues of vote fraud or accuracy in counting in the aftermath of the Florida 2000 debacle. The electoral college method for selecting the American president is likely to remain intact for the foreseeable future, a puzzlement to many of the nation's citizens, as well as an object of derision for foreign observers.

NOTES

1. See, for example, Wallace S. Sayre and Judith H. Parris, *Voting for President* (Washington, D.C.: Brookings Institution, 1968), esp. 48–56.
2. The classic statement of the relationship is found in Maurice Duverger, *Political Parties,* trans. Barbara and Robert North, 2d ed. (London: Methuen, 1959).
3. E. E. Schattschneider, *Party Government* (New York: Holt, Rinehart and Winston, 1967).
4. Gordon S. Black and Benjamin D. Black, "Americans Want and Need a New Political Party," *The Public Perspective* 4 (November/December 1992): 3–6. .
5. Anthony Downs, *An Economic Theory of Democracy* (New York: Harper and Row, 1957).
6. John F. Bibby and L. Sandy Maisel, *Two Parties — or More?* (Boulder, Colo.: Westview, 1998), 56–64.
7. Ibid., 58.
8. *Fusion* is a term meaning that two or more political parties may support a common candidate in the general election. New York is one of the few states where fusion is permitted. Anti-fusion laws are considered a major impediment to third parties, preventing minor parties from coalescing around a candidate and robbing them of the legitimacy that may result from joining the major parties in supporting a common nomineee. See Theodore J. Lowi, "Toward a Responsible Three-Party System: Plan or Obituary?" in *The State of the Parties,* ed. John C. Green and Daniel M. Shea, 3d ed. (Boulder, Colo.: Rowman & Littlefield, 1999), 171–89.
9. Leon D. Epstein, *Political Parties in the American Mold* (Madison: University of Wisconsin Press, 1986), 173.
10. Austin Ranney, "Political Parties, Reform and Decline," in *The New American Political System,* ed. Anthony King (Washington, D.C.: American Enterprise Institute, 1980), 213–48.
11. See Howard Reiter, *Selecting the President: The Nominating Process in Transition* (Philadelphia: University of Pennsylvania Press, 1985).
12. Bibby and Maisel, *Two Parties — or More?,* 99.
13. See, for example, Paul S. Herrnson, "The Revitalization of National Organizations," in *The Parties Respond: Changes in American Parties and Campaigns,* ed. Sandy Maisel, 2d ed. (Boulder, Colo.: Westview, 1994).
14. Larry Bartels, "Partisanship and Voting Behavior," *American Journal of Political Science* 43 (September 1999), 35–50

15. Gerald M. Pomper, "Parliamentary Government in the United States," in *The State of the Parties,* ed. John C. Green and Daniel Shea, 3d ed. (Lanham, Md.: Rowman & Littlefield, 1999), 251–70.

16. David Menefee-Libey, *The Triumph of Campaign-Centered Politics* (New York: Chatham House, 2000). See also John H. Aldrich, *Why Parties?* (Chicago: University of Chicago Press, 1995), who argues that such candidate-centered organizations have actually helped to make parties more effective in the governing process.

17. Walter Dean Burnham, *The Crisis in American Politics* (New York: Oxford University Press, 1982). See also, Walter Dean Burnham, "Electing Not To," *Boston Globe* Focus section, 6 September 1987.

18. Eric Uslaner, *The Decline of Comity in Congress* (Ann Arbor: University of Michigan Press, 1993). For discussions of how increased polarization has led people to distrust government, see David C. King, "The Polarization of American Parties and Mistrust of Government," in *Why People Don't Trust Government,* ed. Joseph S. Nye Jr., Philip D. Zelikow, and David C. King (Cambridge, Mass.: Harvard University Press, 1997), 155–78; and E. J. Dionne Jr., *Why Americans Hate Politics* (New York: Simon and Schuster, 1991).

19. Theodore J. Lowi, "Toward a Responsible Three-Party System? Plan or Obituary?" in Green and Shea, *State of the Parties,* 171–89.

20. Ibid.

21. Sayre and Parris, *Voting for President,* 73.

22. There is comparative evidence that the use of majority runoff results in greater party system fragmentation. See Matthew Soberg Shugart and John M. Cary, *Presidents and Assemblies: Constitutional Design and Electoral Dynamics* (Cambridge: Cambridge University Press, 1992), 206–22.

23. See Arend Lijphart, "Unequal Participation: Democracy's Unresolved Dilemma," *American Political Science Review* 91 (March 1997), 1–14.

24. See G. Bingham Powell Jr., "American Voter Turnout in Comparative Perspective," *American Political Science Review* 80 (March 1986), 17–43. Note that Americans seem turned off by ideologically divided parties (see n. 18 above) and participate less. In other countries, ideological differences produce greater turnout. Eric M. Uslaner explains this by noting that Americans don't seem to be able to disagree politically without being disagreeable. See his essay, "Is the Senate More Civil than the House?" in *Esteemed Colleagues: Civility and Deliberation in the Senate,* ed. Burdett A. Loomis (Washington, D.C.: Brookings Institution, 2000), 33–55.

CHAPTER 7

The Electoral College and Campaign Strategy

William G. Mayer, *Northeastern University*
Emmett H. Buell Jr., *Denison College*
James E. Campbell, *State University of New York–Buffalo*
Mark Joslyn, *University of Kansas*

THE PURPOSE OF this chapter is to sum up what we know, think, and suspect about the effects of the Electoral College on campaigns and campaign strategy. Our conclusions are organized under three headings: the distribution of campaign resources, coalition building, and the problem of unanticipated consequences. First, we conclude that the Electoral College does prompt candidates to concentrate their campaign resources on a relatively small number of competitive states. While most alternatives to the present system would provide incentives for distributing campaign resources more evenly geographically, no system would encourage campaigns to treat all voters equally. Second, we conclude that the Electoral College encourages coalition building to occur within the two major parties that dominate presidential campaigns. Popular elections with a majoritarian requirement — either attained through a two-stage runoff or by the instant runoff — could hinder the capacity of campaigns to develop broad coalitions. Third, we are wary of our capacity to anticipate the full set of consequences — either for how campaigns are conducted or for other aspects of our political systems — that might result from changing our electoral system. Recognizing the possibility and even the likelihood of deleterious unanticipated consequences should prompt caution in reforming or abolishing the Electoral College.

THE DISTRIBUTION OF CAMPAIGN RESOURCES

One of the clearest impacts of the Electoral College on American politics is its effect on the distribution of campaign resources, such as personal appearances by the candidates and television and radio advertising. Presidential campaigns have a clear tendency to concentrate their resources on a relatively small number of competitive states — states that both candidates have some legitimate prospect of carrying — while ignoring states that appear solidly to favor one camp or the other. Given the winner-take-all system used for awarding each state's electoral votes, a candidate who is already well ahead in a particular state gets no bonus for carrying that state by an even wider margin — nor does the losing candidate derive any benefit for narrowing his margin of defeat from, say, 40 percent to 20 percent.[1] Hence, candidates will tend to ignore or "take for granted" states where they are either very far ahead or very far behind. Massachusetts residents, for example, often observed that they literally did not see a single television ad for either major-party candidate during the entire 2000 general election campaign. By contrast, residents of Illinois often complained about being inundated by presidential campaign ads. The difference is explained, of course, by the fact that Massachusetts was always counted as a very safe state for Gore, while Illinois was seen by both campaigns as a competitive, "battleground" state.

This effect has also been measured in a more systematic fashion. In a study of the 1960 election, Stanley Kelley found that John Kennedy and Richard Nixon both spent 74 percent of their total campaign time in twenty-four "doubtful states"; in the final three weeks before Election Day, these same twenty-four states were the scene of 88 percent of the candidates' campaigning.[2] According to figures compiled by Jimmy Carter's campaign in 1976, eleven states did not receive a single visit during the general election campaign from either Carter or his vice-presidential runningmate, while twelve other states received just one visit.[3]

Some scholars have alleged a second type of bias in the current electoral college system: a bias in favor of large states.[4] We will not attempt to sort through this particular controversy here, but will simply offer two summary observations. First, when the distribution of measurable campaign resources (money, public appearances by the candidate) is examined, large states do, on the whole, get a larger than proportionate share. That is to say, if one state has three times as many people as a second state, the first state will generally get *more* than three times as much money and attention as the second state. Second, it is unclear, however, if this effect occurs because the current electoral college system is inherently biased in favor of large states, or because large states tend to be more competitive.[5]

It is less easy to generalize about what the distribution of resources would look like under any of the major alternatives to the current system. At first glance, one might think that the most equitable distribution would occur under a pure popular vote system. Since all votes count equally, regardless of geographic location, candidates would, presumably, allocate their resources in direct proportion to the number of votes available in a given state or locality.[6] Thus, for example, candidates would probably spend a lot more time and money in New York City than in Montana — simply because there are more people in New York than in Montana. But the amount of time or money *per voter* would be equal.

Not everyone agrees with this conclusion. Immediately after the 2000 election, when most newspapers and magazines ran articles about the future of the Electoral College, one of the major criticisms directed against a popular vote system was that it would lead the candidates to do all their campaigning in a very small number of high-density areas, while entirely ignoring the rest of the country. One such article noted,

> According to many political experts, candidates [in a popular vote system] might divide the country into 10 major media and cultural markets. . . . Those nodes would encompass some 135 million people, or about half the U.S. population. But they would cover no more than 10% of the land mass. The vast interior would be excluded, from the western half of Virginia down to the Gulf Coast and across the Midwest into the Mountain States. That means farmers and ranchers in the Nowhere Zone would get short shrift for their concerns — and rarely see a Presidential prospect. Candidates "wouldn't need to worry about putting nuclear waste in Nevada," says Steve Frank, president of the National Federation of Republican Assembles, a conservative grass-roots group. Adds Scott Reed, who managed Bob Dole's 1996 bid for the White House: "You'd be hunting ducks where the ducks are, and leaving large swaths of the country essentially untouched."[7]

It is hard to know what to make of this argument, given the rather abbreviated form in which it has been presented. To begin with, the article exaggerates, at least by implication, the amount of attention that Nevada and lots of other small states get under the current system. More importantly, if half of the U.S. population is located in one of these ten "megalopolises," the obvious rejoinder is: the other half is not located there. Moreover, high-density areas tend to have diverse, heterogeneous populations, including some groups that are inclined to support Republicans and others that are tilted toward the Democrats — which suggests that no candidate could count on winning an overwhelming percentage of the vote in these ten areas. So it seems likely that this particular objection is greatly overstated, and that candidates would still spend a lot of time and money outside these ten high-density areas.

The one way that a popular vote system might lead to this sort of maldistribution of campaign resources is if there are "economies of scale" in campaigning. Do we have any reason to believe, for example, that $10 million spent in a media market with 10 million people will buy more in the way of exposure or persuasion than a similar amount of money divided among ten different media markets, each of which has one million residents? No one we know of has ever systematically investigated this question, but at the very least, one can say that there is no obvious reason to think that such economies exist.

If, for various reasons, one wishes to retain the electoral college format but promote a more even distribution of campaign resources, it does seem likely that either the proportional or districted systems would move further in that direction. A proportional system, in particular, would give campaigns the incentive to invest resources more widely, since relatively small shifts in the statewide vote percentages might enable a candidate to win more electoral votes. This would be particularly true in large states, but the basic principle also applies to the smallest states, with their three electoral votes.

A districted system would probably produce the same sort of general outcome, though to a lesser extent. Much like the current system, campaigns would write off some districts as uncompetitive and would concentrate on those that appear to be at least potentially winnable by either candidate. The advantage the districted system might offer, however, is that even in states that are safe for one candidate or the other, one or more congressional districts might be competitive. In the November 2000 election, for example, the Bush campaign never had a realistic chance of carrying the state of New York and, hence, did almost no campaigning there. Under a districted system, however, a number of individual New York districts clearly would have been up for grabs, thus giving both candidates an incentive to do some campaigning in the Empire State. It is also likely that there would be substantial spillover effects from this campaigning. If Bush hoped to win some of the districts in the New York City suburbs, for example, his campaign would probably have to advertise on television stations that would reach the entire New York metropolitan area. Similarly, if Bush or Cheney made a personal appearance in the New York suburbs, newspapers and television from all over the area would probably cover the event.

So the present system does lead to what most observers would call a geographical maldistribution of campaign resources, and most of the other alternatives would probably do somewhat better in this regard. But two important caveats need to be added to this argument. First, no matter what vote-counting system is used and no matter how the population is spatially distributed, no campaign treats all voters equally. Rather, campaigns are directed at what might be called the "potentially movable" category: those voters who are not so solidly in one camp or the other as to make all efforts at persuasion futile. These voters get most of the attention, while the hard-core, "yellow dog" partisans are ignored or taken for granted. (This is, in a sense, a corollary of the median voter theorem.) Such tactics explain, for example, why at the end of almost every recent presidential campaign, black leaders have claimed that they were ignored by the Democrats, while conservative white Christian voters say they were taken for granted by the Republicans. There is a good deal of truth in both charges, though not for the reasons frequently alleged. Black voters sometimes get ignored by the Democrats not because the Democratic leadership is racist or insensitive, but because the black vote is already so strongly in the Democratic camp that neither party sees any great payoff in competing for it.

Second, even if we could agree that campaign resources are distributed unequally under the present system and that some other system would result in a more even distribution, is this enough reason to drop the Electoral College?

Campaigns provide several benefits to the political system as a whole. They help educate the electorate, even if this is not their principal intention, and they help stimulate voter turnout. But it's not clear that making marginal improvements in these sorts of benefits is a good enough reason to undertake such a significant change in the Constitution.[8]

COALITION BUILDING

One of the most important consequences of electoral systems in general is the effects they have on coalition building: on the incentives or disincentives they provide for parties and candidates to form alliances before or after the election. Here, too, there is widespread agreement about the tendency of the current system: it provides a strong, perhaps irresistible, push toward the maintenance of a two-party system in the United States. Since third parties rarely have any realistic shot at winning the presidency, many of those inclined to vote for an independent or third-party candidate finally conclude that a vote for their top choice would only be "wasted," and that their interests would be better served by voting for one of the major-party contenders. Thus, most recent third-party candidates have seen their support in the national polls peak during the summer or early fall, and then decline precipitously as Election Day draws nearer.[9]

There is less agreement, it should be added, on whether or not this is a good thing. The traditional view, to which most of the members of this panel subscribe, is that the United States has been well served by having a two-party system. Both parties, according to this argument, tend to present broad-based, moderate platforms, designed to appeal to a diversity of groups and interests. Partisan rhetoric aside, the parties are not that far apart on most issues and either party can win an election without posing a fundamental threat to the survival of the Republic.[10] More recently, however, the American two-party system has been attacked for being too narrow, for underrepresenting minority groups and interests, and for stifling the voices of those who might offer more serious challenges to mainstream ideas and policies.[11] In either case, the current Electoral College is one bulwark of the two-party system.

How would coalition building work under the alternatives we have been considering in this project? The proposal with the most radical consequences for the established parties is clearly the majority popular vote with a contingent runoff election. Under this system, it seems highly likely that a sort of two-stage election process would eventually develop, much like the system currently used in France. A large number of candidates would enter the first stage, since there is no obvious disincentive, for either the candidates or their supporters, for doing so. When no candidate succeeded in winning a majority the first time around, there would be a second election between the top two finishers, with the eliminated candidates from round one offering their endorsement and support to one of the two finalists, based on ideological compatibility or promises of future preferment.

Such would be the general outlines of the new system. A number of other details, however, are more difficult to anticipate:

1. Would the major parties continue to nominate candidates? And would these candidates enjoy any substantial advantage over other contenders? In France, one political party or another has formally nominated most of the candidates in the first election, and so might the case be in the United States. Alternatively, it might turn out that both candidates and public come to see the first election as, in effect, the entire nomination process. Suppose, for example, that in the lead-up to the 2004 campaign, John McCain, Bill Bradley, John Kerry, and Jesse Jackson all announce that they intend to be candidates in the first-round election, no matter whom their party nominates. If enough candidates pursue this course of action, and some of them are successful at it, winning a major party nomination might come to be seen as a quite unimportant and dispensable formality. That is to say, virtually everyone who aspired to the White House would run in the first election, without bothering to seek party approval, and the job of reducing that initial field to a manageable number of alternatives would be performed by that election, rather than by political parties. (This is essentially what occurs in a number of cities that have nonpartisan election systems, such as Boston.) In this case, parties would clearly be weakened, at least at the presidential level, for they would be deprived of what is perhaps the most important function they currently perform.

2. How many "major" candidates will run in the first round? As the initial field of candidates grows larger, candidate strategies are likely to take on a very different character. If only three or four significant candidates participate in the first round, each will probably conclude that he or she needs about 40 percent of the vote to make it into the second round, and thus will be compelled to go after a fairly broad, diverse coalition of voters. But if the first round includes seven or eight major contenders, the candidates and their strategists may conclude that they can get to the second round by winning as little as 20 or 30 percent of the vote. Rather than appealing to the electorate as a whole, candidates might find it more useful to go after a small but reliable constituency, particularly one defined in racial, geographic, or ideological terms.[12] For those who think that one of the best features of the current system is its tendency to foster moderate, broad-based candidates and parties, this would be a significant shortcoming.

3. What kind of bargaining would occur after the first election? In the French system, most of the candidates who run in the first round represent parties with a fairly well-defined position on the ideological spectrum. As a result, the first election generally has the effect of producing one candidate from the Right and one candidate from the Left, with all the defeated candidates and parties falling in rather naturally behind the candidate who most closely reflects their ideology. But if there are more candidates in the first round, and fewer have been endorsed by a political party, the results of the first election might set off a furious round of bargaining, where the losing candidates openly shop their support between the

two finalists, looking for a position in the new administration or concessions on major policies. Should the latter occur, it is almost inevitable that many voters and commentators would find such a process distasteful and even corrupt.[13]

How would presidential campaigns work under an instant-runoff system? Since nothing like this system exists anywhere in the United States, nor is it in widespread use elsewhere in the world, any answer we might give is highly speculative.[14] Again, it does seem likely that such a system would substantially lower the barriers facing third-party and independent candidates and thus lead (for better or for worse) to some weakening or modification of the two-party system.

Once the campaign gets underway, candidates would likely face two conflicting pressures. On the one hand, some candidates, particularly frontrunners, would find it very difficult to criticize the other candidates — even if these criticisms are clearly merited. Consider, for example, the predicament of a candidate who has 40 percent of the vote in the latest polls. If he attacks candidates who have only 10 or 15 percent, he runs the risk of angering their supporters and thus making it less likely that they will list him as their second or third choice.[15]

On the other hand, the instant-runoff format would probably generate intense and bitter rivalries between candidates who are running close in the polls, especially if they are appealing to the same types of voters. By removing candidates from the bottom up, the instant runoff treats candidates very differently according to the rank order of their finish and thus magnifies the effect of very small differences in the initial vote. Suppose, for example, that there are two candidates with very similar ideologies, one of whom has 25 percent in the polls while the other has 23 percent. Clearly, the candidate with 23 percent would have an enormous incentive to attack his slightly better-situated rival — and if this sort of campaigning proved at all effective, the candidate with 25 percent would quickly begin to fire back.

How these two forces would balance out in any given election is difficult to predict, but again there are some discomforting scenarios:

1. In some cases, the instant-runoff system might create a dynamic where the early frontrunners are separated, and the electorate ultimately comes to prefer one or more of the second-tier candidates simply because their faults and weaknesses have not been as widely exposed. (Something like this seems to have occurred in a number of hotly contested, multicandidate primaries, such as the Democratic Senate primary in Wisconsin in 1992.)[16]

2. If two candidates in an election take very similar positions and appeal to the same general kinds of voters, the assumption behind the instant runoff is that each candidate's supporters will list the other candidate as their second choice. But if the battle between these two candidates becomes bitter, there may occur a kind of "divisive primary" effect, where each candidate's supporters come to see the other candidate as more of an enemy than an ally.[17]

This suggests that if we are interested in dumping the Electoral College entirely for some kind of popular vote system, the least disruptive alternative, at least from the perspective of the party system and the established party coalitions, would be the plurality rule method, where a single election would be held and whoever gets the most votes wins. Though some members of this panel thought that this, too, might pose a threat to the two-party system, most felt that this method, similar to the one currently used to elect members of Congress, would also provide a strong disincentive to third-party and independent candidates.

UNANTICIPATED CONSEQUENCES

As the preceding discussion should indicate, any attempt to think about the effects of "reforming" the Electoral College comes up against one very important problem: the further one moves away from the present system, the more difficult it becomes to anticipate the full set of consequences. More limited reforms, such as using a districted system, would probably not have radical consequences for campaign strategy.[18] But more limited reforms, by their very nature, also would not satisfy most critics of the Electoral College. Awarding electoral votes on either a districted or proportional basis, for example, would not eliminate the possibility that a candidate could lose the popular vote but win a majority in the Electoral College. In fact, it might make that outcome more likely.[19] Plans that do eliminate the Electoral College, by contrast, are also likely to produce other important changes in the American political system, many of which will be difficult to predict.

Anyone contemplating wholesale changes in the Electoral College would be well advised to give particularly close attention to recent changes in the presidential nominating process. In the late 1960s and early 1970s, a group of "reformers" within the Democratic party succeeded in almost completely rewriting the basic rules governing delegate selection and convention decision making. They did this in the interest of pursuing greater intraparty democracy and, in many respects, they achieved their goal. After 1972, more people than ever before were involved in the presidential nomination process, party processes were considerably more accessible to outsiders and dissidents, established party leaders had much less control over both delegates and candidate selection. But in addition to these intended goals of reform, there were also a whole series of "unanticipated consequences." A dramatic increase in the length of the nomination race, a sharp rise in the number of presidential primaries, a nomination calendar that has been become increasingly "front-loaded:" none of these was expected or desired by the party reformers, yet they did occur as a direct result of the new rules.[20]

The moral of the story is that the consequences of major institutional change are always difficult, perhaps impossible, to anticipate fully. Still, some such consequences will often occur. This does not mean that institutions should never be changed. But we would argue that it does create a general argument in favor of the status quo. Longstanding institutions ought not be discarded for light or transient causes. In the end, this may be one of the compelling reasons to retain the Electoral College.

NOTES

1. Actually, two states — Maine and Nebraska — currently use a districted system, but the statement in the text does describe how about 98.5 percent of the Electoral College votes are awarded.
2. Stanley Kelley Jr., "The Presidential Campaign," in *The Presidential Election and Transition 1960–1961,* ed. Paul T. David (Washington, D.C.: Brookings Institution, 1961), 70–72.
3. For the actual data, see Larry M. Bartels, "Resource Allocation in a Presidential Campaign," *Journal of Politics* 47 (August 1985): 930–31. For similar data from the 1988, 1992, and 1996 campaigns, see Daron R. Shaw, "The Effect of TV Ads and Candidate Appearances on Statewide Presidential Votes, 1988–96," *American Political Science Review* 93 (June 1999): 359–60.
4. It is important to note that the bias alluded to here concerns which states the candidates visit and in which they advertise. This is a separate issue from another much discussed question: whether voters in large, medium, or small states have disproportionate weight in deciding who will become the next president. The latter issue is discussed in chapter 11.
5. On both of these points, see especially Steven J. Brams and Morton D. Davis, "The 3/2's Rule in Presidential Campaigning," *American Political Science Review* 68 (March 1974): 113–34; Claude S. Colantoni, Terrence J. Levesque, and Peter C. Ordeshook, "Campaign Resource Allocation under the Electoral College," *American Political Science Review* 69 (March 1975): 141–54; and Bartels, "Resource Allocation in a Presidential Campaign."
6. For a considerably more nuanced analysis that comes to much the same conclusion, see Eric R. A. N. Smith and Peverill Squire, "Direct Election of the President and the Power of the States," *Western Political Quarterly* 40 (March 1987): 29–44.
7. Paula Dwyer and Paul Magnusson, "The Pitfalls of One Person, One Vote," *Business Week,* 27 November 2000, 48–49. The same argument is also made, albeit more briefly, in Yuval Rosenberg, "Building a Better Election," *Newsweek,* 20 November 2000, 20; and Ben Wildavsky, "School of Hard Knocks," *U.S. News & World Report,* 20 November 2000, 52.
8. Indeed, it is far from clear that we even want campaigns to treat all voters equally. At the most basic level, campaigns are designed to help people decide how to cast their votes. In that sense, campaigns are supposed to focus very unequally on the undecided and those with weak commitments; hard-core partisans don't need campaigns. But there are other dimensions to campaigning where a greater case for equality can be made. When candidates target a particular state or group, they not only make personal appearances and buy television advertising aimed at that group, they also generally make special commitments and promises to the group. As indicated by the above quotation from Steve Frank, when residents of small-population states such as Nevada express concern about how they will fare under a popular vote system, they are not anxious about whether Nevada's economy will lose trivial amounts of advertising revenue or that Nevada voters will be insufficiently informed when they cast their ballots. Rather the concern is that the candidates will not take Nevada's interests into account when making major policy decisions, such as deciding on the location of nuclear waste facilities. Similarly, black leaders would like the parties to pursue black voters more vigorously not because it might make those voters marginally better informed, but because it might lead the candidates to make more generous promises on issues of concern to blacks, such as affirmative action and welfare reform.
9. The best example is John Anderson in 1980, who had more than 20 percent in the polls between May and July, but his support fell to 14 percent in August and September, and then to just 6 percent on Election Day.
10. For a particularly vigorous defense of this position, see John Wildenthal, "Consensus after LBJ: The Role of the Electoral College," *Southwest Review* 53 (Spring 1968): 113–30; and Judith

Best, *The Case Against Direct Election of the President: A Defense of the Electoral College* (Ithaca, N.Y.: Cornell University Press, 1971).

11. See, for example, Douglas Amy, *Real Choices/New Voices: The Case for Proportional Representation Elections in the United States* (New York: Columbia University Press, 1993); and Robert Richie and Steven Hill, *Reflecting All of Us: The Case for Proportional Representation* (Boston: Beacon Press, 1999).

12. Nelson W. Polsby has made the same argument about the way that the proliferation of primaries and the emphasis placed on early results has affected the nature of candidate strategies in the presidential nomination process. See *Consequences of Party Reform* (New York: Oxford University Press, 1983), 64–71.

13. The closest parallel to this sort of bargaining in American political history took place in the presidential election of 1824, before the emergence of a stable two-party system. The electoral vote that year was split among four major candidates: Andrew Jackson, who won 99 votes; John Quincy Adams, who won 84; William Crawford, 41; and Henry Clay, 37. Since no one candidate received a majority in the Electoral College, the task of choosing the president devolved upon the House of Representatives, which, under the provisions of the Twelfth Amendment, could only consider the top three finishers in the electoral vote. This made Clay's support a very valuable commodity, especially since he was then the Speaker of the House. Clay eventually endorsed Adams, who won the presidency and who then appointed Clay his secretary of state. Though there is no evidence that Clay and Adams struck an explicit deal on the matter, from the moment that Clay was appointed, the Jackson partisans claimed that Adams had won his office through a "corrupt bargain." This charge haunted Adams throughout his four years in office and, according to many accounts, undermined his effectiveness.

14. Though "transferrable vote" electoral systems were once used in a large number of American cities, the only city that still uses this system is Cambridge, Massachusetts. But Cambridge uses it only to elect an eight-member city council, with all members elected at large. In terms of the issues we are considering here, this creates a quite different strategic dynamic. If two liberal candidates are running for president, the inescapable bottom line is that only one of them can win: they are unavoidably competitors. But if two (or more) liberal candidates are running for the Cambridge city council, it is possible for *both* of them to get elected so they may not see themselves as direct competitors and may even cooperate on such things as get-out-the-vote drives.

15. Perhaps the closest parallel to this sort of situation in recent American politics was the way that Bush and Clinton treated Perot during the 1992 general election campaign. By the time Perot rejoined the race, in early October, it was clear that he had no real chance to win the election (the first Gallup poll after his reentry showed him with just 10 percent of the vote). Equally important, the polls also showed that Perot had a rather amorphous following that, if it deserted Perot, might plausibly go to either of the major party candidates. Since it was widely expected that Perot's vote would decline further as Election Day drew nearer (as has happened to every other significant third party candidate in modern times), both Bush and Clinton gave Perot pretty much a free ride during the fall campaign. In the first debate, for example, Clinton criticized Bush and the Republicans on 23 separate occasions, while Bush attacked Clinton and the Democrats 17 times. But Perot was criticized only five times by Bush and just twice by Clinton.

16. For a description of the Wisconsin Democratic Senate primary of 1992, see *Congressional Quarterly Weekly Report* (12 September 1992), 2735–36; and (7 November 1992), 16.

17. According to the divisive primary hypothesis, the same sort of effect sometimes occurs under the present system. That is to say, if two Democrats fight a pitched battle for their party's presidential nomination, the supporters of the losing candidate may develop strong negative feelings about the winner and thus be less inclined to support him during the general election. See, among others, James I. Lengle, "Divisive Presidential Primaries and Party Electoral Prospects, 1932–1976," *American Politics Quarterly* 8 (July 1981): 261–77; Priscilla L. Southwell, "The Politics of Disgruntlement: Nonvoting and Defection among Supporters of Nomination

Losers, 1968–1984," *Political Behavior* 8 (1986): 81–95; and Emmett H. Buell Jr., "Divisive Primaries and Participation in Fall Presidential Campaigns: A Study of 1984 New Hampshire Primary Activists," *American Politics Quarterly* 14 (October 1986): 376–90.

Under the present system, however, there is, at least, a three- to five-month "cooling-off" period between the end of the primaries and the general election, during which the supporters of the losing candidate can get over their initial disappointment and begin to view the general election contest in more dispassionate terms. For evidence that this actually occurs, see Lonna Rae Atkeson, "From the Primaries to the General Election: Does a Divisive Nomination Race Affect a Candidate's Fortunes in the Fall?" in *In Pursuit of the White House 2000: How We Choose Our Presidential Nominees,* ed. William G. Mayer (New York: Chatham House, 2000), 294–98. The problem with the instant-runoff format is that there is no cooling-off period: voters register their second and third choices at the same time they make their first choice.

18. The districted system might, however, have radical consequences for other aspects of American politics. In particular, it would almost certainly increase the stakes in congressional redistricting.

19. According to some counts, Jimmy Carter might have lost the 1976 presidential election to Gerald Ford under a districted system, even though Carter beat Ford by a quite healthy margin — 2.1 percent — in the popular vote.

20. For evidence on this last point, see Michael G. Hagen and William G. Mayer, "The New Politics of Presidential Selection: How Changing the Rules Really Did Change the Game," in Mayer, *In Pursuit of the White House 2000: How We Choose Our Presidential Nominees,* 1–55.

CHAPTER 8

Electoral College Reform and Media Coverage of Presidential Elections

Matthew R. Kerbel, *Villanova University*
Michael Cornfield, *George Washington University*
Marjorie Randon Hershey, *Indiana University*
Richard Merelman, *University of Wisconsin–Madison*

TO PARAPHRASE STEVE MARTIN, media coverage of elections isn't pretty. People who have devoted their time to studying election coverage overwhelmingly find it lacking on several important fronts. Coverage is widely condemned for being filled with stories of the horse-race prospects and strategic machinations of the candidates.[1] It has been criticized for spending too much time on superficial elements of candidates' personalities and foibles and too little on their issue positions, ideological leanings, programs, and records.[2] Some see the collective pattern of coverage as having the effect of confusing citizens, obscuring the information they need to make intelligent electoral decisions, even discouraging them from voting. Although, to be sure, responsible coverage does exist, and certainly across all media one may find evidence of issue frames and substantive discussion, aggregate election coverage leaves much room for improvement.

Given this state of affairs, the prospect of electoral reform offers tantalizing possibilities for realizing constructive changes. Journalists, editors, and news producers might approach a major change in the way we elect our president as an opportunity to rethink coverage patterns that rate unenthusiastic reviews from academics who study their work and from a public that, if ratings and circulation figures are any guide, are tuning it out. Quite possibly, changes in the electoral process would drive modifications in the way journalists report elections.

In this chapter, we present our conclusions about how media coverage could be altered should any of the proposed reforms to the Electoral College become reality. These conclusions reflect our deliberations on a wide variety of issues regarding media coverage of presidential elections. We discuss the possibility that electoral college reform would make coverage less horse race-oriented, more citizen-centered, more or less relevant to state and local concerns, and more inclined to emphasize a different type or array of candidates. We also ponder possible changes in election night coverage, consider whether media organizations would lose political power as a consequence of reform, raise the topic of coverage by emerging media, and address whether electoral reform would provide a natural framework for promoting media reform.

Overall, we were not particularly encouraged by the prospects for improvement in media coverage, largely because we believe the forces that shape it would likely be untouched by the reforms being considered in this volume. However, we believe that the possibility of electoral reform creates an interesting opportunity for media reformers, and we address that here as well.

HORSE RACE AND STRATEGY

Two members of our group recently completed analyses of coverage of the 2000 election,[3] and our findings were consistent with one another. We found that issue coverage was present in only about one-third of election stories in major print and broadcast media, taking a back seat to stories about the political strategies employed by the candidates and the status of the campaign horse race. Indeed, during the final phase of the campaign, strategy and horse-race coverage overwhelmed all other reporting. This is consistent with what we know about recent past elections, and is a pattern so ingrained that we were skeptical that even significant reforms in the Electoral College could modify it.[4]

There are several driving forces behind horse race–heavy, strategy-centered campaign coverage, none of which is dependent on the structure of the electoral system. One is to win and maintain an audience, which reporters, editors, and producers consider difficult to do with material about candidates' ideas and records.[5] Another is the dynamic nature of strategic news, which changes more frequently than issue positions — or, as one group member put it, "How many times can you write that Al Gore is a strong environmentalist?" Furthermore, the culture of political reporting leads correspondents to find news in the strategic maneuvering of the campaign.[6] We assume that none of these conditions would change even if the electoral system changed — that one would essentially have to eliminate the horse race entirely in order to reduce coverage of poll figures and strategy. Simply altering the rules — even in meaningful ways — would likely change the content of strategic news, but not the fact of it.

Worse, it's easy for us to imagine how a change in the electoral rules would invite a new level of strategic coverage, as reporters drawn to the game of politics indulge in reporting on how the game changes when candidates no longer have to vie for votes on a state-by-state basis, or need to adhere to a different set of Electoral College rules. Since political reporters struggle to find news that is different and dramatic, the implications of electoral change should provide an ongoing supply of material, at least until the new methods become commonplace.

At that point, we simply anticipate that adjustments in the way candidates behave to deal with the new rules will themselves become part of the strategic story line.

Similarly, we anticipate that any electoral change would compound the tendency for reporters to look inward for material, framing campaign stories in terms of self-references. Any changes in procedure that generate changes in campaign strategy by definition change the way reporters and campaign officials interact as so much strategy is targeted toward sustaining and controlling media coverage. It's easy for us to imagine any reform generating an enduring story line about differences in how the press covers campaigns, before and after reform, and we don't see how that contributes to effective democratic processes. Although we are divided on the value of horse-race coverage — some of us feel it provides a useful function — we are united in our sense that strategic coverage amounts to empty calories, and that self-referential coverage similarly does little to educate the viewer or reader on matters of value to effective decision making. So we would view this outcome as an unwelcome one that perpetuates a problematic trend in coverage.

CANDIDATE VERSUS CITIZEN PERSPECTIVES

Typically, strategic campaign frames focus on the candidate. Arguably, a more beneficial variant of strategic coverage would focus on the citizen, in which reporters, in keeping with the efforts of the civic journalism movement, approach the campaign the way the public rather than the candidates see it.[7] If the rules of the game were such that candidates, in an effort to win election, found themselves appealing for votes by broadening their messages, would reporters be motivated to cover this strategic initiative the way voters would appreciate it — in terms of the message being used to gain favor with the electorate?

One reform that might produce this situation is the instant runoff, where voters would rank-order their preferences. This system forces candidates to become acceptable to a broader share of the electorate and thus prompts them to craft their messages to appeal to a wider audience. With candidates from more parties motivated to participate in the process on the promise of a greater competitive position, it would be in the strategic interest of major candidates to explain to reporters why they should be acceptable second choices to those who might not support them as a first choice. Consequently, with major candidates emphasizing issue positions as a way of gaining strategic advantage in a multicandidate field, reporters could cover this strategic turn in terms of the candidates' platform or issue stands. Should this happen, strategic coverage could shift from the tactical to the substantive — from a candidate to a citizen perspective. In contrast, the runoff reform and the plurality system might not provide an opening for coverage from a citizen perspective, because we assume candidates operating in these systems would not face credible challenges from minor candidates and would therefore maintain conventional strategies for reaching voters.

But would this alternative really generate substantive coverage? Would candidates appeal for second-place votes by making policy distinctions with opponents, and if they did, would reporters find a story in it? Some group members voiced skepticism on these points:

> As a campaigner appealing for a voter's second choice, why would I consider issues my best bet? Why wouldn't I be just as likely to stress my personality characteristics or my generic association with "working people" or "taxpayers"? It may be harder to cite a horse-race appeal as a reason for someone to give me a second-place vote, but then it isn't usually the candidates who use the horse-race frames, but rather the journalists. The simple fact of appealing for second-place or first-place votes should be ample justification for news reports to continue horse-race coverage, if a more complicated version of it.

However, when you consider that the instant runoff would give viability to third-party candidates, it is possible to argue that major-party candidates would be forced into a policy discourse in order to differentiate themselves from sectarian candidates with whom they would be in competition for second-place votes. This would widen the issue and ideological spectrum of the campaign, with potentially positive ramifications for the electorate. But, again, would the media rise to the occasion and emphasize the substantive distinctions we would expect candidates would have to draw — or would they simply cover the confusion that could ensue from a system that might make Florida's famous butterfly ballot look simple? One participant wasn't sure whether they would — or could:

> The media would surely have to work harder to report on and illuminate the wider ideological spectrum, whether it be in citizen strategy forms or straight issue, candidate, or party coverage. The shift certainly would provide the press an opportunity to move closer to a "deliberative" mode of coverage.[8] But can the media properly describe, clarify, and analyze this wider spectrum of candidates so that voters can be engaged, and the rankings not be made to seem too challenging to them?

Members were divided on their response to this question. One thought the answer was yes, arguing that a wider ideological spectrum would produce more interest in the campaign and more uncertainty about the outcome. These factors are optimal conditions for media impact,[9] suggesting a possible motivation for the press to experiment with new approaches to coverage.

But another member saw this as unlikely because of commercial pressures to play it safe. The more familiar story line would center on how people were acclimating to a ballot unlike any previously used in this country, and on the candidate-centered maneuvering necessary to turn out the appropriate vote. If news organizations behaved as they presently do, it may be asking too much of them to make an ongoing story out of ideological distinctions.

NATIONAL VERSUS LOCAL FOCUS

Since one obvious ramification of any reform that eliminates the Electoral College is that campaigning would no longer be a state-by-state affair, we considered whether the ensuing nationalization of presidential politics would shift the locus of coverage as well. Two issues are relevant here. One is the matter of whether the horse race would become more difficult to report if the statewide polls that are now so central to the effort are no longer indicators of the likely outcome. The other is the issue of whether a more nationalized story would serve to distance readers and viewers from politics, reducing their motivation to participate.

On the matter of polling, we felt that there would probably be little change in the way reporters went about their work, save for the way the horse race is covered in the final days of a campaign. To the extent that national polling informs most political coverage until the very end of the process, when most analyses begin to focus on likely electoral vote distributions, eliminating the Electoral College should have no effect. It may even be easier for reporters to cover the last stretch of the contest, because statewide polling is typically less reliable and consistent than national polling. For those using emerging media, we assume statewide polls would likely still be available on the Internet, at least from states where polling exists for races further down on the ticket, and sites like CNN.com typically offer guidance on how to interpret the data. Should the Electoral College be modified to allow for the proportional allocation of electors, statewide polls could be used as they are today; only the interpretation would be different.

The matter of whether a national focus would diminish interest in political news is more difficult to determine. It could potentially increase attention to important national issues. But, as we speculated, there may not be additional attention to issues at all, leaving the news audience with more national political stories and less items of immediate concern to their locality. One group member put the issue nicely:

> I find myself in an odd quandary. On grounds purely of democratic theory, it does seem to me imperative to seek political equality in counting votes, insofar as that is possible. This argues against the Electoral College in most of its forms, and in favor of a "national" solution either in plurality or majority form. But I fear that such a movement would have harmful effects on media, in that a more "nationalized" format would reduce voters' local and state frames of reference. That could lessen their already low motivation to follow and learn from the campaign.

We agree that such a development would be detrimental to democratic discussion, but we weren't all certain that it would occur. A reasonable alternative possibility contends that the present system does focus attention on regional and local concerns, but they are primarily political concerns about things such as state and local allocation of resources, in keeping with the dominance of horse-race and strategic election frames. Under a popular-vote system, candidates will still make strategic decisions about resource allocation, and while they might be different decisions — for instance, George W. Bush might well have allocated more time and money in Texas to run up his vote total — they would still have regional implications and would be covered as such. From a strategic standpoint, even a national election would effectively be a series of regional elections, and political reporters would likely latch on to this angle, as well as to the inevitable comparisons to how regional allocation of resources would have been different had the rules of the game not changed.

Simultaneously, a move to a popular vote would not alter the importance of key state and local elections, which constitute a sizable percentage of media coverage. Even if reporting on the presidential race moved away from the grassroots, we have every reason to believe that coverage of gubernatorial, senatorial, congressional, and significant local races would remain the same. Our hope and expectation is that, if nothing else, voters could still find relevance in coverage of those races occurring closer to home. And given that most newspapers have found that they can compete with network television news only by providing a significant local focus, this might make the impact of the change even less dramatic.

Coverage of Third-Party Candidates

We did agree, however, that instant runoff, along with the proportionality and plurality reforms, would focus newfound attention on challengers who now get little press, if for no other reason than they would suddenly find themselves in an improved competitive situation. What might this mean for who gets covered? One participant thought it would enhance an existing bias toward challengers who know how to play to the media. In 2000, this could have meant more attention for John McCain and Ralph Nader, particularly under either runoff scenario, where a candidate like Nader would have considerably more power to shake things up.

But it is worth remembering that the McCain phenomenon occurred during the primaries and would have been untouched by any changes to the Electoral College. As one participant pointed out, "It might be worthwhile to consider that presidential election coverage now begins in force (I cringe at the thought) better than a year and a half before Election Day. Perhaps Ralph Nader would receive more press attention by virtue of his ability to force a runoff if one was provided for. But what of John McCain, who never made it out of the primaries? My sense is that his coverage would not change." Either way, and especially if the doubters are correct, this could be an appropriate moment for those who study media coverage of politics to listen to the words of one member who urges scholars to appeal directly to the media to take up the challenge of reforming their coverage.

ELECTION NIGHT

Network television received a great deal of heat for the way it mangled its election night 2000 coverage by awarding Florida, at various points, to Gore, then to Bush, then to nobody. In the aftermath of this fiasco — one group member labeled it "heinous" — network officials have pledged to be more careful when making predictions, and it appears certain that their pledges will receive a fair amount of scrutiny. Under the circumstances, we felt it appropriate to consider how any of the Electoral College reforms could influence election night coverage.

The most obvious change would happen with a popular vote system. Gone would be the big map with the red and blue states — or if it remained, it would be simply a quaint reminder of an old election night ritual. In its place: a single tote board and the task of accurately pooling and reporting data from 3,300 counties nationwide. But the removal of states as the unit of analysis for determining the winner would not, in our combined opinion, reduce the strong competitive pressure to call the election quickly and — in light of recent events — accurately. It would simply require network news organizations to modify the procedures they use to gather and interpret voting data, and even these changes might not have to be as dramatic as they initially appear to be.

How news personnel would adjust to a change to popular vote tallies is a matter of speculation. Typically, vote data are collected at the precinct level and reported to county, then state, officials. Because states run and regulate elections, even a move to the popular vote system would retain a statewide emphasis when it comes to crunching the numbers. What is less clear to us is whether news organizations would wait to hear from the states, an unlikely choice considering how long this would take and how much they value making early calls. But one obvious alternative — to get data directly from the county level — is fraught with difficulties such as overlooking or double-counting jurisdictions.

Media organizations with national and global audiences might feature the swing counties known in advance to political insiders for their voting histories. They might also feature counties where there are reports of irregularities — a news story in its own right. Media organizations with local audiences might feature their own swing counties to give viewers a sense of how their region is contributing to the total vote. It is also possible that news organizations might be tempted to use computer-based models to predict national vote projections, to use swing precincts to build national vote projections, or to rely on a nationalized version of the exit polls that form the basis of today's early projections.

It seems unrealistic to believe that changing the electoral system would cause network news organizations to put aside their heated competition to report the results fast, or to return to the days of manual counting when the cumbersome task of tallying real votes supplied the basis for election night projections. It also may be unrealistic to assume that changes in the electoral system would encourage networks to heed the call of reformers and wait to report vote totals before all the polls are closed — although any meaningful change would provide an excellent opportunity for scholars and media critics to shine public attention on this issue.

It is far more likely that the media would simply adjust to new realities. One member, who spent time at WashingtonPost.com, was impressed with the effort involved in developing computer programs and database files to keep online vote totals up to date. With this sort of investment in being comprehensive and fast, and with the commercial pressures to do the same, we believe that even the most dramatic departure from the present electoral college system would not change the prevailing dynamics of election night in the newsroom. It's even possible that a national vote count would still be approached using statewide exit poll projections, with the analysis shifting away from the colorful map to the likely margin of victory in each state as a share of mounting national totals. Under this scenario, sources of data would remain the same; all that would change would be their interpretation. And we would remain at risk for the sort of bungled calls that characterized the 2000 campaign, a product of the rush to be first.

MEDIA CONTRIBUTIONS TO ELECTORAL CHANGE

While considering the likely impacts of changes to the electoral process on the media, we thought it important to address some of the potential impacts of the media on efforts toward electoral reform. We found ourselves raising questions we couldn't answer, but felt it valuable to consider them, for they speak to media power and potential changes in the spoils that might follow if the selection process were altered.

A number of matters came to mind. It's not hard to imagine that the large conglomerates that Alger has dubbed "megamedia" would lobby hard in defense of their interests if a plan to modify the Electoral College ever generated steam.[10] It is possible to imagine scenarios in which organizations such as Disney, Time-Warner/Turner, and other giants might feel they would lose clout through reforms that take electoral power away from the heavily urbanized states where they are based. To the extent that concentration of media power continues, and is based in large cities that presently receive a lot of attention (and campaign promises) from candidates who need the electoral votes of the states where they are located, would these organizations feel better able to influence Congress if the current electoral college system were maintained? If, for instance, the Electoral College were modified along the lines of the proportional plan, reducing the influence of larger states, would media organizations based there anticipate their influence declining as well and marshal their resources to stop it? Considering that government action can directly affect their interests through such things as antitrust suits or tax law chaı ges, the matter of who gets elected and how they get elected is not a trivial one.

An interesting complication to this pattern revolves around how media outlets with direct interests at stake might editorialize about pending electoral changes. Would we see editorializing for or against a particular change that was not tacitly shaped by the commercial interests of the organization? A broader version of this question rests with what the role of editorializing in general should be when dealing with a major change that has implications for the profit margins and business conditions of the major media, and whether editorial writers would or should address the potential ramifications of Electoral College reform for their parent organizations.

NEW MEDIA

Several ideas were raised in relation to emerging media and the proposed reforms. Admittedly, we are just beginning to learn about how Internet use is changing political participation, as access to cyberspace and patterns of computer usage remain quite fluid.[11] At one level, questions about how the proposed reforms would be affected by Internet use can be answered with a modification to any similar question about the Internet: an effect will be there, but no one can say what it will be. Should the Electoral College be abolished or reformed at this period in our history, a significant electoral change would be taking place in concert with the emergence of a technology whose influence we cannot predict. There would have to be some interaction between the two, but it is impossible to know what it would be.

We can, however, take note of a couple of anecdotes that might instruct us about where to look as we try to assess what the interaction will be. One has to do with the speed with which the mass public can get involved in a conflictive electoral situation — a matter relevant to our discussion because we can anticipate that systemic changes in the electoral process will alter the dynamics of political competition. One member commented that mass awareness of a hotly contested 1984 Indiana congressional election developed gradually, in contrast to the rapid public awareness of recent political events. The difference, of course, is the speed with which information travels today. Consider the case of the rapid rate at which people became aware of peculiarities in the Florida presidential vote in 2000 — and responded to it.

> In today's media environment, many more people around the world started learning about the problems in south Florida before the polls closed. I started getting e-mails from strangers in the late afternoon (probably because I work for a project with "Democracy" in the title). In short, media surveillance of elections has been jacked up tremendously by cable, satellite, and the Internet, which enables average citizens/voters to register complaints and comments with unprecedented velocity.

However, a less optimistic participant added that the enhanced ability for people to find out about the Florida situation did not decisively alter the outcome of the election.

We also noted the vote-swapping that took place via the Internet to speculate that emerging technology coupled with electoral reform might empower more citizens to participate in politics. In 2000, a number of people who wanted to support Ralph Nader but feared that their vote would benefit George W. Bush — their third choice after Nader and Al Gore — took to the Internet to participate in an ingenious vote-swap arrangement. Nader voters in competitive states pledged to cast their vote for Gore having found, on the Web, a Gore voter in a noncompetitive state who would in turn vote for Nader. This arrangement used media technology to circumvent one of the dilemmas posed by the Electoral College — that popular votes are not created equal. One contributor to this chapter looked at how this arrangement arose out of political desire and was made possible by technological capability, and found reason for optimism about the new media and electoral reform:

> The political junkie would be empowered by a combination of the Internet and the right electoral reform to have more impact on a presidential election. In addition to swapping (intentions to) vote, online activists could send money and make phone calls in those congressional districts or states where their actions would have the greatest effect.

However, we were not united in our optimism that actions like the Nader vote trade will enable us to transcend the difficulties of our present media environment, simply because they may not amount to much more than a footnote. A skeptical member wondered how many political junkies are out there, noting that the number of swapped votes did not come close to giving Nader the 5 percent share of the popular vote he was seeking. These divisions of opinion on the ability of emerging technology to alter the media landscape are consistent with what little we yet know about media like the Internet. New media provide a tantalizing possibility — but not a probability — for boosting the prospects for reforming coverage.

CONCLUSION: CAN POLITICAL REFORM GENERATE MEDIA REFORM?
Apart from what we might hope will come from new media, we are limited in our expectations for change in the way traditional media cover politics and elections, regardless of which Electoral College reform might ultimately emerge. Independent of the outcome of the pending debate on the electoral process, we have strong reason to suspect that coverage after the fact will look much as it did in 2000, which is to say horse race–centered, strategy-heavy, character-oriented, and ideologically light. We believe that the overall quality of the messages emerging from traditional media will not particularly facilitate democratic discourse and that television networks, burdened by growing commercial pressures, will continue to make quick judgments on election night at the risk of getting it wrong.

We do remain upbeat in our belief that if structural changes in coverage are not likely to follow from structural changes in the political system, we can at least use this moment to revisit the efforts of those in the civic journalism movement and others who assert that reform need not be limited to electoral processes. If following 2000 we have a moment when it is realistic to consider Electoral College reform, why not use that moment to address the drawbacks of how the media cover national elections? Media scholars and critics could potentially lead the way in this effort, proactively drawing attention to changes that need to be made.

Keeping in mind the power of the forces that shape media coverage, we offer the possibility that a historic electoral change, such as to a direct popular vote system, could at least temporarily enhance people's attention to the presidential race and thereby provide a window for discussing coverage reforms. A moment of dramatic change such as this would as surely direct attention to how the media respond to the new system as the coverage debacle of 2000 produced a wave of public soul searching by media brass. Moments like these come rarely, and would be opportunities for reformers — including scholars who traditionally do not seek the role of the public intellectual — to get out their message.

We are under no illusions about how the media would respond to electoral vote reform. As long as media organizations remain private, profit-seeking enterprises, and as long as they believe that their bottom lines will be best served by coverage that casts itself as a game or in terms of character, we recognize that it will be difficult to imagine a situation where the media would take significant reform suggestions seriously. We realize that the civic journalism movement, in the words of one member, "has not exactly mesmerized folks with its potential." But dramatic reform to the electoral process would shake up a lot; it would provide media reformers with an opportunity. Perhaps, then, the most exciting prospect about the relationship between electoral reform and media reform is the promise of what change could bring. Through the flux and excitement of change, we cautiously find hope for improvements in coverage of politics and elections that have escaped us thus far.

NOTES

1. See, for instance, Thomas E. Patterson, *Out of Order* (New York: Knopf, 1993); and Marjorie Randon Hershey, "The Campaign and the Media," in *The Election of 2000*, ed. Gerald M. Pomper (New York: Chatham House, 2001).
2. Marion Just et al., *Crosstalk* (Chicago: University of Chicago Press, 1996).
3. Hershey, "Campaign and the Media"; and Matthew R. Kerbel, "The Media: Old Frames in a Time of Transition," in *The Elections of 2000*, ed. Michael Nelson (Washington, D.C.: CQ Press, 2001).
4. A good discussion may be found in Diana Owen, "The Press' Performance," in *Toward the Millennium: The Elections of 1996*, ed. Larry J. Sabato (Boston: Allyn and Bacon, 1997).
5. Additionally, campaigns are covered by *political* reporters, who are far more inclined to see the campaign in terms of the strategic maneuvering of candidates then in terms of their ideas or proposals. Consequently, it is difficult to convince them that issue coverage could generate an audience. See Doug Underwood, "Market Research and the Audience for Political News," in

The Politics of News, The News of Politics, ed. Doris Graber, Denis McQuail, and Pippa Norris (Washington, D.C.: CQ Press, 1998): 171–93; Herbert Gans, *Deciding What's News* (New York: Random House, 1979); and Doris A. Graber, *Mass Media and American Politics* (Washington, D.C.: CQ Press, 1998).

6. Matthew R. Kerbel, *Edited For Television: CNN, ABC, and American Presidential Elections* (Boulder, Colo.: Westview, 1998).

7. A good review of civic journalism may be found in Michael Schudson, "The Public Journalism Movement and Its Problems," in *The Politics of News, The News of Politics,* ed. Graber, McQuail, and Norris, 132–50.

8. For instance, as described in Benjamin Page, *Who Deliberates: Mass Media in Modern Democracy* (Chicago: University of Chicago Press, 1996), and, recently, Jonathan Mermin, *Deliberating War and Peace: Media Coverage of U.S. Intervention in the Post-Vietnam Era* (Princeton: Princeton University Press, 1999).

9. See John Zaller, "The Myth of Massive Media Impact Revived: New Support for a Discredited Idea," in *Political Persuasion and Attitude Change,* ed. Diana C. Mutz, Paul M. Sniderman, and Richard A. Brody (Ann Arbor: University of Michigan Press, 1996).

10. Dean Alger, *Megamedia: How Giant Corporations Dominate Mass Media, Distort Competition, and Endanger Democracy* (Boulder, Colo.: Rowman & Littlefield, 1998).

11. A valuable source on the topic of emerging media is Russell Newman, "The Global Impact of New Technologies," in Graber, McQuail, and Norris, *Politics of News,* 238–51.

CHAPTER 9

Citizen Participation and Electoral College Reform

Robert M. Stein, *Rice University*
Paul Johnson, *University of Kansas*
Daron Shaw, *University of Texas*
Robert Weissberg, *University of Illinois*

THE ELECTORAL COLLEGE, the method by which we select the president of the United States, is one of our oldest continuing national political institutions. Since the founding of the Republic we have continuously elected presidents under the terms of Article II, section 1 of the Constitution. Divining the Electoral College's political impact has evolved into a cottage industry where speculative tentative findings are the norm. Nevertheless, amid all this quarrelsome discussion there seems to be one unquestionably accepted morsel of conventional wisdom: as currently organized, the Electoral College is inimical to wider citizen participation. Going one step further, this engendered apathy is a democratic "problem" insofar as democracy rests on an active citizenry. It would seem to follow then, at least for fans of expanded citizen participation, that the Electoral College should join history's dustbin alongside the poll tax, literacy requirements, religious qualifications, male-only suffrage, and similar long-banished, undemocratic evils. Yet for all the rhetoric, we know little about how the Electoral College impacts citizen participation. This paucity of knowledge owes in part to the Electoral College's longevity. There has been little opportunity to experiment with other methods of electing the president.

Superficially, the factual component of this position seems eminently logical: given that outcomes in countless states are virtually preordained, the incentive to vote must be close to zero in half or more of the nation. Moreover, why should any candidate waste his or her high-priced mobilization efforts to transform a rout into a humdrum calamity? Or buy a landslide when 60 percent does nicely? It then would seem to follow that abandoning our ancient arrangement, or at least the unit-rule system on the state level, would usher in a New Democratic

Era. Then, candidates would vigorously compete in every nook and cranny, the civic life of once moribund one-party states would be invigorated, and former apathetics would be reborn in the mode of *homo civicus*.

Is the Electoral College responsible for the low levels of citizen participation that has characterized American presidential elections? Does our present electoral system distort "the popular will"? Would alternative electoral systems stimulate citizen participation and increase responsiveness to the average citizen (dubbed "the median voter" by political scientists)? Such questions seem to be central to evaluations of the Electoral College and to proposals for electoral reform.

While our goal is to bring our understanding of electoral systems and citizen participation to bear on an assessment of the Electoral College and alternatives to it, we have chosen to impose some constraints on the extent of our investigation. Specifically, we limit our analysis to assessing the extent of voter turnout under various presidential electoral systems. This is not to suggest that other forms of participation than voting are unimportant or beyond the influence of any of the electoral reforms under consideration.[1] Our reason is simple. Voting is the mode by which we select the president. It might be expected that the electoral reforms discussed in this volume should influence whether citizens vote. Should our findings demonstrate such an impact, others might investigate whether these proposed reforms influence the incidence of other forms of political participation.

In the following section, we review the literature on political participation, identifying the main theories and determinants of voter turnout. We identify several factors that influence voter participation and that might be altered by changes in presidential election systems. Then, we identify the attributes and features of each proposal, including the current Electoral College, that are most relevant to voter turnout, and — drawing on empirical research on voting — we evaluate several hypotheses about the relationship between each proposal and voter turnout and behavior. Our conclusion is that reforming or even eliminating the Electoral College will not appreciably alter the level or nature of citizen participation in presidential elections.

Central to reforming the presidential selection process is the belief that greater levels of participation (i.e., voter turnout) are beneficial to the quality of American democracy. The Electoral College is seen by some as contributing to low levels of citizen efficacy and participation, and that this condition is viewed as problematic.[2] We question both the theoretical and empirical validity of this proposition. After finding that voter turnout will be little increased by electoral reform, we revisit the thesis developed during the early stages of the behavioral revolution in political science that maximization of voter turnout is not preferable for the health of American democracy.[3] We explain why the maximization of voter participation is not a necessary component of an effective method for choosing our president.

THEORIES OF VOTER PARTICIPATION

When electing the president, the most relevant form of citizen participation for study is voting. The individual's decision to vote and the aggregation of these decisions (i.e., voter turnout) defines the behavior we expect to be influenced by changes in the procedures for electing the president. The literature on voter turnout identifies several theoretical and empirical models that explain the incidence of voter participation.[4] To summarize that literature, there seem to be three main reasons why individuals may choose not to vote: "Individuals may choose not to participate because they can't, because they don't want to, or because nobody asked."[5]

Many studies of voter turnout focus on whether or not citizens want to participate — whether or not citizens believe voting is instrumental to achieving economic or noneconomic (e.g., psychological) benefits. Individuals who have preferences they believe cannot be fulfilled through balloting simply choose not to vote, perhaps pursuing these preferences through venues outside of politics. The standard socioeconomic model posits that voting and other forms of political participation are driven by individual resources such as time, money, and skills, which enhance psychological orientations that predispose individuals to vote.[6] "Because high-status individuals are located in social environments which encourage and enforce positive attitudinal and participatory norms as well as civic skills, they are more likely to participate in politics than are low-status individuals."[7] High-status individuals have the ability and/or predisposition to overcome constraints that prevent low-status individuals from voting. Because voting is thought to be a low-cost and low-benefit activity, the more formidable constraint on voting may be psychological.[8] Researchers have repeatedly found that a lack of trust in government and efficacy with voting is significantly related to lower levels of voting.[9]

Individuals are often persuaded to vote because they were asked to vote by a candidate or political party or a friend. This effect is stressed by what is known as the mobilization model; this model asserts that participation is a response to contextual cues and political opportunities structured by an individual's environment. Two kinds of cues are stressed: first, the presence of a large number of candidates appealing for citizens' votes, and second, campaign spending, media messages, grassroots campaign activities, and discussions with friends and neighborhoods. Individuals' psychological motivations and their resources are relevant to the mobilization explanation of voter turnout but occupy a different position in the explanatory model of voter turnout. Mobilization effects (i.e., voter contacts with candidates, parties, the media, or other persons) interact with a voter's psychological predispositions and resources (i.e., socioeconomic status) to influence the decision to vote. For example, higher status voters are likely to have greater access to media outlets in which political parties and their candidates advertise (e.g., follow politics in the news). Consequently, mobilization factors might be thought of as mediating variables between an individual's socioeconomic status and voting.

Some citizens may want to vote and be asked to vote but still find that they cannot. Thus, other important determinants of voter turnout are the legal restrictions states place on access to the ballot, including restrictive voter registration laws and absence of opportunities to vote on and before Election Day.[10] It has been estimated that turnout would increase nearly 9 percent with a relaxation of registration laws that constrain voting among mobile populations.[11] However, other studies provide evidence that greater opportunities to ballot on or before Election Day (e.g., allowing absentee and early voting) bring about only a limited increase in turnout; they suggest the effects of these enhanced balloting opportunities are marginal.[12]

What is the relative importance of each of the aforementioned determinants of voter turnout? One important assessment concludes that the decline in voter turnout is not primarily a matter of increased voting costs because the registration system, the chief source of costs to U.S. voters, has actually become less stringent. Instead, the solution to the turnout problem lies with reversing the decline in the perceived benefits of voting. Changes in demographics (i.e., a younger, less married, and less church-going electorate) have driven a significant portion of the electorate to become less connected, informed, and interested in politics. Moreover, the same demographic trend has pushed up the proportion of the electorate who believe government is not responsive to their needs and interests and who believe their vote doesn't matter.[13] If this assessment is correct, it is a lack of perceived benefits from voting and not of costs of voting that deter many from participating in national elections.

The literature on voting behavior suggests that voter turnout can be altered through changes in the benefits (and, to a lesser extent, the costs) that are associated with balloting or through external motivations to mobilize voters. The benefits associated with balloting include the pecuniary and psychological preferences individuals express through balloting for different candidates. The costs of voting are associated with access to the ballot, specifically restrictive registration and balloting requirements. Mobilization indirectly affects the costs and benefits associated with balloting. The persuasive activities of candidates and political parties and contextual influences that define elections (e.g., competitiveness of elections, number of contesting candidates) can provide external influences that mobilize citizens to vote.

This review of the literature on voter participation leads us to conclude that proposed changes in the way we elect the president may positively influence voter participation by increasing both the perceived benefits associated with voting and the efforts of candidates and parties to mobilize voters. These hypotheses guide our assessment of each proposal's potential effect on voter participation.

EXPECTED EFFECTS OF ELECTORAL CHANGES ON VOTER TURNOUT
Increasing the Perceived Benefits to Voters?

The popular election of the president presents several potential opportunities for altering voters' incentives to ballot. The most obvious expected effect is that voters will believe their vote counts more than it does under the status quo system of the Electoral College and that this perception will motivate turnout. Efficacy is the expected psychological predisposition that motivates voters to participate in a national popular election for president. Under the current system for electing the president, voters in smaller states are thought to believe they have a diminished influence on electing the president compared to their counterparts in larger states (because their states have too few electors to swing the election). This is true even when competing presidential candidates contest smaller states. Shifting to a popular vote for president presumably increases the incentives to vote by altering a voter's belief that they can influence the outcome of the election.

Empirical evidence for this hypothesis is wanting. First, there is substantial evidence to suggest that the marginal value of a voter's ballot increases only minutely under a system in which the president is elected by a popular vote.[14] Even if voters exaggerate the value of their vote under a popular vote scheme, there is no empirical evidence that the perception by citizens that their vote is valuable affects their tendency to actually vote.[15] Moreover, the influence of citizens' feelings of trust, efficacy, and perception of responsiveness on voting is believed to be mediated by a set of social institutions and experiences that promote these psychological attachments.[16] The popular election of the president does not create these social experiences for voters. In spite of strong public sentiment for the popular election of the president, there is no evidence to suggest that voters who prefer the popular election of the president would perceive increased benefits from voting in such a system and thus be more likely to participate in presidential elections.

Looking inside a voter's mind is always speculative and difficult. Minimally, we would expect voter participation among the most informed segments of the electorate to respond positively to the popular election of the president. This effect is probably small if not trivial. The most informed and attentive voters are already predisposed to vote. Replacing the Electoral College with the popular election of the president is not likely to be perceived by inattentive and less informed voters and will have only a trivial influence on the likelihood of voting among the most informed voters.

One variation of the national popular election — the addition of a requirement that a subsequent runoff election be held if no candidate receives a majority in the initial balloting—would further reduce the likelihood that popular elections would enhance voter turnout. A nontrivial proportion of the general electorate (in some elections, a majority) does not have a preferred second choice candidate.[17] The literature is clear that interest in runoff elections is depressed among voters whose most preferred candidates have been eliminated from the runoff election. Turnout rates fall off considerably between general and runoff elections as the number of candidates winnows to the top two finishers.

Another variation in the national popular election — having an instant-runoff election through the provision of a single transferable vote — might stimulate voter turnout. The reason is simple. Instant runoffs "may encourage greater voter participation since some refrainers [i.e., persons who see little benefit to supporting the candidates of the leading parties and who normally do not vote] may feel they have a candidate to enthusiastically support with their first-choice vote."[18] Unfortunately evidence to support this speculation is weak and anecdotal. Since the adoption of an instant runoff in 1970, voter turnout for municipal elections in Ann Arbor, Michigan, has been consistently higher, but only when there were more than two credible candidates contesting for a least one elective office. Thus an instant-runoff election for the president may only increase turnout when there are three or more competitive candidates contesting the presidency — a condition that the instant runoff might make more likely.

Still, there is little theoretical reason for voters to believe that the act of voting would be more beneficial to them under a popular vote scheme than under the Electoral College, and there is no empirical evidence to support the hypothesis that citizens would be more likely to vote under such systems. If voter turnout is to be increased by electoral reform, the most likely way for this to happen is for certain reforms to increase party and candidate mobilization of voters. We look first at how electoral reform could encourage parties and campaigns to employ their resources in ways that enhance voter turnout. Then we look at how electoral reform might mobilize voters simply by increasing the number of candidates who could ask citizens for their vote.

Mobilization through Party Resource Allocation

Some evidence suggests that how candidates and their political parties conduct their campaigns can influence turnout.[19] Researchers have long demonstrated that voter turnout increases with the level of campaign spending and other resource allocations (e.g., candidate visits). The Electoral College encourages candidates to allocate their resources disproportionately to the most populous states, especially those having the most intensive competition. Consequently, under the electoral college system, parties fail to mobilize voters in less populous and less competitive states, depressing turnout in such parts of the country.

Theorists writing on resource allocation under the Electoral College have argued "rational campaigners would allocate their resources to states in proportion to the size of the state's electoral vote blocs raised to the 3/2's power — an allocation that would concentrate resources markedly in the most populous states."[20] This theoretical expectation was confirmed for the 1976 Carter presidential campaign when "the concentration of each of these resources was almost exactly as predicted."[21] However, some scholars have found deviations from these patterns that are suggestive of the campaign strategies presidential candidates might pursue absent the large-state bias associated with the Electoral College. One contributor to this chapter has shown that bias in campaign resource allocation of the 1992 Bush campaign toward large states was mitigated by several other factors related to both mobilizing partisan supporters and persuading swing voters.[22] The 1992 Bush campaign allocated resources based on a cost per swing vote for a set of competitive battleground states. Within targeted battleground states resource allocations were based on the costs of advertising per market and access to swing voters. Another analyst reports that the travel decisions of 1980 presidential candidates revealed a strong constituency appeal (e.g., women, blacks, union members, etc.) independent of the state population size.[23]

Such research suggests that the replacement of the Electoral College might lead presidential candidates to abandon a disposition to focus on a few battleground states. Under a popular election scheme, they might employ a different strategy for identifying swing voters (as well as marginal loyalists in noncompetitive states) who can be reached in the most cost-efficient manner. This is likely to result in the substitution of one set of media markets for another. We have no reason, however, to believe that the distribution and location of swing voters will change as a result of the adoption of a new system for electing the president. Furthermore we have no reason to believe that candidates will abandon their strategy of targeting campaign resources to swing voters in areas (i.e., media markets) that afford them the most cost-efficient means of advertising. Therefore the popular election of the president is not likely to increase voter turnout by altering the level or quality of candidate campaigning among their target voters.

Reforming the Electoral College by abandoning the winner-take-all rule and allocating electors proportionately to the popular vote in each state should reduce candidate's focus on the big battleground states. This could have the same sort of minimal impacts on voter turnout that we projected in our analysis of adopting a popular vote scheme.

However, shifting to the district plan (i.e., to a system where a state's electoral votes are allocated by congressional district) would focus presidential campaigns on competitive congressional districts rather than on battleground states. The number of competitive congressional districts is relatively small (perhaps about 20–30 districts nationwide) and not concentrated in any set of states.[24] The district plan would greatly complicate presidential campaign strategies since congressional districts and media markets are not always coterminous or substantially overlapping.[25] Within some congressional districts efficient mass media campaigning (i.e., radio, television, and newspapers) may not be feasible. This might force candidates to utilize other campaign methods, including grassroots' activities, mass mailings, and direct voter contact. These campaign strategies

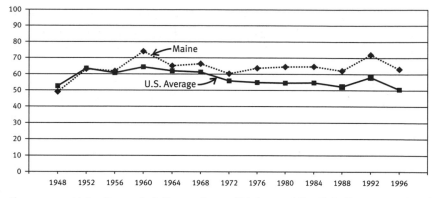

**Figure 9.1   Voter Turnout: A Comparison of Maine and the U.S. States, 1948–96
(in percentages)**

require organizational efforts beyond the current repertoire of candidate or party-centered campaigns. The relevant question is how this change in campaign activity, should it occur, might influence voter turnout.

Since 1824 only three states — Michigan, Maine, and Nebraska — have ever awarded their state's electoral votes on the basis of the votes cast for presidential candidates in each of the state's congressional districts. Michigan used the district allocation method once, in 1892. Maine has used this system since 1972, and Nebraska, since 1992. Maine provides a limited opportunity of testing the relationship between a district method of selecting presidential electors and voter turnout. To examine this link, we've calculated voter turnout in Maine and all other states for each presidential election between 1948 and 2000. If a district method of selecting presidential electors positively influences turnout, we should observe higher levels and/or rates of increase in voter turnout after the adoption of this method of selecting presidential electors, ceteris paribus.

Figure 9.1 graphs voter turnout between 1948 and 1996 for two populations. The diamonds represent the voter turnout in Maine, and the squares represent the average voter turnout in all other states. Between 1944 and 1968 voter turnout in Maine and all other states was almost identical (with the exception of 1960). Since 1972, when Maine adopted a congressional district method of selecting presidential electors, voter turnout in Maine has exceeded the average rate of voter turnout in all other states. Moreover, this gap has increased in each presidential election except 1988. This provides some, albeit circumstantial, evidence for the hypothesis that district selection of electors will increase voter participation. A statistical analysis of this relationship, however, demonstrates that the observed differences are not significant.[26]

It is possible that a district-centered allocation of electoral votes would significantly enhance local/grassroots campaign activities, which could in turn stimulate a nontrivial increase in voter turnout, but existing research is not promising of such effects. Parties, candidates, and special interests have selective incentives to mobilize target populations of voters.[27] These incentives wax and wane with changes in the distribution of social and demographic traits among the American electorate. Certainly, organizing the electorate around congressional districts for purposes of electing the president would increase incentives for parties to increase their activities at the district level. However, it is questionable that within organized interests, including political parties, this can significantly impact voter turnout.[28] Voter turnout in presidential elections declined steadily between 1960 and 1990 in spite of enhanced organizational efforts by state parties over the same period.[29] Perhaps the best evidence for evaluating whether the district plan would enable parties to successfully mobilize voters comes from a study finding that voter turnout is positively affected by local party canvassing (i.e., personal party contacts with voters), but that the impact is marginal and highly qualified.[30]

Another expected outcome from district-centered presidential campaigns is a greater inefficiency in campaigning. Relying on less cost-efficient methods of communicating with voters is likely to drive up the costs of presidential campaigns without any appreciable increase in the scope or effectiveness with which candidates communicate with voters. This might have the perverse effect of reducing voter turnout or minimally raising the cost of campaigns, to the point where candidates limit the scope of the voters they target in their mobilization efforts.

We cannot overlook recently proposed campaign finance legislation and its potential impact on voter turnout via the conduct of presidential campaigns. One provision of the McCain-Feingold Campaign Finance Act would limit soft money contributions to political parties. This would constrain party voter mobilization activities, diminishing voter turnout. However, the McCain-Feingold Act might shift campaign expenditures from political parties to the political action committees (PACs) of organized interests, with unclear consequences for increasing or decreasing voter turnout.

In sum, it is doubtful that the district plan would significantly enhance voter turnout. While the Maine experience suggests that some increase in turnout is possible, the capacity of local parties to enhance voter turnout through their activities is minimal. The increasing costs of campaigning in district-centered elections combined with new restrictions on party resources at the local level may curtail the capacity of local parties to mobilize voters in presidential campaigns conducted at the district level.

Mobilizing Voters by Increasing the Number of Candidates

Several proposals for changing the way we elect the president might increase the number of candidates seeking the office. Although others in this volume disagree (see chapters 5 and 6), we suspect that the popular election of the president under a plurality rule would significantly increase the number of minor and third-party candidates. Under a plurality election method, a larger number of candidates lowers the threshold needed to capture the presidency, increasing incentives for additional candidates to enter the election. Having a popular election of the president using majority rule with a contingent runoff election would also increase the number of candidates, as candidates representing the interests of small minorities might enter the race hoping to win concessions from major party candidates seeking additional support to win the runoff election. We further suspect that many of the candidates for president that would emerge under these election formats would appeal to voters who traditionally do not participate in presidential elections. Consequently, turnout can be expected to increase as the number of candidates for president increases. However, one limiting factor may be that citizens will not be mobilized by third-party candidates having little chance of capturing the presidency. Another limiting factor may be that supporters of third-party candidates may not be readily mobilized to support one of the two major party candidates in the runoff election, even if endorsed by the candidate who had received their vote in the initial election. We suspect that the popular election of the president with an instant runoff would have the greatest effect on voter turnout by increasing the number of candidates for president that directly appeal to traditional nonvoters.

Although we cannot test empirically the speculation that changing the method of electing the president will increase the number of contesting presidential candidates, we can assess the empirical relationship between the number of contesting presidential candidates and voter turnout. Specifically, we can test the proposition that voter interest and participation in presidential elections will increase with more presidential candidates. To test this proposition we report in figure 9.2 the relationship between voter turnout (i.e., the percentage of eligible voters who cast a ballot) in each presidential election between 1872 and 1992 and the percentage of total presidential votes cast for third-party candidates. If candidates from outside the Democratic and Republican parties attract new voters, we would expect total voter turnout to be higher in those presidential elections in which third-party candidates gained a greater share of total votes cast. Such a finding would mean that third-party candidates were attracting new voters to the polls rather than siphoning voters from the two major parties.

Figure 9.2 fails to demonstrate that a significant relationship exists between voter turnout and the presence of third-party candidates on the presidential ballot between 1872 and 1992.[31] There is virtually no relationship between the percentage of votes cast for third-party candidates and the percentage of eligible voters balloting over the period studied. If there is any discernible relationship it appears that turnout actually declines, albeit insignificantly, with a higher percentage of votes cast for third-party candidates. We cannot conclude from these data that any change in the method of electing the president that increased the number of

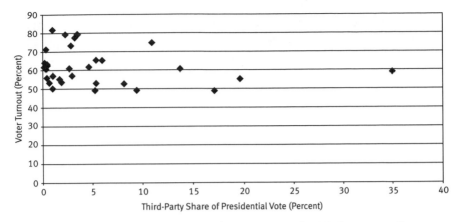

Figure 9.2   Third-Party Vote Share and Voter Turnout in U.S. Representative
Elections: 1872–1992

Source: Brent Boyea, "Moderate Third Parties: Moderate or Policy Pragmatists." Unpublished
manuscript, Rice University, Houston, Texas

contesting candidates would in turn significantly increase voter participation in
presidential elections.

The Uniqueness of the Electoral College

Finally, our skepticism about the efficacy of any proposed electoral reform to
positively influence citizen participation is based on the uniqueness of the presidential election process. The Electoral College is unique and has no counterpart.
Virtually every other election held in the fifty states and more than 80,000 local
governments uses one (and in instances more than one) of the electoral methods
considered in this volume. Yet, on average voter turnout has been higher in
presidential elections than for any other electoral contest. Moreover, presidential
elections occur simultaneously with elections for other federal, state, and local
offices that are conducted under very different rules/procedures from those governing the election of the president. Though it would be specious to reason from
this fact that voter turnout is heightened by the Electoral College, it seems reasonable to expect that voter turnout in presidential elections will be unaffected
by any of the proposed reforms.

THE DUBIOUS VIRTUES OF CITIZEN PARTICIPATION

It is assumed that greater levels of citizen participation are desirable and beneficial
for the health of the American political system. Reforms of the electoral process
that enhance turnout are therefore thought to be justified, even if the change in
turnout is only marginal and costly. A past president of the American Political
Science Association has advocated for the adoption of compulsory voting, ar-

guing that "its advantages far outweigh the normative and practical objections to it."[32] In this section, we examine the logic and empirical evidence for a fully engaged and mobilized electorate. We argue that American democracy with its federalist structure operates best when voter turnout is constrained to those who have sincerely held preferences across electoral choices. A fully engaged and mobilized electorate is not necessary for the health of the Republic and might, under specific circumstances, be counterproductive to democratic aspirations.

The Case for Full Voter Participation

Normative democratic theorists have argued that, in a society with diverse preferences and interests, maximization of participation is both desirable and necessary for the maintenance of democratic institutions.[33] First, failure to achieve maximum participation leaves many preferences unrevealed and potentially unmet. Under majority rule it is expected that the median voter's position will be adopted. Failure of some to participate may skew the outcome of elections and government policies away from the median citizen's preference. The consequences are less public support and compliance with government policies. Chronic levels of nonparticipation erode support for the political system and its institutions penultimate to serious challenges to the legitimacy of political institutions. Policies under a political system with nonparticipation from a majority of the electorate are likely to be inefficient and ineffectual.

Several empirical conditions should be observable among the eligible electorate if these normative prescriptions and empirical predictions about citizen participation are true. We should observe significantly higher levels of dissatisfaction, distrust, and alienation with government among nonvoters. Furthermore, policy preferences should be significantly at variance between those who participate and those who do not. Moreover, there should be a significant and positive correlation between the policy preferences of participants and the actions of government. Conversely there should be a weak or insignificant relationship between the policy preferences of nonparticipants and government policies.

Comparing Voters and Nonvoters

There is little evidence in the literature to support any of these hypotheses. It appears that there are no significant differences between voters and nonvoters on several affective dimensions, including trust in government, perceived responsiveness of government, and satisfaction with the actions and policies of government.[34] Moreover, the policy preferences of voters and nonvoters on a wide range of issues were virtually identical.[35] Also suggestive of the point that maximum voter turnout really doesn't matter is the finding that the outcomes of the 1980, 1984, and 1988 presidential elections would have been the same even if nonvoters had balloted.[36] What makes these findings even more perplexing is that "the core group of people that participate in election after election, time after time is remarkably small."[37] Citizen participation in general and in voting specifically is episodic with different people voting in different elections.[38]

In short, the very conditions necessary to justify maximum electoral participation for the maintenance of democratic institutions appear not to be operative. What explains this apparent disconnect between theory and reality? What do these findings suggest about the importance of citizen participation for the healthy operation of democratic political institutions? Moreover, how can so few voters (i.e., less than half the electorate) produce an electoral outcome identical to what would have occurred if all voters balloted?

An important study of nonvoters offers some answers to these questions.[39] First, it rejects the stereotypic image of the nonvoter as "a decidedly downcast lot...insufficiently motivated to participate in politics."[40] Though some portion of the nonvoting electorate (approximately 18 percent) fits this image, the overwhelming majority of nonvoters are engaged in and knowledgeable about politics, candidates, and the actions of government. Their choice not to vote is voluntary and conscious, and not solely determined by limited resources and contextual obstacles to voting (e.g., restrictive registration laws for mobile voters). Nonvoters are often thought of as people who never enter the political arena, but they are better understood as individuals who enter and exit the electorate with greater regularity (and reason) than core or habitual voters. For such citizens the irregularity of voting is partially a function of candidate and party mobilization of voters, but we think another explanation may also be operative. This explanation centers on the marginal or intermittent voter. For such voters, nonvoting is itself a form of political behavior.

The Role of the Marginal Voter

In the literature on voting much is made of the role of the average or median voter — the person who defines the democratic choice in mass elections. But does the median voter change as a function of who does and who does not vote in specific elections? The research discussed above suggests that there is a class of voters (and nonvoters) who move in and out of the electorate but whose preferences and choices are not significantly different from those unengaged in any single election.

The behavior of citizens in the public sphere may be similar to that of consumers in the private market.[41] Consider the role of the consumer and his behavior in purchasing cars. Most cars last several years, and between purchases individuals need not concern themselves with knowing anything about the costs and benefits of cars. But when a consumer is in the market to buy a car, he is relatively informed and knowledgeable. In fact, the market for cars is driven by a small percentage of the population (about 20 percent each year). These consumers are informed and attentive to the advertisements of car companies. When they leave the market, they are replaced with another 20 percent of the buying public who similarly are informed and energized to make utility-maximizing choices. The important point of this example is that there is little year-to-year difference in either the composition of the car-consuming public or the choices they make. The attentiveness and knowledge of the marginal consumer "acting in their own self-interest help create an efficient market."[42] Moreover, the marginal consumer produces a positive externality for nonconsumers by making decisions and choices that are proximate to those nonconsumers would make if they invested the time and sources in becoming informed about the market choices available.

We suspect that voter turnout and the outcomes of elections can be described in terms similar to the marginal consumer thesis. Buying cars is not entirely like voting for candidates for public office. The purchase of private goods and services has specific properties that drive the utility-maximizing behavior of individuals in ways that are fundamentally different from voting and political participation. Drawing an analogy between car buying and voting is useful, however, to explain why limited voter participation may not be problematic for the health of democracy.

Like car buyers, voters enter and leave the electorate with some regularity. Recall that an individual voter's participation waxes and wanes over time. This variation is partially a function of voter mobilization by candidates and parties.[43] To this explanation we add a modest addendum. At different points in time, voters — like car buyers — may be in the market for a particular elective office and hence be more attentive to advertisements of candidates and their parties contesting for these offices. It is the need to vote at a specific point in time and for a specific office and/or candidate that makes voters more susceptible to the messages of candidates. Their attentiveness to the candidates' messages enables these voters to make utility-maximizing choices. Nonvoters ride free on the benefits that accrue from the electoral choices of marginal voters because they too would make the same (or approximately the same) choices were they attentive to campaign messages and had they voted.

American federalism, with its three distinct levels of government, creates a market for political participation. Each level of government has a set of unique responsibilities as well as a shared set of functional responsibilities. Most citizens have a basic knowledge of the functional responsibilities of each level of government.[44] For most voters, exclusive of the small proportion of habitual participants, voting is like shopping for cars. People participate in those electoral contests for which they have a substantive interest. Voters with school-age children are expected to turn out for school-board and school-bond elections with greater regularity than for presidential or mid-term congressional elections. Voters over 65 who receive Social Security and Medicare benefits should be more attentive and interested in national political campaigns.

Voters are drawn to elections for those levels and units of government whose functional responsibilities are most germane to their interests and needs. This is hardly a heroic hypothesis. Moreover, it is not inconsistent or at variance with the popular mobilization thesis. To the contrary, candidates and parties are most efficacious in mobilizing voters for electoral contests in which the voters have strong stakes and interests. These voters are motivated to acquire information about contesting issues and candidates in order to identify the choice that maximizes their preferences. Their choices are not at variance with the preferences of nonvoters.

Under our marginal voter scenario, modest voter turnout in any election is not a problem for representative democracy. Voter participation is expected to be informed and rational; that is, voters possess the information necessary to match their preferences and needs with the available candidates and/or electoral choices that maximize their utility. The decisions of these marginal voters are not at variance with the preferences of nonvoters. In fact, the latter obtain a free ride from voters, who produce outcomes that are similar to what nonvoters would have produced had they voted.

Thus far, our discussion has focused on the consequences and meaning of low voter turnout. Another perspective on this question asks whether there are unintended and unexpected consequences of maximum voter turnout?[45] Higher turnout brings to the ballot box peripheral voters, who are unlikely to have voted without significant help from the candidates and parties and who are "just as fickle inside the voting booth as they are about getting to it."[46] The fickleness of peripheral voters leads them to defect from their weakly held preferences (i.e., party identification) at rates much greater than core voters. Peripheral voters are not sufficiently interested in the outcome of any election to invest in maximizing their preferences (however weakly held) through candidate selection. We expect peripheral voters will ballot in the direction of the loudest and most recent campaign message.[47] Moreover, peripheral voters' weakly held preferences and insincere voting choices actually distort the outcome of elections for core and other nonperipheral voters. Though the preferences of peripheral voters are not expected to be at variance with the core voters, it is their mobilization into the electorate that produces defections from these weakly held preferences, thus distorting electoral outcomes for those with sincere and informed preferences. Under these conditions maximization of voter turnout is both unnecessary and potentially harmful to democratic representation. Mobilized peripheral voters are making choices they would not otherwise have made had they voted sincerely.

Our skepticism about the necessity for maximum political participation originates with several anomalous empirical findings in the literature, including the lack of disparity in preferences and attitudes between voters and nonvoters, the fickleness of the peripheral voters' ballot choices, and the intermittent nature of individual voter participation.

SUMMARY AND CONCLUSION

There are several compelling and empirically valid reasons for reforming the way we select the president of the United States. Several chapters in this volume make the case for one or more of these reforms. We cannot, however, find any supporting arguments or evidence to justify reforming the presidential electoral process based on how these reforms would impact citizen participation. We have found no substantial argument or evidence to support the hypothesis that increased voter participation would result from any of the proposed electoral reforms. Moreover, the relevant empirical research in the extant literature suggests that the proposed electoral reforms address maladies and inadequacies in the electoral process that are not germane to voter participation or nonparticipation. In short, the reforms discussed in this volume are largely irrelevant to the nature and scope of voter participation.

We question the logic of proposing electoral reforms that would increase voter participation. In the second half of our chapter we argue that maximum voter participation is neither a necessary condition for a healthy democracy, nor is it desirable. We demonstrate using previous research why maximum voter participation might distort electoral outcomes in ways that undermine democratic principles (i.e., majority rule and the median voter hypothesis). Our point is not to be unnecessarily obdurate about electoral reform or political participation. Rather we think that reforming the presidential selection process may be justified for a number of reasons, but not because it enhances citizen participation.

NOTES

1. For a more extensive discussion of nonvoting forms of political participation, see Jan E. Leighley, "Attitudes, Opportunities and Incentives: A Field Essay on Political Participation," *Political Research Quarterly* 48 (March 1995): 181–209.
2. Becky Cain, testimony at hearing on "Proposals for Electoral College Reform" before the Subcommittee on the Committee of the Constitution of the Judiciary Committee of the House of Representatives, 4 September 1997, Serial No. 87, 19–22.
3. Bernard Berelson, Paul F. Lazarsfeld, and William N. McPhee, *Voting: A Study of Opinion Formation in a Presidential Election* (Chicago: University of Chicago Press, 1954).
4. This discussion draws heavily from Leighley, "Attitudes, Opportunities and Incentives," and Ruy Teixeira, *The Disappearing American Voter* (Washington, D.C.: Brookings Institution, 1992).
5. Sidney Verba, Kay L. Schlozman, Henry Brady, and Norman Nie, "Resources and Political Participation," paper prepared for the 1991 annual meeting of the American Political Science Association.
6. Gabriel Almond and Sidney Verba, *Civic Culture: Political Attitudes and Democracy in Five Nations* (Princeton: Princeton University Press, 1963); Lester Milbrath, *Political Participation* (Chicago: Rand McNally, 1965); Sidney Verba, Norman Nie, and J. Kim, *Participation and Political Equality: A Seven Nation Comparison* (Cambridge: Cambridge University Press, 1978).
7. Leighley, "Attitudes, Opportunities and Incentives," 103.
8. John Aldrich, "Rational Choice and Turnout," *American Journal of Political Science* 37 (March 1993): 246–78.
9. Leighley notes this relationship is plagued by an endogeneity problem: specifically, do efficacy, trust, and civic obligation determine voting, or do voting and other forms of political participation determine and fashion attitudes about government and political participation? In

"Attitudes, Opportunities and Incentives," 106, Leighley states: "One obvious consequence of mis-specifying the relationship between civic orientations and participation is to overestimate the effects of individuals' attitudes on participation."

10. Raymond E. Wolfinger and Steven J. Rosenstone, *Who Votes?* (New Haven: Yale University Press, 1980); G. Bingham Powell, "American Voter Turnout in a Comparative Perspective," *American Political Science Review* 80 (June 1986): 17–44.

11. Raymond E. Wolfinger, David P. Glass, and Peverill Squire, "Residential Mobility and Voter Turnout," *American Political Science Review* 81 (March 1987): 45–66.

12. Robert M. Stein, "Early Voting," *Public Opinion Quarterly* 62 (Spring 1998): 57–70; Robert M. Stein and Patricia Garcia-Monet, "Voting Early, But Not Often," *Social Science Quarterly* 78 (September 1997): 657–77.

13. Teixeira, *Disappearing American Voter,* 56.

14. Aldrich, "Rational Choice and Turnout."

15. Paul R. Abramson and John H. Aldrich, "The Decline of Electoral Participation in America," *American Political Science Review* 76 (September 1982): 502–21.

16. Michael W. Giles and Marilyn K. Dantico, "Political Participation and Neighborhood Social Context Revisited," *American Journal of Political Science* 26 (February 1982): 144–50; Robert Huckfeldt and John Sprague, "Political Parties and Electoral Mobilization: Political Structure, Social Structure, and the Party Canvass," *American Political Science Review* 86 (March 1992): 70–86; Robert Huckfeldt and John Sprague, "Networks in Context: The Social Flow of Political Information," *American Political Science Review* 81 (December 1987): 1197–1216.

17. George Rabinowitz and Stuart Elaine Macdonald, "A Directional Theory of Issue Voting," *American Political Science Review* 83 (March 1989): 93–121.

18. The Center for Voting and Democracy 2000, www.fairvote.org.

19. Steven J. Rosenstone and John Mark Hansen, *Mobilization, Participation, and Democracy in America* (New York: Macmillan, 1993); Samuel C. Patterson and Gregory A. Caldeira, "Mailing In the Vote: Correlates and Consequences of Absentee Voting," *American Journal of Political Science* 29 (November 1985): 766–88; Samuel C. Patterson and Gregory A. Caldeira, "Getting Out the Vote: Participation in Gubernatorial Elections," *American Political Science Review* 77 (September 1983): 675–89.

20. Steven J. Brams and Morton D. Davis "The 3/2's Rule in Presidential Campaigning," *American Political Science Review* 68 (March 1974): 113–34; Claude S. Colantoni, Terrence J. Levesque and Peter C. Ordeshook, "Campaign Resource Allocations under the Electoral College," *American Political Science Review* 69 (March 1975): 141–54.

21. Larry M. Bartels, "Resource Allocation In a Presidential Campaign," *Journal of Politics* 47 (August 1985): 928–36.

22. Daron Shaw, "The Methods Behind the Madness: Presidential Electoral College Strategies, 1988–1996," *Journal of Politics* 69 (November 1999): 893–913.

23. Darrell M. West, "Constituencies and Travel Allocations in the 1980 Presidential Campaign," *American Journal of Political Science* 27 (August 1983): 515–29.

24. Gary C. Jacobson, *The Politics of Congressional Elections* (New York: Longman, 2001).

25. John R. Alford, Keith Henry, and James Campbell, "Television Markets and Congressional Elections," *Legislative Studies Quarterly* 15 (March 1985): 665–78.

26. A pooled cross section regression analysis with robust standard errors was performed where the dependent variable was voter turnout. The main independent variable was a dummy variable where 1 represented voter turnout in Maine after 1972 (when Maine adopted a district method for allocating presidential electors) and 0 for the years preceding 1972. Other variables were included as controls for national and state trends. The coefficient for voter turnout in Maine after 1972 is not statistically significant, indicating that the rise in Maine's turnout after 1972 was not significantly different from the national trend for the same period.

27. Rosenstone and Hansen, *Mobilization, Participation, and Democracy,* and Aldrich, "Rational Choice and Turnout."

28. Teixeira, *Disappearing American Voter,* 42.

29. James L. Gibson, Cornelius P. Cotter, John F. Bibby, and Robert J. Huckshorn, "Whither

the Local Parties? A Cross- Sectional and Longitudinal Analysis of the Strength of Party Organizations," *American Journal of Political Science* 29 (February 1985): 139–60.

30. Robert Huckfeldt and John Sprague, "Networks in Context."
31. The relationship between voter turnout and third-party vote share is statistically insignificant: B = .014, p = .56.
32. Arend Lijphart, "Unequal Participation: Democracy's Unresolved Dilemma. Presidential Address, American Political Science Association, 1996," *American Political Science Review* 91 (March 1997): 1–13. For a contrary position, see Austin Ranney, "Nonvoting is Not a Social Disease," *Public Opinion* (October/November 1983): 16–20.
33. James Fishkin, *The Voice of the People: Public Opinion and Democracy* (New Haven: Yale University Press, 1995).
34. Teixeira, *Disappearing American Voter,* 89–101.
35. A dissenting view on the policy congruence between voters and policy outputs is provided by: Kim Quaile Hill and Jan E. Leighley, "The Policy Consequences of Class Bias in State Electorates." *American Journal of Political Science* 35 (May 1992): 351–65; Alexander Hicks and Duane H. Swank, "Politics, Institutions and Welfare Spending in Industrialized Democracies," *American Political Science Review* 86 (September 1992): 658–74; Walter R. Mebane Jr. "Fiscal Constraints and Electoral Manipulation in American Social Welfare," *American Political Science Review* 88 (March 1994): 77–94.
36. Teixeira, *Disappearing American Voter,* 93; Stephen Bennett and D. Resnik, "The Implications of Nonvoting for Democracy in the United States," *American Journal of Political Science* 72 (November 1990): 314–33.
37. Rosenstone and Hansen, *Mobilization, Participation, and Democracy in America,* 55.
38. Ibid., 70.
39. Lyn Ragsdale and Jerrold G. Rusk, "Who Are Nonvoters? Profiles from the 1990 Senate Elections," *American Journal of Political Science* 37 (August 1993): 721–46.
40. Ibid., 744
41. Paul Teske, Mark Schneider, Michael Mintrom, and Samuel Best, "Establishing the Micro Foundations of a Macro Theory: Information, Movers, and the Competitive Local Market for Public Goods," *American Political Science Review* 87 (September 1993): 702–13.
42. Ibid., 704.
43. Rosenstone and Hansen, *Mobilization, Participation, and Democracy in America.*
44. Charles M. Tidmarch, Lisa J. Hyman, and Jill E. Sorkin, "Press Issue Agendas in the 1982 Congressional and Gubernatorial Election Campaigns," *Journal of Politics* 46 (November 1984): 1226–42; Robert M. Stein, "Economic Voting for Governor and U.S. Senator: The Electoral Consequences of Federalism," *Journal of Politics* 52 (February 1990): 29–53.
45. James Denardo, "Turnout and the Vote: The Joke's on the Democrats," *American Political Science Review* 74 (June 1980): 406–20.
46. Ibid., 418.
47. John Zaller, *The Nature and Origins of Mass Opinion* (Cambridge: Cambridge University Press, 1992).

CHAPTER 10

Election Rules and Social Stability

Erik S. Herron, *University of Kansas*
Ronald A. Francisco, *University of Kansas*
O. Fiona Yap, *University of Kansas*

THERE IS LITTLE PROTEST against elections anywhere in the world. Unless there is a suspicion of fraud or other subversion of public will, open dissidence rarely occurs. Voting, after all, gives a voice to eligible citizens. Why should the aggregation of these voices lead to terror, protest, or other forms of social instability?

Political instability involves the breakdown of a government regime so that it must govern with repression. Social instability involves open and widespread dissidence and protest that question the legitimacy of the regime and its officials. Studies that link elections to political and social stability generally focus on legislatures rather than on the chief executive.[1] Parliaments represent more diverse interests than the executive branch because they contain more democratically elected officials. Further, legislative debate is generally more open and transparent than deliberation in the executive branch. Because legislators represent varied constituencies and views, the adequacy of the means of their selection can contribute to the maintenance or decline of political and social stability.

However, elections for the chief executive may also influence the likelihood of stability or instability because presidents tend to have an independent, national mandate and generally wield substantial powers. While presidential power varies crossnationally, presidents are invested with informal or formal authority to set the policy agenda, propose laws, and check other branches of government.[2]

A presidential system's ability to promote or undermine stability has generally been framed within the argument about the merits and flaws of presidential and parliamentary systems. Critics of presidential systems have pointed to dual legitimacy of the executive and legislative branches, temporal rigidity preventing the ouster of ineffective presidents during their terms, a "winner-takes-all" outcome that may encourage a president to eschew coalition-building, and the

Table 10.1   Number of Countries Employing Electoral Rules under Consideration

	Electoral College	Plurality	Majority runoff	Instant runoff
Number of countries	1	20	49	2

Source: André Blais, Louis Massicotte, and Agnieszka Dobrzynska, "Direct Presidential Elections: A World Study," *Electoral Studies* 16 (April 1997): 441–45.

possibility of populist amateurs gaining office as factors that potentially contribute to instability.[3] However, our concern is not with the debate between presidential and parliamentary systems, but rather with how electoral rules within presidential systems might exacerbate or mitigate social instability.

Election rules that contribute to the perception that the public will has been subverted may undermine social stability. Rules that lead to the exclusion of minority opinions, particularly in societies divided along cultural, religious, racial, regional or other lines, can lead to instability. Likewise, rules facilitating the accession to power of politicians with extreme political views are a factor. Further, presidential election rules interact with legislative election rules, influencing the number of political parties, their ideological diversity, and the level of support they provide the president in parliament.[4] The interaction of presidential and parliamentary election rules may also influence the effectiveness of policymaking, bringing about political instability and ultimately social instability. Election rules themselves are not direct causes of instability, but some rules may precipitate it.

A recent cross-national analysis of presidential election rules shows that each of the four major alternative proposals considered in this book are currently used in at least one country (see Table 10.1).[5] Most popularly elected presidents are selected by majority rule with a runoff, which is "majority runoff" in the table. Plurality rules are the second most popular form of election rules for presidents. Two countries (Ireland and Sri Lanka) use the single transferable or alternative vote, which is labeled the instant runoff in this volume. Only the United States still uses an electoral college,[6] as Argentina and Finland recently discarded such systems.[7] We will assess how each factor contributing to instability listed above may be influenced by the four forms of electoral rules proposed for presidential elections.[8]

SUBVERSION OF THE PUBLIC WILL

The perception that the will of the public has been subverted can arise if fraud (or a belief that fraud has occurred) is widespread or if the winning candidate claims a mandate not supported by the election results. The former could occur under any set of electoral rules, but the nature of electoral fraud may differ depending upon the rules.

All elections are subject to random and systematic error. Random error occurs when ballots are miscounted or erroneously discarded, precinct officials apply different standards of voter identification, or other mistakes are made that do not systematically benefit certain parties or candidates. Ultimately, random errors should cancel each other out at the national level. Systematic errors can be introduced through ballots that confuse or mislead voters and fraud at the local or national level.[9] Systematic fraud may involve candidates or parties receiving more votes or a higher proportion of votes than were legitimately cast because of the following: ballot box stuffing; theft of ballot boxes; alterations in individual ballots; changes of vote tallies by local, regional, or national election officials; or other improper manipulations of the vote.

If fraudulent methods are employed, one might expect to find variation in the forms of fraud based on the election system. Under an electoral college, partisans willing to manipulate elections may concentrate their efforts in regions where their candidate is expected to lose (especially if the margin is small) and that have a relatively high number of electors (e.g., Illinois in 1960). If victory margins are wide, a greater level of fraud may be required to win the electors, increasing the likelihood of detection. Because vote manipulations may not be beneficial in all geographic regions, election observers could concentrate on regions where fraud is most likely to occur. Because the Electoral College reduces the benefits of widespread vote manipulations and increases the probability of detection, it mitigates the risk of social instability arising from the belief that the public will has been subverted through fraud.

Under a plurality system, fraud could be more widespread. Increases in vote totals in any or all precincts would contribute to the candidate's likelihood of victory. The diffusion of fraud would also make it more difficult to prevent. Majority-runoff systems introduce further complexity for those willing to manipulate votes. In both rounds of the election, votes in any precinct could help a candidate win. However, the use of a two-round system raises the likelihood that fraud may be detected, because of the additional round of voting. For example, scholarship comparing first and second round results in Russia's majority-runoff presidential elections suggests that votes were manipulated in the 1996 elections to the detriment of the Communist Party candidate.[10] The instant runoff or alternative vote introduces the possibility of additional forms of fraud. Vote manipulation could occur not only in any geographic area, but also on many parts of the ballot. First-place votes might not be altered; second preferences could be changed to influence election outcomes.

Although some amount of random and systematic error is likely to occur in most elections, the Electoral College provides the most likely environment both for discovering and preventing fraud among the systems we assess. Despite this relative advantage, the American Electoral College introduces a unique form of subversion of the public will: rogue electors.[11] Cases of rogue electors are empirically rare and they have not changed the results of elections. Nevertheless, the Electoral College allows electors to vote for candidates not supported by the plurality of voters in the state (even candidates outside the presidential race). Some states require electors to vote for the candidate winning the state's plurality vote, but this provision is not in the U.S. Constitution.[12] If rogue electors altered election results, the legitimacy of the presidential elections could be questioned, contributing to instability.

The public will can also be subverted if the winner claims a mandate that does not conform with election results. The 2000 U.S. presidential elections yielded a victor who could not claim majority or plurality support in the popular vote. While the election of minority presidents in the past did not directly lead to social instability in the United States, the failure to gain a popular victory along with an electoral victory may undermine a president's ability to govern and indirectly contribute to instability.[13]

The Electoral College may also inflate the victory margin, conferring upon the victor the perception of a more substantial victory than he enjoyed in the popular vote[14] and thus a "contrived majorit[y]."[15] The Electoral College "mandate" can convey greater legitimacy to the winner by implying that his victory was supported by a majority of the population. If the assumption of a clear electoral mandate extends to policies, the chief executive could assert that his policy preferences enjoy majority support and should be enacted regardless of legislative preferences.[16] By asserting a mandate that does not reflect popular vote outcomes, a president could incite opposition that would lead to conflict. In the United States, however, many presidents have failed to garner majority support, but social instability has not emerged as a consequence.

Plurality systems may produce a president with majority support, but the winning candidate needs only to win more votes than the closest competitor. Winners of recent plurality elections in Iceland, Kenya, Mexico, Panama, the Philippines, South Korea, and Taiwan did not receive majority support, although some came close.[17] If a president without majority support in the electorate promotes a partisan agenda, his efforts could be characterized as an attempt to implement policies that contradict the popular will. Because a majority of the population did not support the election of the president, attempts to assert his preferences (through decree or executive orders) could galvanize the opposition and contribute to instability. Conversely, presidents without majority support may strike more conciliatory policy stances in order to be effective.[18]

To win in the first round of a majority-runoff or instant-runoff system, a candidate must obtain majority support among voters. A first-round winner, therefore, may claim an electoral mandate provided by a majority of voters. If elections require a second round, however, the ultimate winner would not enjoy majority support of first preferences. Rather, voters would express lower preferences either through a second round of balloting (in the majority-runoff) or the distribution of their expressed preferences (in the instant runoff). Nevertheless, the winner ultimately acquires majority support to gain office.

The electoral mandate may increase the president's authority vis-à-vis the legislature, allowing him to implement his policy agenda. Nevertheless, majority support may not provide the president freedom to enact policies that are perceived to limit the rights of large minority populations.

MINORITY REPRESENTATION

The failure to represent minority interests in government may undermine social stability, particularly in societies with deep cultural, religious, ethnic, or linguistic cleavages. While the presidency is not designed to be a broadly representative institution because a single individual occupies the office, electoral rules may encourage a president to select a more diverse cabinet under certain conditions. The selection of a more diverse cabinet can send signals to opposition groups that their interests are being considered directly by the executive branch.

An established electoral college and plurality rules are less likely to encourage the selection of a diverse cabinet than are popular majority rule systems (attained by a contingent second round of elections or by the instant alternative vote). Under the former rules, the winning party is neither obligated nor encouraged to choose a cabinet that reflects the views of unsuccessful competitors. While American presidents have tapped members of the losing party to participate in the cabinet, cabinet members' policy views are generally similar to the president's.[19]

But a majority-runoff or instant-runoff system can encourage a greater diversity of views in the executive branch. Majority-runoff rules tend to encourage more candidates to participate in presidential elections than plurality rules or an electoral college.[20] In a two-round system, the third-place finisher can play the role of "kingmaker" by negotiating a position in government in exchange for supporting one of the two top finishers from round one.[21]

The creation of a more representative cabinet is not guaranteed under majority-runoff or instant-runoff systems. When a majority-runoff system produces no clear first-round winner and a strong third-place finisher with relatively disciplined supporters (who might support either of the remaining candidates without an endorsement), the third-place candidate is positioned to negotiate with one of the two remaining players. If these conditions are not present, the third-place finisher is in a weaker position vis-à-vis the other candidates and may be unable to obtain a position in government.

Majority-runoff and alternative vote systems, by (possibly) including multiple parties in the cabinet, could mitigate the winner-takes-all nature of presidential systems. Further, minority members of the cabinet are more likely to be viewed as independent players than minority members under plurality rules or an electoral college.[22] While this process facilitates representation, it could permit extremist politicians to join the government (a point addressed below).

ACCESSION OF EXTREMIST POLITICIANS

When extremist politicians gain power, system performance usually suffers. In legislatures, support for extremist groups is associated with increased incidents of rioting as well as political and social unrest.[23] The more seats controlled by antigovernment parties in a legislature, the higher the probability of policy paralysis and government failure.[24] Some election rules facilitate the accession to power of extremist politicians more than other rules.

Because the Electoral College requires diffuse geographic support as well as broad, national support, it raises barriers to the extremist candidate. Countries with substantial ethnic cleavages have adopted procedures that provide similar safeguards, as does the Electoral College to prevent extremist politicians from becoming chief executive. Although it did not employ an electoral college, Nigeria used an electoral formula in 1979 and 1983 that followed the principle of local and national support to prevent extremists from gaining office. The law required a candidate to gain a national plurality as well as 25 percent of the vote in two-thirds of the states.[25] By using this formula, a candidate required support beyond his own ethnic group to win the presidency. In this way, Nigeria attempted to ensure that extreme policies were not pursued by the winner. The American Electoral College operates in a similar manner, requiring a candidate to enjoy support in many states to win the presidency. Concentrated support in a single region or within a single constituency does not guarantee victory.

Majority-runoff rules and the instant runoff also protect the presidency from extremists. The majority requirement in the first round forces a candidate to have broad electoral support. If no candidate wins the first round, the surviving candidates must attempt to curry favor with their defeated foes prior to the second round of balloting. Under the instant runoff, cooperation is likely to occur prior to the election. Electoral cooperation, promoted by majority-runoff or instant-runoff rules, may moderate policies and insulate the presidency from extremists.

While majority-runoff rules and the instant runoff may reduce the likelihood of an extremist president, they may increase the likelihood of extremist politicians gaining cabinet positions. As noted above, prominent extremists may win cabinet posts in the process of negotiation with one of the top two candidates. Although the president may allow an extremist politician into the cabinet in exchange for support during the campaign, members of the executive branch serve at the behest of the president and may be removed if their political views become discordant with those of the president.

Plurality rules provide extremist politicians with the greatest opportunity to gain the presidency. Although plurality rules should encourage two-candidate competition over time (moderating the views of candidates), multicandidate races may occur. As the number of candidates increases, the minimum bound of the effective threshold declines.[26] That is, when more candidates participate, the proportion of votes needed to win the position drops. If only two candidates compete, one must win a majority (50 percent plus 1 vote) of valid votes to gain office.[27] However, if five candidates divide vote shares evenly, the winning candidate needs only to obtain 20 percent plus one vote to gain the presidency. Further, because support is aggregated nationally, a politician does not need geographically diffuse support to win office under plurality rules. Because of these features, plurality rules provide the least protection against extremist politicians gaining the presidency.

The importance and high profile of the presidential office has prompted many third-party candidates to compete in U.S. elections, despite the institutional incentives for two-candidate competition. The impact of these candidates is generally minimal, but some third-party candidates have influenced which major party candidate won the election (e.g., as Theodore Roosevelt's third-party bid in 1912 split the Republican vote, enabling the Democrat Woodrow Wilson to win with a plurality). Thus, in the U.S. context, it is unlikely that an extremist politician would win the presidency even if other rules were employed.

INTERACTION WITH OTHER ELECTION LAWS

Certain election rules and features of elections (such as the timing of legislative and presidential elections) contribute to the likelihood that a president's party will receive a majority in the legislature. Without a majority or near-majority, presidents are less likely to be able to enact policy initiatives.[28] While gridlock between the legislature and executive may not generate mass protest, it can increase public dissatisfaction with the government and regime. Electoral rules undermining the president's ability to acquire majority support in the legislature increase the likelihood of regime failure or political instability.[29]

The Electoral College discourages many candidates from contesting the presidency because a candidate must have broad support to acquire enough electors to win office. Similarly, single-member-district plurality rules for congressional representatives generally discourage many candidates from contesting seats, although any individual race may have more than two effective candidates. Institutional pressure toward two-candidate competition in each district improves the likelihood that the president's fellow partisans will gain a majority in the legislature, particularly if presidential and legislative elections are held concurrently. In the U.S. context, the election rules work in tandem to promote coattail effects that facilitate governance.[30] The use of plurality rules for the presidency could also produce a presidential majority in the legislature based on the same logic.

By contrast, majority-runoff and instant-runoff rules are less likely to facilitate a presidential majority than those that promote two-party competition.

These rules encourage multicandidate competition that could have spillover effects into legislative elections. Congressional candidates from minor parties might gain electoral support if voters do not perceive that their votes will be wasted. Majority-runoff and instant-runoff systems encourage sincere voting that could influence voter preferences on legislative ballots. Third parties in the United States have been damaged by the "wasted vote" argument (e.g., as happened to John Anderson in 1980).[31] Majority-runoff and alternative vote rules undermine this argument and could divert votes from major to minor parties in both presidential and legislative elections.

By encouraging multicandidate competition, these rules reduce the likelihood of a presidential majority in parliament. While the use of single-member districts in U.S. congressional elections would probably minimize the effect, different presidential formulas and election timing could influence legislative election outcomes. Thus, majority-runoff and instant-runoff rules are less likely to yield a presidential majority in the legislature than electoral college and plurality rules, although the difference may be marginal in the U.S. context. If such electoral rules encourage "divided government," and if divided governments produce stalemates and ineffectiveness, instability could result.

UNINTENDED CONSEQUENCES

Changes in institutional rules inevitably yield both intended and unintended consequences. Proposals to eliminate the Electoral College in the United States generally attack it as an archaic method that prevents American citizens from directly selecting their president. Further, it can yield a president who loses the popular vote. On the one hand, the Electoral College does require candidates to obtain support in many states and limits the chances that extremist candidates will win the office.

The Electoral College also promotes stability in the American context between its flaws are known. Adopting new electoral rules may correct some of the Electoral College's shortcomings, but may introduce consequences that promote conditions that threaten social stability more than the existing system.

The choice of an electoral system is a choice between governance and representation.[32] Governance implies an easily identified mandate with limited opposition, while representation maximizes opposition by allowing most parties to have seats in the legislature. The U.S. electoral system is wholly skewed toward governance. It minimizes representation through the plurality system and winner-take-all rule. Other countries attempt to gain broader representation, often with the tradeoff of less stable governance. So strong is the plurality and electoral college rule in U.S. elections that governance is virtually certain.[33] When Benjamin Harrison won the presidency in 1888 through the Electoral College, he had 100,000 fewer popular votes than did Grover Cleveland. But there was no unrest. In more than one-third of U.S. presidential elections the victor has had no majority in the popular vote, and there was no unrest. Indeed, the closest recent election before 2000 was the Kennedy-Nixon contest in 1960, and despite the closeness and controversy about that vote, there was no social instability.[34] The real trouble was exactly one century earlier. With the plurality and electoral college voting law there has been no governance difficulty in all of these non-majority elections, save one — the 1860 election. This election is a much-studied critical juncture in U.S. history. We examine its dynamics more closely here since it led to the Civil War, the ultimate breakdown in social stability.

THE 1860 ELECTION

The politics of the United States in 1860 teetered on secession of the southern states and civil war. Abraham Lincoln set the stage for the election in his 1858 senatorial campaign debates with Stephen Douglas. In a debate with Douglas in Freeport, Illinois, Lincoln trapped his opponent with a famous question that led to the 1860 presidential election. He asked Douglas whether a U.S. territory could lawfully exclude slavery prior to the formation of a state constitution.[35] Douglas, a Democrat, faced a dilemma. To answer "yes" would lead to opposition of the Democrats in the southern states. To answer "no" would alienate the support of moderate and abolitionist Democrats in New England. Moreover, a negative response would jeopardize Douglas's Senate incumbency against Lincoln. Accordingly, Douglas answered "yes" and the South deserted him.

In 1860 Lincoln won the presidential nomination over William Seward in the emerging Republican Party in its first presidential convention at Chicago. John Bell was nominated by the new National Union Party (an amalgam between the old Whig and American parties). Douglas won the Democratic nomination, but only from the northern wing of the party. The southern wing split off and nominated John C. Breckenridge for the presidency. The unraveling of the Democrats enhanced Lincoln's electoral chances, but there was still cause for concern. Even after the popular vote had given Lincoln a plurality over Douglas and Breckenridge, he worried about the stability and predictability of the Electoral College: "The presidential electors chosen in that election did not meet until December 5, and their ballot would not be officially counted until February 13, which Lincoln regarded as 'the most dangerous time' in the whole election process."[36]

Lincoln won seventeen of the thirty-three states in the election. Had the Electoral College formula been only slightly more proportional, the election would have been thrown to the House of Representatives. It was then unclear whether it was the old or the incoming newly elected House that would vote for the president. In the 1824 presidential election, neither candidate (John Quincy Adams nor Andrew Jackson) had a majority. Therefore the election was sent to the House of Representatives. In this instance it was the old House that chose Adams over Jackson. Should it have been the old House in 1861, Lincoln might well have lost the presidency.[37]

Electoral systems matter. Had we not relied on statewide pluralities in 1860, Stephen Douglas would almost certainly have won the presidency. Had Bell and Breckenridge not been candidates, that is, had the contest been solely between Lincoln and Douglas, Douglas would have won.[38] Tabarrok and Spector (following Riker)[39] conjecture that in a Borda count vote, Douglas would have won, followed by Bell, then Lincoln, and then Breckenridge.[40] Would this have preserved social equilibrium and prevented the Civil War? Perhaps Lincoln's accession under the Electoral College was the precipitating event that caused the breakup of the nation, and this event could have been avoided by another electoral system. But perhaps any candidate elected under any system could not have contained the slavery issue, which was so volatile that the events of 1861–65 were unavoidable. It is idle to speculate. Instead, we return to the issue of governance versus representation and introduce the concept of proportionality.

GOVERNANCE, REPRESENTATION, AND PROPORTIONALITY

Thomas Jefferson intoned in the Declaration of Independence that "governments are instituted among men, deriving their just powers from the consent of the governed." The United States and every other democracy has implemented the method of "consent of the governed" as voting. We note above that there are many different ways to conduct voting and elections. Also, as G. Bingham Powell notes, "Elections are not democracy itself but an instrument of democracy."[41] As a democratic instrument, the Electoral College and the plurality electoral law lead to electoral distortion. To the extent that a proportional measurement of voter choices is different from, say, seats in the Electoral College, distortion occurs. The systems used in the U.S. presidential elections maximize distortion. The institutional designers of the U.S. Constitution did not trust eighteenth-century voters and certainly had no intentions to represent slaves, American Indians, women, or any other groups. Their goal in the first democratic constitution in the world was governance.

There have been many changes in values and concerns between the end of the eighteenth century and the beginning of the twenty-first century. Now groups and minorities seek and deserve representation. Representation is primarily achieved through political parties. In most of the rest of the world, an electoral system allocating seats among members of competing parties is one of the first choices and mechanisms for representation. To attain public officials who mirror or represent the will of a diverse public, many countries adopt "proportional representation," but there are several formulas for allocating seats (or electors) proportionally. For example, Brazil, which uses the U.S. form of government, nonetheless uses a proportional representation electoral law, the greatest remainder system. This system is the best for providing representation for small parties. The d'Hondt or highest-average electoral system is the method of attaining proportional representation that is most used in the world, especially if one considers the Scandinavian adaptation to it — the Sainte Laguë system.[42] The rules for the d'Hondt system are simple:

- One seat is awarded at a time.
- Each party's or candidate's vote total votes are divided by one more than the number of seats already awarded (if A has no seats, the divisor is one, and with 2 seats, the divisor is 3).
- The party or candidate with the highest quotient in each round wins the seat.

Note that the d'Hondt system is designed to reward large parties — one of the many reasons for its popularity in the world. In the system Brazil uses, Pat Buchanan would almost certainly have gained at least one Electoral College seat during the 2000 U.S. presidential race.

The United States is unique in using an electoral college that can seriously undermine proportional allocation through its use of the winner-take-all system in which all votes go to the winner of plurality within each state. How much does this system distort representation as achieved through the d'Hondt system?

In table 10.2 on the following page, we first show the number of Electoral College seats (or votes) for each state. Then, we show the allocation of electors between the parties (Bush and Gore) in the College for the 2000 presidential election under the winner-take-all (or unit) rules that are currently employed. Finally, we show the allocation of electors under the d'Hondt proportional electoral system.

The striking thing about the table is not the summed results. It is the difference between winner-take-all and proportional representation in all the states. The only "state" that had all votes for one candidate is Washington, D.C. Under the d'Hondt system, even Texas awarded Gore twelve seats in the Electoral College. Democratic Texans are then represented and their votes are not wasted. This issue is not the same as minority representation in the ethnic sense. It means that Wyoming Democrats can be relieved that at least one of the three seats of their state in the Electoral College has a Democrat, just as Massachusetts Republicans can feel represented by the four Republican seats from Massachusetts in the Electoral College using proportional allocation.

The bottom line means a great deal, however, in this and most cases. Voting rules matter. Under the d'Hondt system no candidate in 2000 would have received the necessary 270 votes, so the election would have traveled to the House of Representatives. Under statutes clarifying the Constitution, the vote would be in the new House, that is, the newly elected members of the House of Representatives. In 2000 this would have almost certainly led to the election of George W. Bush. Each state gets only one vote. By House rules each state's representatives must vote in a single-state caucus with the outcome decided by majority rule. If there are more Republicans than Democrats, the Republicans win in the state and then cast their one vote for the Republican in the House of Representatives.[43] Since Republicans had majorities in twenty-seven state delegations, Bush would

Table 10.2   Actual and d'Hondt Results for the Electoral College Seats in U.S. Presidential Election 2000

State	Electoral Votes	Bush (actual)	Gore (actual)	Bush (d'Hondt)	Gore (d'Hondt)	Nader (d'Hondt)
Alabama	9	9	0	5	4	0
Alaska	3	3	0	2	1	0
Arizona	8	8	0	4	4	0
Arkansas	6	6	0	3	3	0
California	54	0	54	23	29	2
Colorado	8	8	0	4	4	0
Connecticut	8	0	8	3	5	0
Delaware	3	0	3	1	2	0
District of Columbia	3	0	3	0	3	0
Florida	25	25	0	13	12	0
Georgia	13	13	0	7	6	0
Hawaii	4	0	4	2	2	0
Idaho	4	4	0	3	1	0
Illinois	22	0	22	10	12	0
Indiana	12	12	0	7	5	0
Iowa	7	0	7	3	4	0
Kansas	6	6	0	4	2	0
Kentucky	8	8	0	4	4	0
Louisiana	9	9	0	5	4	0
Maine	4	0	4	2	2	0
Maryland	10	0	10	4	6	0
Massachusetts	12	0	12	4	8	0
Michigan	18	0	18	9	9	0
Minnesota	10	0	10	5	5	0
Mississippi	7	7	0	4	3	0
Missouri	11	11	0	6	5	0
Montana	3	3	0	2	1	0
Nebraska	5	5	0	3	2	0
Nevada	4	4	0	2	2	0
New Hampshire	4	4	0	2	2	0
New Jersey	15	0	15	6	9	0
New Mexico	5	0	5	2	3	0
New York	33	0	33	12	20	1
North Carolina	14	14	0	8	6	0
North Dakota	3	3	0	2	1	0
Ohio	21	21	0	11	10	0
Oklahoma	8	8	0	5	3	0
Oregon	7	0	7	3	4	0
Pennsylvania	23	0	23	11	12	0
Rhode Island	4	0	4	1	3	0
South Carolina	8	8	0	5	3	0
South Dakota	3	3	0	2	1	0
Tennessee	11	11	0	6	5	0
Texas	32	32	0	20	12	0
Utah	5	5	0	4	1	0
Vermont	3	0	3	1	2	0
Virginia	13	13	0	7	6	0
Washington	11	0	11	5	6	0
West Virginia	5	5	0	3	2	0
Wisconsin	11	0	11	5	6	0
Wyoming	3	3	0	2	1	0
Total	538	271	267	267	268	3

Table 10.3   Summary of Potential Influences on Social Stability

	Electoral College	Plurality	Majority runoff	Instant runoff
Limiting vote distortion	Low	Moderate	Moderate	High
Limiting fraud	High	Low	Moderate	Moderate
Minority cabinet representation	Low	Low	High	Moderate
Limiting extremist presidents	High	Low	High	High
Presidential majority in the legislature	High	High	Low	Low

likely have won. The irony of the House vote is that small states have even greater power than they do in the Electoral College. In a House of Representatives presidential vote, North Dakota has equal power with California, New York, and Texas. The ultimate institutional solution to the absence of an electoral college majority thus produces the greatest electoral distortion.

For this and many other reasons, no one is interested in having the election decided by the House of Representatives. As comparativists, we find the U.S. system sorely deficient on representation. As the table above shows, the d'Hondt system led to no majority in the Electoral College. But why insist on a majority, when we use a *plurality* rule in virtually every other election in the United States? After all, the Electoral College is not a legislature. It exists only to elect one person. If the rule were the standard *plurality*, then Gore would win the presidency by one vote — matching his close "victory" in the popular vote.

ASSESSING THE ALTERNATIVES

In this chapter we have identified features of electoral rules that could contribute to social instability. We noted that election results rarely lead directly to mass protest and political violence, especially in the American context. The American Civil War, following the 1860 election, was not directly caused by the electoral system used to elevate Lincoln to the presidency.

How do the four main proposals for election rules compare with one another by their contributions to social instability? Table 10.3 summarizes our arguments, comparing the Electoral College, plurality system, majority runoff, and instant runoff by their relative influence on five factors: limiting vote distortion, limiting fraud, encouraging minority cabinet representation, limiting the likelihood of extremist accession, and facilitating a presidential majority in the legislature. The rankings are ordinal and are derived from our analysis in this chapter. Each electoral formula is provided a rank of "low," "moderate," or "high" by its expected contribution to stability, relative to the other proposals under consideration.

The instant runoff should limit distortions between the popular vote and election outcomes more than other election rules by allowing voters to express multiple, rank-ordered preferences that are included in the vote tally. The winning candidate must garner a majority of votes based on the preferences expressed by voters. For these reasons, the instant runoff is the electoral system least likely to produce a winner without a popular mandate. Majority-runoff rules encourage sincere voting in the first round but force voters to choose between the top two candidates in the second round. Voters are compelled to vote strategically in the second round, if they choose to participate. While plurality rules do not provide the range of choice of the instant-runoff or majority-runoff systems, the winning candidate must gain plurality support at the national level. The system encourages strategic rather than sincere voting but precludes the accession of a president with fewer votes than his closest competitor. The Electoral College, by contrast, allows candidates to gain the presidency without even gaining plurality support at the national level. Based on this criterion, the instant runoff is the most desirable system and the Electoral College is the least desirable system.

We noted that different election rules may facilitate the reduction of fraud. The Electoral College should increase the likelihood of detection by concentrating fraud in certain regions. Majority-runoff rules provide incentives for fraud to be dispersed nationally, but increase the possibility of detection because of the two-round system. The instant runoff further complicates the successful commission of fraud because voters express multiple preferences. Plurality rules facilitate fraud more than other rules because ballots are simple and fraud can be geographically diffuse. Based on this criterion, the Electoral College is the best system and plurality rules are the worst choice.

Majority-runoff rules, by promoting bargaining between the first and second rounds, increase the likelihood of minority representation in the cabinet. The instant runoff may also encourage bargaining for second preferences, increasing the probability of coalitions in the cabinet. The Electoral College and plurality rules provide no incentives to place minority politicians in the cabinet. Based on this criterion, majority-runoff rules are the best choice; the Electoral College and plurality rules are least optimal.

The Electoral College, majority-runoff, and instant-runoff rules should limit extremists accessing the presidential office because candidates require broad support to win the position. Plurality rules, by contrast, potentially facilitate extremist victories because candidates need only obtain a national plurality to win office. Based on this criterion, any alternative is preferred to plurality rules.

Because they encourage two-party competition, both the Electoral College and plurality rules should facilitate presidential majorities in the U.S. Congress. The majority-runoff and instant-runoff systems promote multicandidate competition that could erode presidential majorities in the legislature over time. Based on this criterion, both the Electoral College and plurality systems are preferred to majority-runoff and instant-runoff systems.

The comparison of election rules makes clear that none of the alternatives promote all conditions supporting social stability. The selection of institutional rules involves tradeoffs among each system's benefits and costs.

We must further ask, in the U.S. context, which of the criteria promoting stability is most salient? That is, should we weigh one of the characteristics more heavily in our decision about the optimal method of selecting the U.S. president? We indicated that facilitating governance and promoting representation are critical elements of elections in the United States. Obtaining presidential majorities in the legislature is our main criterion contributing to successful governance.

Gridlock between the executive and legislative branches undermines policy-making. While we do not argue that presidents should have complete freedom to enact their preferred policies, presidential majorities in the legislature contribute to the likelihood of policy successes. Both the Electoral College and plurality rules fared the best with this criterion, even in the face of recent electoral results that have produced divided governments.[44]

While the selection of minority members of the cabinet could contribute to a perception of broad representation in the executive branch, we noted that this may be an illusion. Cabinet members in the United States serve the president and can be removed at his discretion. Presidents have selected diverse cabinets in terms of ethnicity, gender, and party affiliation, but this diversity does not overcome the basic feature of the presidency — only one person serves as president. While the U.S. Congress has 535 members who can represent different views of their constituents, the presidency is not designed to be a broadly representative institution.

CONCLUSION

In the United States, elections are not likely to cause social instability. Even when we consider how presidential election rules could contribute to instability, we find no compelling reason to alter the existing Electoral College. First, the Electoral College rates high for governance. Second, no alternative is clearly superior to the Electoral College on all criteria for social stability. Third, institutional change often yields unintended consequences.

However, if we were to change the electoral rules for the presidency, some alternatives are better than others. If we could abolish the majority rule in the Electoral College that can invoke the House contingency procedure and have a proportional allocation (rather than unit rule) electoral law, such reforms might be acceptable. We are confident that American citizens could understand and approve these rules with good and simple explanations by the government and the press.

In our view, though, the easiest and most effective reform is the excision of the Electoral College and reliance on the popular vote in a plurality electoral law. Plurality rules are simple, they correspond with congressional election rules, and they promote presidential majorities. The Electoral College was designed to remove a presidential vote from mistrusted voters, but such a cautionary practice is no longer necessary. The Electoral College does overrepresent small states — the smallest get the boost of three seats instead of one. This is, however, not wholly significant when two states have over thirty seats and California has fifty-four. If the Electoral College were to be reformed, in our view, it would be better to follow all other democracies and remove the institution itself rather than to tinker with its components.

NOTES

1. A. J. Milnor, *Elections and Political Stability* (Boston: Little, Brown, 1969); G. Bingham Powell, "Party Systems and Political System Performance: Voting Participation, Government Stability and Mass Violence in Contemporary Democracies," *American Political Science Review* 75 (December 1981): 861–79; William Mishler and Anne Hildreth, "Legislatures and Political Stability," *Journal of Politics* 46 (February 1984): 25–59.

2. Shugart and Carey compare the power of presidents for most presidential systems. Matthew Soberg Shugart and John M. Carey, *Presidents and Assemblies* (Cambridge: Cambridge University Press, 1992), 155. Frye provides ratings of presidential power for post-communist states. Timothy Frye, "A Politics of Institutional Choice: Post-Communist Presidencies," *Comparative Political Studies* 30 (October 1997): 523–52.

3. Alfred Stepan and Cindy Skach, "Constitutional Frameworks and Democratic Consolidation: Parliamentarism Versus Presidentialism," *World Politics* 46 (October 1993): 1–22; Juan J. Linz, "Presidential or Parliamentary Democracy: Does it Make a Difference?" in *The Failure of Presidential Democracy,* ed. Juan J. Linz and Arturo Valenzuela (Baltimore: Johns Hopkins University Press, 1994).

4. Mark P. Jones, *Electoral Laws and the Survival of Presidential Democracies* (South Bend, Ind.: Notre Dame University Press, 1995); Gary Cox, *Making Votes Count* (New York: Cambridge University Press, 1997).

5. We will assess the existing U.S. Electoral College, plurality, majority-runoff, and alternative vote systems.

6. Some countries, such as Italy, use an electoral college consisting of members of parliament and other officials to select a president, but these are not presidential systems.

7. André Blais, Louis Massicotte, and Agniezka Dobrzynska, "Direct Presidential Elections: A World Summary," *Electoral Studies* 16 (December 2000): 441–55.

8. Since no other countries use the Electoral College, none have the modifications of the Electoral College considered elsewhere in this book (the district plan, proportional allocation, or the national bonus plan).

9. Such as the infamous "butterfly ballot" in Florida's Palm Beach County during the 2000 presidential race in the United States.

10. Valentin Mikhailov, "Kolichestvo demokratii [The Quantity of Democracy]" *Armageddon* 3 (May-June 1999): 134–53.

11. Some states require electors to cast a vote for the candidate winning a plurality.

12. Electors are required by state law to vote for specified candidates in Alabama, Alaska, California, Colorado, Connecticut, Florida, Hawaii, Maine, Maryland, Massachusetts, Michigan, Mississippi, Montana, Nebraska, Nevada, New Mexico, North Carolina, Ohio, Oklahoma, Oregon, South Carolina, Vermont, Virginia, Washington, Wisconsin, Wyoming, and the District of Columbia. Local requirements and potential punishments vary by state. National Archives and Records Administration, "Frequently Asked Questions on the Electoral College," www.nara.gov/fedreg/elctcoll/faq.html#wrongvote.

13. In four presidential races, the winner failed to earn more popular votes than his closest rival. Only the 1860 election was followed by substantial social instability, a point addressed here.

14. Judith Best, *The Case Against Direct Election of the President: In Defense of the Electoral College* (Ithaca, N.Y.: Cornell University Press, 1975).

15. Richard Gunther and Anthony Mughan, "Political Institutions and Cleavage Management," in *Do Institutions Matter? Government Capabilities in the United States and Abroad*, ed. R. Kent Weaver and Bert A. Rockman (Washington, D.C.: Brookings Institution, 1993).

16. Robert Dahl, "The Myth of the Presidential Mandate," *Political Science Quarterly* 105 (Fall 1990): 355–72.

17. The winning candidates garnered between 39 percent and 46 percent of the vote.

18. For instance, Chen Shui-Bian ran on a platform promoting Taiwan's independence during the 2000 presidential elections, but moderated this policy after taking office.

19. For example, Republican William Cohen served under Bill Clinton, and Democrat Norman Mineta is in the George W. Bush cabinet.

20. Mark P. Jones, "Electoral Laws and the Effective Number of Candidates in Presidential Elections," *Journal of Politics* 61 (February 1999): 171–84.

21. In the alternative-vote system, negotiations between candidates would take place prior to the first round. Candidates that are likely to finish in first or second place may work with candidates with less support to attract second preference votes. Donald L. Horowitz provides a hypothetical example of this process in Sri Lankan politics in *A Democratic South Africa? Constitutional Engineering in a Divided Society* (Berkeley: University of California Press, 1991).

22. For example, Aleksandr Lebed was able to negotiate a position in Boris Yeltsin's administration in exchange for his open support of Yeltsin during the second round of the 1996 presidential race.

23. Powell, "Party Systems and Political System Performance."

24. Michael Taylor and V. M. Herman, "Party Systems and Government Stability," *American Political Science Review* 65 (March 1971): 28–37.

25. A majority was required if only two candidates competed. See Horowitz, *A Democratic South Africa.*

26. See Rein Taagepera and Matthew Shugart, *Seats and Votes* (New Haven: Yale University Press, 1989) or Arend Lijphart, *Electoral Systems and Party Systems: A Study of 27 Democracies, 1945–1990* (Oxford: Oxford University Press, 1994) for a discussion of the effective threshold.

27. Assuming that voters may only select one of the two candidates on the ballot. In some countries, such as Russia, voters may choose "against all." If this were an option, the winner could gain a plurality of the votes.

28. Jones, *Electoral Laws and the Survival of Presidential Democracies;* Shugart and Carey, *Presidents and Assemblies.*

29. Jones, *Electoral Laws and the Survival of Presidential Democracies.*

30. Taagepera and Shugart, *Seats and Votes* (91), indicate that the mean number of effective parties based on vote share in the House from 1910 to 1970 was 2.08; the mean number of effective parties in the Senate was 2.15 for the period 1912–70. According to Shugart and Carey, *Presidents and Assemblies* (220), the median effective number of candidates in U.S. presidential elections is 2.1. The standard formula for the effective number of parties is $1/p_i^2$. The proportion of seats received by each party is squared, summed, and inverted, yielding a scale that approximates a count of "effective" political parties.

31. There is strong evidence that the wasted vote argument affects voter decisions. Many of John Anderson's supporters defected to other candidates in 1980, while H. Ross Perot retained a higher level of loyalty from his supporters in 1992. The "results suggest strongly that at least some voters responded to the wasted vote argument." Paul R. Abramson, John H. Aldrich, Phil Paolino, and David W. Rohde. "Third-Party and Independent Candidates in American Politics: Wallace, Anderson and Perot," *Political Science Quarterly* 110 (Fall 1995): 363.

32. Kenneth A. Shepsle, "Representation and Governance: The Great Legislative Tradeoff," *Political Science Quarterly* 103 (Fall 1988): 461–84.

33. Unlike other countries, the U.S. system almost always generates a "majority" mandate for elected candidates. See G. Bingham Powell Jr., *Elections as Instruments of Democracy: Majoritarian and Proportional Visions* (New Haven: Yale University Press, 2000), 71–81.

34. Brian J. Gaines, "Popular Myths About the Popular Vote-Electoral College Splits," *PS: Political Science and Politics* 34 (March 2001): 71–75.

35. William H. Riker, *The Art of Political Manipulation* (New Haven: Yale University Press, 1986), 1–9.
36. David Herbert Donald, *Lincoln* (New York: Simon and Schuster, 1995), 260.
37. Alexander Tabarrok and Lee Spector, "Would the Borda Count Have Avoided the Civil War?" *Journal of Theoretical Politics* 11 (April 1999): 287.
38. Ibid, 262.
39. William H. Riker, *Liberalism against Populism: A Confrontation between the Theory of Democracy and the Theory of Social Choice* (San Francisco: W. H. Freeman, 1982).
40. Tabarrok and Spector, "Would the Borda Count Have Avoided the Civil War?"
41. Powell, *Elections as Instruments of Democracy,* 155.
42. This system uses odd-numbered divisors, thus hastening seats for small parties.
43. What happens to states like Illinois that have House delegations evenly split between Democrats and Republicans? Unless someone defects from the party, neither candidate can obtain a majority of the state delegation, but since a majority is required, the state must abstain.
44. While the Electoral College and plurality rules should facilitate presidential majorities, concurrent elections and the use of single-member districts in congressional elections would likely minimize the effects of majority-runoff or the alternative vote in the United States.

CHAPTER 11

The Electoral College and Social Cleavages: Ethnicity, Class, and Geography

Robert L. Lineberry, *University of Houston*
Darren Davis, *Michigan State University*
Robert Erikson, *Columbia University*
Richard Herrera, *Arizona State University*
Priscilla Southwell, *University of Oregon*

THE ONLY GAME in town to elect the president of the United States is the Electoral College Game. Electoral systems distribute and redistribute political power. Changing the rules, of course, changes the game, helping the prospects of success for some and hurting the prospects for others. The question is "who is helped and who is hurt?" In this chapter, we are concerned with those broad groupings called "social cleavages" by political scientists and sociologists. Division among groups remains strong in the United States. Analyzing the 2000 elections, Gerald Pomper noted that "in addition to geographical and party lines, the American electorate was polarized along social lines."[1] These cleavages, as he calls them, are reflected in the following point spreads among various groups (the first group in each pair being more Democratic):

- the poor and the rich, a 14 point difference
- nonbelievers and frequent churchgoers, 25 points
- residents of large cities and rural areas, 14 points
- blacks and whites, a staggering 48 points

In 2000, nine-tenths of black Americans, two-thirds of Hispanic Americans, and 54 percent of Asian Americans voted for the candidate who won the popular vote but lost the Electoral College and the presidency. The income break appeared at the family income category of $30–50,000, with those at that level splitting their votes between Bush and Gore almost exactly. Those below it gave solid majorities to the Democrats, and those above gave solid majorities to Republicans.

These 2000 patterns of voting by race, class, and geography have persisted for years. Brooks and Manza remark that "political conflicts arising out of social cleavages based on race, class, religion, or linguistic divisions have been a central concern in the sociological study of politics." Their studies of voting by four major types of cleavage (race, gender, religion, and class) from 1960 to 1992 reveal that the divisions among groups have remained pretty constant since the presidential election of 1960.[2]

We define *social cleavages* as political differences based on (1) social class; (2) race and ethnicity; and (3) geography.[3] The first two of these are the "grand cleavages" of American politics, as well as in the politics of most industrial and postindustrial nations. The third is one of the oldest conflicts in American politics, one uniquely linked to the spatial character of the Electoral College. In this chapter, therefore, we examine American presidential elections in terms of race, class, and geography.

We will look first at elections in the United States in comparison to those in other democratic countries, particularly with an eye toward assessing turnout, perhaps the largest deficiency in achieving equal protection for poorer and minority voters. In the process of considering alternative ways of electing the American chief executive, we will first focus on the Electoral College, dealing along the way with one of the most deeply ingrained bits of conventional wisdom about American politics — that the present system advantages minorities. We will also consider the potential impacts of alternative electoral configurations.

We begin with the presumption of the United States Constitution and United States Supreme Court that "equal protection" of the vote is the key test of a voting system (see *Baker v. Carr; Wesberry v. Sanders;* and *Bush v. Gore*). The "equal protection" clause of the Fourteenth Amendment, and the Supreme Court's reference to that clause in its election-deciding case of *Bush v. Gore,* applies only to the intrastate equal protection of voting strength. We assume here that the logic and defense of equal protection as a voting standard should apply to the nation as a whole.

AMERICAN ELECTIONS IN COMPARATIVE PERSPECTIVE

American elections in general, and presidential elections in particular are, by comparison with other countries, enormously complex and confusing. With 450,000 elected officials in 80,000 local governments, plus referendums in many states, American elections are at least numerous, if not downright bedazzling.

Aside from their sheer complexity (or possibly related to it), American elections differ from those in other democratic countries by (1) the relative distance between popular participation and popular control of policy;[4] (2) the indirect connection between the popular vote and the election of the chief executive;[5]

and (3) their stunningly low turnout rate. The turnout rate in American elections deserves particular attention in the context of the questions we address in this chapter.

Americans are not, in politics at least, a very participatory people. Turnout in presidential elections these days hovers around 50 percent of potential voters. Among 53 democracies meticulously quantified by LeDuc and colleagues, only Zambia (!) had a lower turnout for its presidential election (our 51.5 percent in 1992 vs. Zambia's 50.0 percent).[6]

There are many correlates of turnout in modern, democratic elections: education, income, ethnicity, gender, plus factors characteristic of the electoral process itself such as the complexity of registration systems. When political scientists examine the correlates of turnout among various democracies, they use fairly sophisticated models of turnout patterns and determinants. Mark Franklin reports that turnout rates vary more between countries than within countries. Of course, indicators of social class and race figure prominently in accounting for high or low turnout. Still, he reports, country is a better predictor than social characteristic in predicting turnout. As Franklin puts it, "It matters whether one is rich or poor, educated or uneducated, interested in politics or not, but none of these things matter as much as whether one is an Australian or an American."[7] The usual suspects in explaining differences in voter participation — education, income, political interest — predict popular participation less well in non-American nations than in the United States. Thus, "individual level differences are very similar across Eastern and Western Europe, although rather greater in the United States, where education accounts for a 41 percent difference in turnout levels, whereas age, income, and political discussion have effects that exceed 30 percent."[8]

Turnout differences among groups are impressive. African Americans and newer ethnic groups, of course, have low turnout rates compared to the group Texans call "Anglos." (African Americans, though, vote more heavily than their socioeconomic characteristics alone would predict.) Class is a key factor, too (though education seems stronger than income in predicting voting), and — completing the loop — because less educated and minority voters tend to vote Democratic, poor turnout in the United States significantly disadvantages Democrats. Economists Ron Shachar and Barry Nalebuff report, after examining a state-by-state model of presidential voting from 1948 to 1986 that "Republicans have a 32-percent higher propensity to vote than Democrats do. This suggests that if voting had been mandatory and, hence, the propensities to vote had been equalized, then all of the Republican presidents elected in the last 50 years would have lost their first election."[9]

In short, *skimpy turnout is, to a surprising degree, unique to the United States and significantly more connected to social cleavages here than elsewhere.* There are plenty of culprits in this low-turnout-in-general, very-low-turnout-among-the-disadvantaged scenario. Of course, our cumbersome registration system is one problem, although African Americans are 1.5 times more likely to register than whites when other variables are controlled.[10] Even eliminating the effects of registration by permitting Election Day registration increases voting turnout by only about 7 percent.[11]

There is another class of reasons why Americans in general, and the poor and minorities in particular, are weak participators. It would be no surprise to the constitutional drafters that the link between elections and policy in the United States is weak. Franklin strongly suggests that the weakness of American electoral turnout is a function of the relatively weak connection between electoral outcomes and actual policies.[12] There is an enormous political science literature on this question, far too voluminous for us to summarize here. In one twist on this issue, John Hibbing and Elizabeth Theiss-Morse suggest that Americans see policies as fairly coterminous with their preferences but the election process as out of step with public preferences.[13]

In the mosaic of reasons for America's low turnout and the sharp dropoff of turnout by minorities and the poor, the Electoral College may be little more than a blip on the radar screen. There is, however, abroad in the land, a hypothesis that the Electoral College advantages minorities (and perhaps by implication, the poor).

Let's look at this dragon and see if it can be slain.

THE ELECTORAL COLLEGE AND MINORITY VOTING POWER

Unlike any other democracy, the United States uses the quaint constitutional system called the Electoral College, in which some are more equal than others. Here, states are assigned a number of electoral votes equal to their number of senators and representatives in Washington (and D.C. gets three). By custom — by now a part of the "unwritten constitution" — the slate of electors whose votes are counted is the one pledged to the plurality winner in each state. The "unit rule" or "winner-take-all" principle has meant that, with only two exceptions today (Maine and Nebraska), all the electoral votes of a state are cast for the plurality popular winner regardless of the scope of the popular victory. It is this distortion of the popular result that produced the vote paradox of 2000.

The Conventional Wisdom

One of the most widespread beliefs about the Electoral College is that it actually advantages minorities (particularly African Americans). A standard exposition of this conventional wisdom is in the venerable text on presidential elections by Nelson Polsby and Aaron Wildavsky.[14] The Electoral College, they contend, advantages voters in two kinds of states, the small ones and the large ones. Small states gain from the overrepresentation given them by the Constitution's guarantee of no less than three members, that is, because each state has two senators and at least one representative, no matter how small the state. These are states such as Wyoming and Vermont. They are also states with low minority populations and traditionally high Republican concentration. (The "whitest" state in the country is Vermont, with 97 percent white, followed by West Virginia and New Hampshire, with 96 percent of their voting-age population white.)

The Electoral College, Polsby and Wildavsky contend, also advantages large, populous urban states, and hence minorities. The argument goes like this. It is "primarily the larger states, through the unit-rule principle, which benefit from the Electoral College."[15] Here, then, is where minority voting enters the Electoral College door. "The large states," they argue, "are also the home of many organized minorities, especially racial and ethnic minorities, and this has traditionally meant that presidential candidates have had to pitch their appeals to these groups, or at least to not drive them off."[16] And since, they claim, the adoption of a direct popular vote for the president would "reduce the importance of the larger states," the implication is that those popular elections would actually reduce, rather than enhance, minority voting power.[17]

Apparently, the confused conventional wisdom is as follows: (1) small states benefit from the extra boost given them by the guarantee of a minimum of three electors, but (2) large states benefit from the unit rule; and (3) since large states tend to have more minorities, minorities gain by the electoral college system.

Questioning the Conventional Wisdom

No one has done more to sort through the political power deriving from the Electoral College than Lawrence Longley. In two books, one with Alan G. Braun and one with Neal Peirce, Longley has quantitatively weighed electoral power state-by-state.[18] Longley calculates the electoral value of each state under various voting schemes (the current electoral college system, a proportional division of votes, and a congressional district basis). Under the electoral college scheme, some of the conventional wisdom holds. There is a curvilinear relationship between size of state and voting power. The very smallest states have added voting strength because of the extra weight of the three-elector minimum rule. The larger the state, the more electoral power it will have.[19] As a graph, the line of state electoral power looks a bit like a checkmark. Two elements of the conventional wisdom about the Electoral College are supported by this analysis: the very smallest states and the very biggest states reap advantages from the system.

The deal-breaker upsetting the conventional wisdom, however, has to do with the numbers and, by implication, the power of African Americans (and other minorities) in the states. It is simply not true that blacks are disproportionately concentrated in the most favored states. Among the states that have a black population more than one percent above the national average, *blacks are more concentrated in states (principally in the South) that are less favored by the quirks of the Electoral College.*[20]

By any measure, Longley finds that the Electoral College has consistently disadvantaged blacks. As with Anglos, being a black in a state with exaggerated electoral power is far more important than solely being black. Put another way, "a black voter living in California [the most favored state] has approximately two and one half times the chance of affecting the electoral outcome that a black voter in Montana has."[21]

There are limitations to Longley's analysis. One limitation is that the raw number or percentage of a group is not the same thing as its voting-age population, or of its voting-eligible population. (Minority groups have younger populations; they have larger nonnaturalized populations.) Another limitation is that the voting power of a group depends on many things not considered by Longley. One ignored factor in a group's voting power is its turnout. Another such factor is its cohesion. If minority groups essentially voted randomly, or distributed themselves in the same way as nonminority voters, these factors would not matter. In practice, minority groups in the United States (as we saw earlier) vote anything but randomly. African Americans may not be single-issue voters, but they are single-party voters. African Americans cast about 90 percent of their votes for Democrats, and Hispanics cast about two-thirds of their votes for Democrats. While such cohesion enhances group power in direct popular elections, it may not help and can even hurt groups under the electoral college system, where cohesive groups are valued only in those circumstances where they can "swing" competitive states to one candidate. In noncompetitive states, cohesive minorities are "stand-patters" who can be ignored, taken for granted, or given symbolic benefits. No group in the United States contains more stand-patters than blacks, whose consistent Democratic voting reduces the need for candidates to respond to their interests unless they can swing a crucial state in their direction.

Another limitation on Longley's analysis is its excessive focus on African Americans, now a diminishing share of the American population. The case of Hispanics — the nation's fastest-growing and soon to be largest minority — is both different and similar. Hispanics are more concentrated in a small number of states than are blacks. Five major "gateway states" (Arizona, California, Illinois, New Mexico, and Texas) have for decades received the overwhelming share of Mexican immigrants — California alone receiving 40 percent of all immigrants from Mexico.[22] Only nine states have double-digit Hispanic percentage voting populations, while eighteen states have double-digit African American voting populations. Only Hawaii, with its 61 percent, and California, with 12 percent, has double-digit Asian populations.

Overall, the principal limitation of the Longley analysis — as well as its principal strength — is its simplicity. The strength of a state is measured mathematically in the Electoral College and the percentage of voters with this or that characteristic is correlated with that measure. Still, it tells us essentially nothing about how groups in fact vote, or how much they vote. Being big enough and cohesive enough to swing an election does not mean that you ever actually swing an election.

The Concepts of Pivotalness and Vote Value

We need other concepts here, ones that indicate the actual probability of affecting the Electoral College result. One such concept is pivotalness.[23] Though there is, generally, no rational reason to vote, given how limited one's chances are of affecting an election outcome, people do vote. In what must have been one of the most tedious studies of elections ever done, Shachar and Nalebuff modeled everything from the Electoral College weight of each state to the weather to predict modern presidential elections. Central to their analysis is the notion that, in a close election, one voter can be pivotal, however small the chance.[24] They covered presidential elections from 1948 through 1988. In an electoral college system, though, a voter who voted in each of these eleven presidential elections had not even a mere eleven tiny chances of affecting the outcome. Her chances depended on the state in which she lived. Hence the concept of "double pivotalness." They put it like this: "For a vote to change the result of a national election, there must be 'double pivotalness.' The vote has to change the state outcome, and the state's electoral votes must then change the national result."[25] To swing an election, you have to be a swing voter (or group) *and* live in a swing state. Needless to say, your chances of making much of a difference are pretty trivial. Shachar and Nalebuff report seventeen states where a voter's chance of being a pivotal voter — though very low — was relatively high.[26] None of these seventeen states is a high-minority or a large state. Hawaii, Rhode Island, Vermont, Delaware, New Hampshire — none of these or others on the list would fit the concept of an Electoral College vote aiding minorities.[27]

There is another way of looking at the effect of the Electoral College on minorities and, by implication, the poor: vote value. In the freakish Electoral College, some votes are cheap, others are expensive. Here, too, conventional wisdom is only partly correct. It is correct to say that *California is advantaged by the electoral college system; Californians, though, are not.* It takes fewer Vermonters to select an elector than it takes Californians to select an elector. It will be helpful here to construct a simple measure of vote value, using data provided by University of Michigan demographer William Frey (whose mantra is "all politics is regional"). Table 11.1 on the following page shows the data, and reveals the extent to which states differ in the number of voters per Electoral College vote.

Frey's measure has two advantages because it takes into account a couple of quirks in the Electoral College that contribute to inequalities in vote value across states. First, it is a measure of *the voting-age population*, not the total population of the state that is used to allocate the electors in the College. Second, it is based on the *voters of the state in the year of the election*, rather than a decade ago when the number of electors was determined.

Table 11.1   The Electoral College–Ethnicity Mix in States Having
Low and High Vote Value, 2000

	Voters per Elector (in 1000s)	Group Share of Voting Population (in percentages)			
		Hispanic	Asian	Black	White[a]
Low Value					
Florida	471	15	2	14	70
Texas	464	27	3	12	58
California	461	28	12	14	70
Georgia	453	3	2	27	68
Arizona	453	19	2	4	72
New York	418	13	6	17	67
New Jersey	416	12	6	14	70
North Carolina	414	2	1	20	75
Michigan	409	3	2	13	82
Illinois	408	9	3	14	74
Virginia	405	4	4	19	73
High value					
Wyoming	119	5	1	1	92
Alaska	143	4	4	4	75
Vermont	153	1	1	1	97
North Dakota	159	1	1	1	94
South Dakota	181	1	1	1	92
Rhode Island	188	6	2	5	88
Delaware	194	3	2	19	76
Montana	223	2	1	1	93
Hawaii	227	2	61	3	31
Idaho	230	6	1	1	91

Source: Data from William H. Frey, "Regional Shifts in America's Voting Age Population: What Do They Mean for National Politics?" Institute for Social Research, University of Michigan, 2000, Appendices A and D. See www.psc.isr.umich.edu/pubs/.

Note: Percentages do not sum to 100 because American Indians are not shown and because the Black category includes Hispanic blacks.

a. Non-Hispanic white

We list the eleven states (Georgia and Arizona tie for tenth place) whose votes are least valuable to the individual voter and ten at the opposite end of the continuum. In the top half of the table, each elector represents 400,000 or more voters. In the bottom half, each elector represents between 119,000 and 230,000 voters. Coincidentally, given its prominent role in 2000, the most disadvantaged state is Florida, where each elector represents 471,000 voters. The Florida resident who wanted to quadruple her voting power would be advised to move to Wyoming, where only 119,000 voting-age residents select an elector.

We also list Frey's tabulation of the vote share of America's three major ethnic groups by state. Only the most rudimentary knowledge of American demography would be needed to guess that Vermont, South Dakota, Alaska, Idaho, and other high-vote-value states are not heavily minority. Low-vote-value states such as New York, Virginia, North Carolina, and Georgia are high-minority-residency states. If minorities wanted to increase their political strength in the United States, they would be advised to move en masse to states where they are not now.

Minorities are not concentrated at either end of the low-high vote-value spectrum. Seven states (plus the District of Columbia) have more than 20 percent African American voting populations, all in the South, where vote value is medium. Three states, Texas, California, and New Mexico, have more than 20 percent Hispanic voting-eligible populations, and two of them are among the lowest vote-value states. Minorities tend, therefore, not to be concentrated in states that are advantaged by the mathematical quirks of the Electoral College, or in the states that profit from the unit rule.

The same is true, to a lesser degree, of the poor. Poverty is more evenly spread among the states than is ethnicity. Still, the mean percentage of the population below the poverty line in 1998 was 13.3 percent in eleven low-vote-value states and 12.9 percent in high-vote-value states.

We can summarize the evidence on the Polsby-Wildavsky conventional wisdom quite simply: there is no evidence for it. A fairly simple and straightforward analysis by Longley cuts off the legs of the hoary conundrum that minorities benefit from the Electoral College. A more sophisticated analysis of pivotal voting found that pivotalness is a function of all sorts of things — closeness of the election, for example — but not of where minorities are concentrated. And, minorities are disproportionately concentrated in states with low vote value.

Stake in heart. The dragon is slain.

PRESIDENTIAL ELECTIONS OF THE FUTURE: A BETTER WAY?

American elections are almost certain to change in the future, and issues of race and ethnicity are only likely to become more prominent. There may be more electronic voting, for example, and differences in technological sophistication may overlap and exacerbate existing educational and ethnic cleavages.

If "all politics is local," demographic shifts will reshape the electoral landscape. Demographer William Frey created a typology of states suggesting the demography-vote nexus.[28] In the 2000 election, the most contested states were those with white demographic advantages. His "interior battleground states" (Pennsylvania, Ohio, Michigan, Illinois, Missouri, and Wisconsin) are overweighted with "white working wives," "white senior citizens," and "white forgotten majority men." These groups constitute a majority in the "interior battleground states." The elections of the future may have as their battleground those states that Frey designates as "melting pot states" (New York, New Jersey, Florida, Texas, California, New Mexico, and Hawaii). In these states, whites are less prominent.

In the coming presidential elections, "minority politics" will increasingly hinge on Hispanic politics. The fastest-growing minority in the United States, of course, is the Hispanic population. Jorge Durand, Douglas S. Massey, and Fernando Charvet provide some analysis of what has happened to Mexican immigrants.[29] Those who migrate from Mexico once went primarily to Texas, then to Texas and California, and then to a few other "gateway" states. In recent decades, though, the population of Mexican immigrants has significantly dispersed. As Durand and his colleagues report, "by the mid-1990s, nearly one-third of all Mexicans were settling somewhere other than gateway states. Trends since 1950 once again suggest the emergence of Florida, Idaho, Nevada, New York–New Jersey, and Utah as destinations, but they also hint at the emergence of Georgia, Minnesota, North Carolina, and Oregon as poles of attraction. As a result, *immigrant destinations are now more diverse than ever.*"[30] Hispanic voters differ from black voters in two important respects: they are far less likely to vote and they are far less solidly Democratic.

The Electoral College disadvantages for minority voters are likely to increase. Minority populations are accelerating faster than the nonminority population. Because the census occurs only once a decade, the further from the census point (years ending in a zero), the less closely state population growth will be reflected in electoral vote allocations toward the end of the decade. Fast-growing states (Nevada is the fastest) are penalized regardless of their minority/majority mix. Fast-growing minority populations are also penalized.

HARRY AND LOUISE LOOK AT ELECTING THE PRESIDENT

When President Bill Clinton presented his much-discussed national health care reform plan early in his tenure, opponents of the plan pulled out every stop in their efforts to derail it. Of all of these efforts, perhaps the most effective was a television commercial, sponsored by the health care industry, in which a middle-class couple, "Harry and Louise," sitting in their kitchen, rummaged through the voluminous health care proposal and then pontificated: "There's got to be a better way." So it is with the American election system. The Supreme Court coined the famous phrase "one man, one vote" in deciding that unequal-sized districts for state legislatures were unconstitutional under the Fourteenth Amendment's Equal Protection Clause. Again in 2000, another Supreme Court reached for the Equal Protection Clause to decide Florida's election for the Republicans. It is odd that adherence to a system of equality within states could comfortably exist with a system that permitted so much inequality between states and their voters.

How would Harry and Louise look at the existing Electoral College and the main alternatives to it, especially if they focused on the possible inequalities and the biases that attend these systems. What if they — like John Rawls — focused on the fairness of the system to the minorities and poor people who are under-represented in positions of power in the American national government?[31] How would they regard maintaining the current Electoral College?

They would probably see as a mere myth the notion that the Electoral College was some thoughtfully debated, well-crafted, finely honed, and fairly balanced concoction of the Founding Fathers. As Forrest McDonald points out, "The convention worked out the Electoral College system in a matter of three days. Suddenly the constitutional order clicked into place."[32] No longer deluded by the myths of the virtues of the Electoral College, Harry and Louise would see that our current method advantages states with mountains and deserts in them. Residents of states with small populations are the only ones consistently advantaged by the system. Even voters in the largest states — while benefiting from the unit rule — have a poor vote value. The Electoral College has effectively reduced the franchise of minority Americans, even though a mythology has developed that it advantages them. Harry and Louise would say that one of the most significant changes that the United States could make to improve electoral equality would be to abolish the Electoral College.

Harry and Louise would also reject reforming the Electoral College. They would probably see some virtue in the proportional allocation system that reduced the iron grip of the unit rule applied in most states. Under proportional allocation of electors within states, the "winner take-all" aspect of the Electoral College would be replaced by the fairer principle of "winner takes his share." But they would see two deficiencies in proportional allocation. First, the proportional plan would exaggerate even more the power of small states and diminish the power of large states.[33] These small states (the Wyomings of American geography) are states with the smallest minority populations. Second, the proportional allocation plan would often produce a "winner unclear" result. In five elections since 1960, no candidate would have received a majority of electors if we employed proportional allocation, and these elections would have been decided in the House of Representatives.[34] The House is another place in American politics where minorities are underrepresented. And the one voter per state rule of the House contingency procedure would greatly advantage the small states where minorities seldom reside.

Harry and Louise would regard the district plan as possibly the worse method for minorities and the poor. First, the redistricting of congressional districts after every census would become even more contentious, and it is unlikely that districts would be carved up in ways that advantage minorities. Second, under the district system, some districts would become the battleground districts, as we now have battleground states, and it is unlikely that these would be places of high minority concentration. Just as minority House members are overwhelmingly elected from mostly-minority districts, the same heavily minority districts would vote overwhelmingly Democratic. They would be easier to ignore by both parties and locked up in districts with little chance of ever being pivotal. Quite likely, the outcome of the presidential election would come to mirror the division of the parties in Congress. With the decline of competitive districts in Congress, the effect would be to lock congressionally noncompetitive districts into the presidential election process and provide a certain Republican advantage.[35] Thus, Kennedy's victory in 1960 and possibly Carter's victory in 1976 would have been reversed, becoming Republican victories under the district plan.[36] And in 2000, Bush's narrow (271–266) Electoral College victory under the state unit rule would have become a more decisive (288–250) Electoral College victory under the district plan.[37] Again, the main reason that the district plan favors Republicans is that racial minorities are often concentrated in specific congressional districts in a way that dilutes their capacity to exercise voting power on behalf of the party they most strongly support.

For Harry and Louise, abolishing the Electoral College would make more sense than reforming it. They would say that the fairest thing to do is to elect our president by popular vote.[38] Minorities would be better served under popular vote methods than by the current system in two ways. First, all votes would count equally, regardless of the state where the vote was cast or the racial (or class) characteristics of the person who cast the ballot. Second, cohesive blocks of minority votes (like those cast by blacks) would be more crucial to popular vote totals; black voters in noncompetitive states (or districts) could no longer be ignored. Among its many weaknesses, the Electoral College encourages parties and candidates effectively to write off states they are unlikely to win (or lose). Oddly, in 2000, this included the three largest states — California, Texas, and New York. (Texans in 2000 would scarcely have known that a national election was going on from the amount of advertising they saw about the national candidates and parties.) In 2000, 53.4 million Americans of voting age lived in these three electorally orphaned big states. What George W. Bush could ignore in the campaign, he could ignore after the election as well. The *New York Times,* for example, noted that even early in President Bush's term, this well-traveled new president had visited twenty-five states, but California was "not even penciled into Mr. Bush's engagement book."[39] A national election would engage voters in all states. Candidates could not overlook the racial minorities in such states that could cast decisive votes in a national popular election.

Would Harry and Louise prefer any particular popular voting method? Considerations of whether to employ the plurality rule, a majority rule with a distinct contingent runoff election, or a majority rule with an instant-runoff election would probably focus on the how these rules would influence the development of parties and candidates that are particularly hostile or sympathetic to minorities (and the poor). For example, the rule of having a contingent runoff between the top two vote-getters in order to attain a majority was originally designed in southern states to discourage black influence in state elections. A candidate supportive of black interests and supported by racial minorities could get a plurality in state elections running against a field of candidates opposed to or indifferent to black interests. The black-preferred candidate could then be picked off in the runoff election. However, it is unclear if such outcomes would still occur today in a national presidential election. The two candidates surviving into the runoff would both have strong incentives to appeal to the large number of minority voters who could contribute to their victory in the runoff.

The instant runoff is a curiosity in the United States, and its complexity may diminish its attractions. But there is a possibility that this method could aid minorities by facilitating the development of parties and campaign organizations focusing on minority issues. Under the instant-runoff system, one could envision a Jesse Jackson making a prolonged run for the presidency (even if he could not emerge from the primaries as the Democratic candidate). Minorities could name Jackson as their first choice on the single-transferable-ballot while naming the Democratic candidate as their second choice. This could encourage the Democrats to be more responsive to minorities — both to keep black Democrats who might shift allegiance to Jackson and to be named at least the second choice of Jackson supporters (getting his votes transferred to them when Jackson was eliminated under the instant-runoff voting scheme). Such an election might also increase minority turnout. But while instant runoff could benefit minorities in this way, it could also benefit parties and candidates hostile to minorities in the same manner — and it's difficult to predict the full implications of such an innovation.

Having a direct popular vote under the plurality rule may have the least such effects. It is a commonplace of modern political science that plurality elections discourage third parties.[40] In a plurality election, a number of parties and candidates both supportive and hostile to minority interests may initially organize campaigns, but as Election Day approaches, voters turn their attention to the parties with the highest probability of winning, which would doubtless be relatively inclusive parties, appealing to many interests and groups — including minorities.

CONCLUSION

The Electoral College is America's national political lottery. The quirky geography of the electoral college system is, like lightning, freakish. Small states, of course, benefit; large states also benefit, but voters in large states do not. Nowhere do minorities and ethnic groups benefit. Minority and poor voters face many disadvantages in the American economic and social system, the presidential electoral system being only one of them. In the political system, their principal disadvantage is their low turnout. The current system of electing presidents represents essentially a piling-on of electoral disadvantages. If equality of voting opportunity is to remain an American goal, there must be, as Harry and Louise would say, a better way. Although Harry and Louise may not be certain which popular election method would best serve the interests of minorities, any popular election method would at least provide more equal voting power to citizens regardless of race, class, and geography.

NOTES

The senior author is deeply indebted to Craig Goodman, who provided assistance and counsel every step of the way. He is also indebted to Karl Eschbach, Rebecca Morton, and Susan Scarrow for countless leads and references.

1. Gerald Pomper, "The Presidential Election," in *The Election of 2000,* ed. Pomper (New York: Chatham House, 2001), 137.

2. Clem Brooks and Jeff Manza, "Social Cleavages and Political Alignments: U.S. Presidential Elections, 1960 to 1992," *American Sociological Review* 62 (December 1997): 937.

3. Gender is a broad social grouping, too, but we minimize gender as a "social cleavage" worth looking at in this analysis. Margaret Conway reports that women vote at slightly higher levels than men in presidential elections (though at slightly lower levels in congressional elections). See her "Gender and Political Participation," in *Gender and American Politics,* ed. Sue Tolleson-Rinehart and Jyl J. Josephson (Armonk, N.Y.: M. E. Sharpe, 2000). The state-by-state differences in the male-female ratio are so minuscule that it is difficult to see how altering the presidential election could affect the political power of women.

4. Mark Franklin, "Electoral Participation," in *Comparing Democracies: Elections and Voting in Global Perspective,* ed. Lawrence LeDuc, Richard G. Niemi, and Pippa Norris (Thousand Oaks, Calif.: Sage, 1996), chap. 8.

5. André Blais and Louis Massicotte report that 26 democracies that have presidencies directly elect their presidents, while 27 do not. Of those 26 directly electing a president, only the United States has a voting system they describe as "elected by an electoral college bound by a popular vote." See their chapter in LeDuc et al., *Comparing Democracies,* 51.

6. LeDuc et al., *Comparing Democracies,* 8–9.

7. Franklin, "Electoral Participation," 218.

8. Ibid., 218–19.

9. Ron Shachar and Barry Nalebuff, "Follow the Leader: Theory and Evidence on Political Participation," *American Economic Review* 89 (June 1999): 529. This is, however, an economist's "counterfactual" which defies imagining in the real world. Mandatory voting is not in practical terms mandatory anywhere. Presumably in any real election, the next real voter to vote would be the one statistically next most likely to vote, and not the mean nonvoter. Still, the point is vividly made.

10. Loretta E. Bass and Lynne E. Cooper, "Are There Differences in Registration and Voting Behavior between Naturalized and Native-Born Americans?" Bureau of the Census, Working Paper no. 28, February 1999, p. 9.

11. Craig Leonard Bryans and Bernard Grofman, "Election Day Registration's Effect on U.S. Voting Turnout," *Social Science Quarterly* 82 (March 2001): 170–83.

12. Franklin, "Electoral Participation."

13. John Hibbing and Elizabeth Theiss-Morse, "Popular Preferences and American Politics: What Americans Want Government to Be," *American Political Science Review* 95 (March 2001): 145–54.

14. Nelson Polsby and Aaron Wildavsky, *Presidential Elections,* 10th ed. (New York: Chatham House, 2000), 245–53.

15. Ibid., 246. The principal citation for this claim is George Rabinowitz and Stuart MacDonald, "The Power of the States in Presidential Elections," *American Political Science Review* 80 (March 1986): 65–87.

16. Polsby and Wildavsky, *Presidential Elections,* 246–47. There is no evidence cited for this claim. Polsby and Wildavsky do cite a similar argument made in Allen P. Sindler, "Presidential Election Methods and Urban-Ethnic Interests," *Law and Contemporary Problems* 27 (Spring 1972): 213–33.

17. Polsby and Wildavsky, *Presidential Elections,* 247.

18. Lawrence Longley and Alan G. Braun, *The Politics of Electoral College Reform* (New Haven: Yale University Press, 1972), and Lawrence Longley and Neal Peirce, *The Electoral College Primer 2000* (New Haven: Yale University Press, 1999).

19. See Longley and Braun, *Politics of Electoral College Reform,* 115.

20. Ibid., 158.

21. Ibid.

22. Jorge Durand, Douglas S. Massey, and Fernando Charvet, "The Changing Geography of Mexican Immigration to the United States, 1910–96," *Social Science Quarterly* 81 (March 2000): 1–16.
23. Shachar and Nalebuff, "Follow the Leader."
24. Pivotal power is also curvilinear. Voters in different states have different pivotal power in the sense that the per capitalized probability that one state can pivot the election is a function of state size. If states were divided into a number of equally populated units with an equal number of electoral votes, all would, by definition, have the same pivotal power. But large states have extra pivotal power because a state with, say, 24 electoral votes, has more than eight times (24/3) the pivotal power of a state with 3 electoral votes. Thus, politicians weigh the interest of one 24 electoral vote state more than eight 3 electoral vote states. The catch is that the eight states with three electoral votes have fewer people than the large electoral vote states. The losers are the states in the middle of the population distribution. If large states and small states vote differently, these differences will, to some degree, wash out.
25. Shachar and Nalebuff, "Follow the Leader," 535.
26. Ibid., 527. For what it's worth, the probability of a single vote swinging an election for all but these 17 elections is smaller than 10 to the −36th power.
27. This economic analysis of pivotalness may not be as reality divorced as it may seem to the nonsocial scientist. *USA Today* and the *Miami Herald* undertook a recount of the fabled Florida ballots. Under one set of standards, Al Gore won Florida by 3 votes. If that scenario is correct — and it is as reasonable as many others — those three real voters were truly Shachar and Nalebuff's doubly pivotal voters.
28. Willam Frey, "Regional Shifts in America's Voting-Age Population: What Do They Mean for National Politics?" Report no. 00-459, Population Studies Center, Institute for Social Research, University of Michigan, 2000. The data in table 11.1 are from the Frey report.
29. Durand, Massey, and Charvet, "Changing Geography of Mexican Immigration."
30. Ibid., 11. Italics added.
31. John Rawls, *A Theory of Justice* (Cambridge, Mass: Harvard University Press, 1971). In his monumental theory of justice, Rawls argues that inequalities of primary goods — such as voting power — are justified only if they advantage the least advantaged. The " 'least advantaged" are those whose social circumstances include poverty or minority status that limit their capacities to achieve their life plans.
32. Forrest McDonald, *The American Presidency: An Intellectual History* (Lawrence: University Press of Kansas, 1994), 162.
33. Longley and Braun, *Politics of Electoral College Reform*, 116.
34. Polsby and Wildavsky report the results under proportional allocation for 1960 to 1996. See *Presidential Elections,* 251. The first chapter of this volume reports these results for 2000.
35. A stronger case, though, could be made for the district system if one preferred that minorities get *some* votes counted, rather than *no* votes counted. If Hispanics in Arizona, for example, who dominate District 2, vote for a Democratic candidate, and win, then some Hispanic votes are translated into an electoral vote for Gore, while under the present system, none are because the Republicans won the state. The district system may permit a minority group's votes to approximate their numbers more closely, but it also makes redistricting even more important.
36. Polsby and Wildavsky, *Presidential Elections,* 251.
37. See Clark Bensen, "Presidential Election 2000 Congressional District Preliminary Study," at www.polidata.org.
38. Their argument would be buttressed by recent work by Andrew Gelman and Jonathan Katz, "How much does a vote count? Voting power, coalitions and the Electoral College," available at www.polmeth.ufl.edu/papers/01/gelman01.pdf. Gelman and Katz show that voting power is greater under a popular-plurality system than an electoral college system.
39. Richard L. Berke, "Bush is Devoting Scanty Attention to California," *New York Times,* 15 April 2001, 16.
40. See Blais and Massicotte, in LeDuc et al., *Comparing Democracies,* 67, for evidence.

CHAPTER 12

Reaching a Collective Judgment

Paul Schumaker and Burdett A. Loomis

SO WHAT DO ALL the assessments in the previous chapters add up to? What is the best system for selecting our president? Unfortunately, this book cannot answer this question — and we suspect no book can. All we can provide are the collective judgments of the thirty-seven political scientists involved in this project. This chapter summarizes our judgments about the Electoral College and the main alternatives to it, but our conclusions are less important than the collective judgments of the American public and its political representatives. Our aspiration is to provoke informed deliberation by citizen groups and within our political institutions on the issue.

COUNTING OUR VOTES

To provide a quantitative summary of our collective judgment on the Electoral College and its alternatives, all participants read executive summaries of each group's analysis and then cast their ballots. In this section we aggregate these individual assessments in various ways to determine whether defining our collective judgment is dependent on the methods employed to count our ballots.

One method for reaching a collective decision that is prominent in the discipline of political science, though seldom used elsewhere, is the approval ballot.[1] Rather than forcing voters to choose among various alternatives, approval balloting allows participants to vote for each option that they approve of, while rejecting all others. Under approval balloting, a voter can choose none, some, or all of the possible candidates, policies, or — as in the issue before us — electoral systems. When our participants cast such approval ballots, the results were as follows:

Electoral College	24	District plan	12
Popular-plurality	16	Bonus plan	11
Proportional allocation	14	Popular-majority	8
Instant runoff	13		

Table 12.1 Ranking the Electoral College and Alternatives to It: The Votes of 37 Project Participants

Assigned rank	Electoral College	District plan	Proportional allocation	Bonus plan	Popular- plurality	Popular- majority	Instant runoff
First	15	5	2	2	8	3	2
Second	6	7	4	7	6	3	4
Third	6	3	13	5	3	2	5
Fourth	2	5	5	9	3	6	6
Fifth	3	2	7	2	7	8	6
Sixth	1	8	2	8	6	11	6
Last	4	7	4	4	4	4	8
Borda count	102	155	144	153	140	173	171

Note: This table shows how many participants ranked each system as best (first), second best, and so forth. A few participants ranked their three (or in one case, four) least preferred alternatives as tied for last. Such ties in rankings were assigned the score of "sixth" in this table and the score of "6" in calculating the Borda count.

Approval balloting shows that the Electoral College is our most widely supported electoral system. As the only system supported by the majority of us, it appears to be the best system available for electing our president, in our collective judgment. Nevertheless, thirteen of us disapprove of the Electoral College, and there is considerable support for the various alternatives as well.

While approval voting has many virtues, it is not a definitive method for achieving a collective decision. One difficulty with approval voting is that it does not take into consideration *the degree* to which participants approve or disapprove of particular options.[2] Thus, it is important to consider electoral methods that take into account each voter's rank-ordering of options. Perhaps a different picture of our collective judgments will emerge if we tabulate our votes using methods based on how participants rank-ordered their preferences.

Table 12.1 summarizes our rank-orderings among the seven systems considered here. The first row reports the number of first-choice votes for each system. The second row reports the number of second-choice votes for each system, and so forth. These data can be used to reach a collective decision using the Borda count method.

The Borda count is another method frequently employed by political scientists and touted by other academicians (particularly economists and mathematicians)[3] as the best system for reaching a collective judgment. It takes fully into account the rank-ordered preferences of each participant, summing up these rank-ordered preferences to reach the collective judgment. If everyone in our project ranked the Electoral College as his or her first choice, its Borda count would be 37 (1 x 37). If everyone ranked the popular-majority system last (or seventh), its Borda count would be 259 (7 x 37). So the smaller an option's Borda count, the higher is its rank in a collective judgment. The last row of table 12.1 reveals the Borda counts for each of our alternatives. Again, the Electoral

College is indicated as our collective choice, with the popular-plurality and the proportional-allocation systems again emerging as the most highly regarded alternatives. Notice, however, that approval voting and the Borda count lead to different outcomes in choosing among the other alternatives.

While academics are fond of approval voting and the Borda count, these voting systems have not been much discussed as alternatives to the Electoral College — and thus we have not considered the implications of adopting them as ways of counting presidential votes. Our concern is to evaluate the Electoral College and the most prominent alternatives to it. But as a final prelude to that discussion, it is instructive to use our participants' rank-order ballots to see whether and how our collective choice would be altered if we used these systems to determine that choice.

An electoral college approach to collective choice would of course involve a federal rather than an individual process. Just as the Electoral College initially requires elections within states, prior to summing state results to get a choice for the country as a whole, an electoral college approach for this project would initially involve each group making a determination of its choice and then aggregating the group decisions into our collective choice. Only a couple of our groups have explicitly indicated their collective choice; for example, our institutionalists (who wrote chapter 5) declared that the popular-plurality method was their first choice, with the present electoral college system being their second choice. But the top choices of each group can be determined from the ballots of the individuals within each group.[4] Here are the outcomes within each group:

- our theorists choose the Electoral College
- our federalists choose the Electoral College
- our institutionalists choose the popular-plurality system
- our party specialists choose the Electoral College
- our campaign experts choose the Electoral College
- our media specialists choose the Electoral College
- our experts on citizen participation choose the Electoral College
- our comparativists (specializing in stability) choose the popular-plurality system
- our specialists on social cleavages choose the popular-majority system

Since the Electoral College won in six of our nine groups, it looks to be our collective choice under this method. However, only if we used the rules of the House contingency procedure — granting one vote to each group — would we declare the Electoral College a 6-2-1 winner. Under electoral college rules, we would grant each group two electors (for being groups with equal standing to one another in our project) and an additional three to five electors depending on their populations. We would then give all the electors allocated to each group to the group's top choice. The Electoral College would still win, 43-11-7, as neither the small differences in the size of our groups nor the granting of extra voting power to the smaller groups affected our outcome.

There is one noteworthy feature of this result. The popular-majority system, which finished last in both the approval vote and the Borda count, came in third under the electoral college system. Just as the Electoral College awards electors to third parties that are strong in a region but have little support in the country as a whole, so this system would provide a more prominent role for the popular-majority system due to its strong support among our group specializing in social cleavages.

There was considerable diversity of preferences within each group, but the electoral college approach with a unit rule overlooks such diversity. The smallness of our electorate precludes us from compiling our results using the district plan to represent such diversity within an electoral college system. To apply a district plan, we would have to partition our groups into districts, but there would be much arbitrariness in how we would create such districts and not much to be gained from the exercise.[5] Using the proportional allocation method to deal with this diversity is also not very meaningful. In apportioning electors within groups, we would presumably end up having one elector casting a vote for each individual in the group, and the result for those ballots would be the same as for the popular-plurality system considered below. The only difference would be that each group would have two extra electors (for being equal groups in the project) and these electors would vote for the top-ranked (or two top-ranked) systems by the group. No matter what formula was used for allocating such electors to achieve proportionality, the Electoral College would win, and the popular-plurality system would come in second under this system.[6]

To determine the winner under a popular-plurality method, we would simply have to look at the top row of Table 12.1.[7] The Electoral College, as it currently exists, is the first choice of fifteen of us. The popular-plurality alternative came in a fairly distant second with eight first place votes. The district plan came in third with five first-place votes. The other systems got two or three first-place votes each. The relatively strong showing of the district plan here shows the key limitation of the popular-plurality method. We have bimodal attitudes about the district plan. Some of us like it a lot, but others dislike it immensely. The popular-plurality method takes into account only the strong support for the system by some and ignores the strong reservations about the system by others. Just as an extremist candidate could do well if we had a popular-plurality rule for choosing the president, divisive plans — like the district plan — can do well if we apply this decision rule to our collective choice in this project.

We are now in position to see what our collective choice would be had we adopted a bonus plan as our decision rule. We would start with the results from our Electoral College-style procedure. As previously indicated, this resulted in 43 votes for the Electoral College, 11 votes for the popular-plurality system, and 7 votes for the popular-majority system. We now know that the Electoral College also won the popular plurality, so we simply give some number of bonus votes to the 43 votes already won by the Electoral College under the electoral college procedure. In this case, the number of electoral votes granted doesn't matter. In any decisive election, the number of bonus votes won't matter.

To determine our collective choice if we adopt the majority rule with a contingent runoff, we need results from two separate votes. Because we had an initial vote at the beginning of the project, we use its result to determine the possibility of an initial winner under the majority rule. The first choices of our thirty-seven participants in the initial balloting were as follows:

Electoral College	11
District plan	7
Popular-plurality	6
Proportional allocation	4
Instant runoff	4
Popular-majority	3
Bonus plan	2

With less than 30 percent of the vote, the Electoral College had far less than a required majority, but it would be a finalist in head-to-head competition in our second round of voting, pitted against the district plan. Although we did not ask our participants to choose between the Electoral College and the district plan in the second round, we can use their rank-order ballots to determine who would have won in a head-to-head competition. The result: the Electoral College wins with 26 votes, while the district plan gets only 11 votes.

The rank-ordering of our individual preferences in our final balloting also allows us to conduct an instant runoff. We do this by dropping those systems with the least first-place votes, in this case the proportional allocation plan, the national bonus plan, and — ironically — the instant-runoff plan. Distributing the second-place votes of those who supported these plans to the remaining choices, we get the following result:[8]

Electoral College	18
Popular-plurality	9
District plan	6
Popular-majority	4

Since there is still no majority, we next drop the popular-majority plan, and transfer the votes of its supporters, and finally receive a decisive result.

Electoral College	19
Popular-plurality	12
District plan	6

Table 12.2   Collective Ranking of the Electoral College and Alternatives Using Different Voting Methods

Voting system	First	Second	Third	Fourth	Fifth	Sixth	Last
Approval voting	Electoral College	Popular-plurality	Proportional allocation	Instant runoff	District plan	Bonus plan	Popular-majority
Borda count	Electoral College	Popular-plurality	Proportional allocation	Bonus plan	District plan	Instant runoff	Popular-majority
By group: Unit rule	Electoral College	Popular-plurality	Popular-majority				
By group: Proportional	Electoral College	Popular-plurality	District plan (tie)	Popular-majority			
Bonus plan	Electoral College	Popular-plurality	Popular-majority				
Plurality rule	Electoral College	Popular-plurality	District plan	Popular majority	Instant runoff (tie)	Bonus plan (tie)	Proportional allocation
Majority rule	Electoral College	District plan					
Instant runoff	Electoral College	Popular plurality	District plan				

One difference between the contingent-runoff system and the instant-runoff system is that the supporters of the less preferred options were not forced to choose between the Electoral College and the district plan under the instant-runoff system. Had they been forced to make that choice under the contingent-runoff system, most would have opted for the present Electoral College. But supporters of the current system might have feared the supporters of the least preferred systems were some sort of reformers who would vote against the Electoral College (by supporting the district plan) in the contingent runoff. To get the votes of these reformers, perhaps supporters of the Electoral College would have made some sort of concession to these participants.[9]

Our results are summed up in table 12.2, which reports the order of finish of each electoral system under the different methods that we have thus far employed to achieve a collective choice. Under every system we have examined, the Electoral College is our top collective choice. This result points to a basic truth: when one alternative has much more support than any other option, it really doesn't matter what electoral system is adopted. Only when communities are strongly divided does the method of counting votes make a difference.[10]

There is much more division about what is the best alternative to the Electoral College. This is, of course, precisely the result that is predicted by pluralists and that provides a challenge to progressives. As in the public at large, as revealed by various polls, most political scientists prefer another system to the Electoral

College.[11] But the multiplicity of alternatives creates divisions among those who would challenge the existing system and prevents focusing enough energy to mount a successful challenge to the Electoral College.[12]

Opponents of the Electoral College may look at the results thus far and say that the best alternative to rally around — least in the collective judgment of political scientists — is the popular-plurality system. But the slim differences in the Borda count for that system and proportional allocation, coupled with the different rankings of alternatives under different counting methods, prompts us to withhold that judgment. Is there some procedure that we can recommend to discover the best alternative — one that opponents of the Electoral College might rally around in order to mount a sustained challenge to the existing system?

Many philosophers instruct us that when making evaluations such as this, the most effective method is not to hold one option up against an ideal, but to compare one alternative against another using agreed-upon criteria.[13] Public choice theory also instructs us that the best method of reaching a collective choice is to decide between alternatives in pairwise comparisons. Condorcet, a French philosopher and mathematician in the late eighteenth century, proposed that if one alternative is the majority choice over all other choices in a series of head-to-head comparisons, that alternative is the rational collective choice.[14] In the terminology of public choice theorists, it is the Condorcet winner.

Pitting the Electoral College against each alternative to it in head-to-head competition (based on the rank-order preferences of our participants), reveals that the Electoral College is our Condorcet winner, defeating each alternative by a margin of at least 2 to 1. But beyond that, things get muddier, though we can break our alternatives into two groups. The popular-plurality, the proportional allocation, and the district plan comprise one set of alternatives and they always defeat the other set of alternatives — the popular-majority system, the bonus plan, and the instant runoff — in head-to-head competition. But within the top group, the infamous "voting cycle" appears. In head-to-head competition, the popular-plurality system defeats the district plan (20–17), but it loses to the proportional allocation plan (18–19). The proportional allocation plan is not the Condorcet winner among the alternatives, however, as it only ties the district plan (18–18, with one participant abstaining because he ranked the two systems equally). The important point is that the popular-plurality system, which seemed to be the leading alternative, is not thought the better choice by most of us when we make head-to-head comparisons between it and the proportional allocation plan.

In short, we cannot provide a collective choice among alternatives to the Electoral College. We suspect that our deadlock on this issue reflects the broader division and uncertainty that exists among political activists concerning the challengers to the Electoral College. As in the country as a whole, most of us do not regard the Electoral College as the best system of selecting a president, but we are far from agreeing on a replacement. Failing such agreement, the Electoral College remains an acceptable status quo.

Voting provides the sort of quantitative assessment about our collective judgments that cannot be ignored. But in the chapters that comprise the bulk of this volume, we have provided our qualitative assessments, and these provide the ideas (rather than simply the numbers) that are the real basis for making both individual and collective judgments about political matters. In the next two sections, we summarize these assessments concerning first the Electoral College and then the alternatives to it.

THE ELECTORAL COLLEGE AS REIGNING CHAMPION

The case for the Electoral College begins with the recognition that it was part and parcel of the U.S. Constitution, our most basic social contract for governing.[15] More than any other constitutional feature, it has survived numerous challenges and has provided the basic rules for selecting presidents for more than two centuries. Successful candidates under its rules have won the authority of the office and sufficient legitimacy, both from the public and from political elites, to govern.[16] Only the 1860 presidential election arrived at an outcome that seriously threatened the stability of our social and political systems, but we doubt that any electoral system could have prevented the civil war that followed Lincoln's victory.[17]

The Electoral College meshes with the underlying principles of the Constitution: federalism and the separation of powers. Its most basic federal feature is its allocation of electors. By distributing 436 electors to the states (and the District) on the basis of their populations, it gives great weight to the idea that we are a nation of individual citizens, who should all count equally in holding our presidents accountable through their votes. By allocating 102 electors to the states (and the District) simply because they are states, it also recognizes that we are a nation of states, each of which should also count equally in the presidential election process. Arguments that the Electoral College is unfair in giving more value to the votes of citizens of small states are therefore problematic because they assume that we are simply a nation of individual citizens.[18] As a nation of states, each state has a role to play in the process of electing the most powerful national authority. By giving states qua states this role, presidents and presidential candidates have incentives to be attentive to the interests and rights of states.[19] Given the federal component to the Electoral College, it is entirely appropriate that the states determine how they select their electors. Thus, if some states want to adopt the district plan or the proportional allocation of electors, that is their right.

Developed as an alternative to the congressional selection of the executive, the Electoral College is also consistent with the principle of the separation of powers. Having the legislature select the executive is a key feature of an alternative form of government, the parliamentary system, which integrates the workings of the executive and legislature. But the American preference has been for a government that divides power so that interests dominant in one institution can be checked if they pursue policies harmful to those interests better represented in other institutions.[20] The electoral college system provides a way of electing the president that has developed as independent of the legislature, and the dormancy of the House contingency procedure has enhanced the separation-of-power principle in our government.

But the separation of powers can make governance difficult. Effective governance occurs when there is considerable consensus on policy goals and when opposing interests lack the capacity to cause stalemate.[21] The chief barrier to effective governance is a proliferation of parties, each representing distinct interests and having considerable influence within governmental institutions. Governance is most effective when one party controls both the presidency and Congress and can claim widespread support for its policies. Governance is more difficult when different parties control the presidency and Congress, but if both parties are relatively pragmatic and centrist, they can still govern effectively. Governance is most difficult when control over institutions is fragmented among multiple parties, each representing narrow interests and/or uncompromising ideologies. The Electoral College helps prevent this situation because it promotes a two-party system in which both Democrats and Republicans have strong incentives to be centrist and pragmatic.[22] Although the Electoral College was created before the development of political parties, our two-party system has been nurtured by the Twelfth Amendment and the practice of allocating electoral votes on a winner-take-all basis to the candidate with the most popular votes within each state.[23] The Electoral College limits the role of third parties that would fragment government and diminish effective governance.

Two major criticisms have been leveled against the Electoral College, but both are problematic. The first is that the Electoral College thwarts representation of the country's extensive diversity.[24] By enhancing the role of the two centrist parties, it diminishes the opportunities for citizens who support the goals of third parties to express their preferences effectively at the ballot box. Because of the unit rule, supporters of the weaker party within noncompetitive states go completely unrepresented in the Electoral College. This may be problematic, but such representation is not very germane to presidential elections. Under the American system, the executive is not an institution for the representation of diversity. The president should govern by pursuing policies that reflect the concerns of "the median voter."[25] The president creates and oversees an administration occupied by those who generally share the president's policy goals.[26] Congress is better suited to represent diverse interests, and we might want an electoral system that produces a more representative Congress.[27] But having third parties (and minority parties in one-party dominant states) play a greater role in the selection of the president will not overcome the fact that the president is one person, and our best hope is that he or she will represent most Americans by pursuing a mainstream policy agenda that addresses as many of their concerns as possible. The rules of the Electoral College help elect such mainstream candidates and make unlikely the election of extremist presidents having both intense minority support and widespread opposition.[28]

The second, more frequent criticism of the Electoral College is that it is undemocratic and can distort the public will. The 2000 election reminds us that the winner of the popular vote may not triumph in the Electoral College. Still, this criticism is problematic because it misunderstands democracy and has an oversimplified conception of "the public will."

The "undemocratic" criticism fails in part because the founders did not intend the Electoral College as a device to thwart democratic majorities.[29] They made no provisions preventing states from using popular elections to determine electors, and for almost 150 years all states have employed this procedure. The Electoral College was designed to encourage widespread or supramajoritarian support for presidents. Today, however, the Electoral College permits popular pluralities to determine the winners of statewide contests and requires candidates to gain the votes of a majority of democratically elected electors to win the presidency.[30]

Whatever the criteria for a democratic process, producing "outcomes consistent with the public will" is not among them.[31] Democracy does require popular sovereignty, which means that, because citizens have control over government, they consent to be governed by it. Popular elections are the means by which citizens control government, but there are many kinds of elections, including our electoral college approach. Most electoral systems are probably capable of controlling officeholders, letting citizens oust those who are corrupt, incompetent, or out of sync with the predominant aspirations of citizens. Because no one set of election rules is clearly best, the critical issue for democracy is that agreement exists on electoral rules, which are then consistently followed.

Popular elections under both plurality and majoritarian rules are often viewed as the preferred electoral format because they are said to lead to outcomes consistent with the public will. However, public choice theorists have demonstrated that the concept of a public will is often vacuous, an abstraction intended to signify what most members of the public want, but a concept that is impossible to operationalize precisely.[32] As demonstrated earlier in this chapter, if voter preferences are fairly closely split among several options, the method of aggregating individual choices will influence which alternative appears to be the top collective choice, or so-called public will. In short, we can reach different understandings of the public will depending on the method used to count votes. If the popular-plurality method yields a different outcome than the popular-majoritarian method, which outcome is consistent with the public will? The answer is that there is simply no true "public will," at least not in close elections.

Moreover, in close elections, three practical matters prevent knowing the public will by just counting the ballots. First, nonvoters may have different preferences than voters.[33] If the extent of voter turnout influences who will win — a basic notion accepted by most candidates — then election results can at best tell us the will of the voters, not of the public. Second, counting errors approaching one percent or more can and do occur through both mechanical and human processes.[34] Thus, our conception of the public will in close elections can be distorted by the sort of problems that occurred in Florida. Third, electoral fraud does exist, and such fraud can yield results that distort the public will.[35] In short, in any close election we cannot know the public will and should not fool ourselves that a popular vote will inform us what that will is.

Nevertheless, accurate vote totals are important. In a democracy, electoral rules must be followed, and all fair electoral systems have procedures that minimize counting errors and rules that outlaw fraud. Given its decentralized nature, the Electoral College effectively locates critical counting errors and minimizes incentives for fraud by focusing attention on states where irregularities are suspected. Under the electoral college system, most states produce sufficiently decisive outcomes to render irrelevant questions of fraudulent or miscounted ballots.[36] Efforts to correct counting errors or fraud can thus be concentrated on areas where it matters, such as Florida in 2000.

The electoral college system is scarcely perfect. Its most obvious shortcoming is that it focuses attention on large states where large blocks of electoral votes are "in play." The rules of the electoral college game require obtaining 270 electoral votes, so the attention and resources of candidates, parties, interest groups, and the media are concentrated on those large states where the outcome is in doubt.[37] In noncompetitive and small states, citizens may feel far removed from the election and parties may be inactive, resulting in lower voter turnout.[38] Certain groups of citizens, considered pivotal to the outcome in the large competitive states, receive extraordinary attention from the candidates, thus increasing their participation and influence on the outcome. Presidents may even shower such groups with policy benefits to ensure their continued support in subsequent elections.

One contention in political science is that minorities and the urban poor may be such especially influential groups. Because these groups are otherwise relatively powerless in our political life, this could count as another merit of the electoral college system. But questions remain about the validity of this thesis.[39] For example, blacks may be such committed Democrats that they are either taken for granted or ignored by candidates, even when they comprise a crucial voting bloc in large competitive states. And the stereotype of blacks as residents of large urban centers within competitive states misses the reality that many blacks may be ignored because they live in middle-sized and noncompetitive southern states. While Hispanics are becoming increasingly dispersed throughout the states, they are least likely to reside in smaller states where the value of the vote is greatest.

The Electoral College was designed to generate widespread support for presidents from most states in our infant nation. But the current system may not reinforce the kind of supramajoritarianism that was initially envisioned. Now candidates may ignore those groups that they see as unnecessary blocks of voters under our electoral rules. The Electoral College's major weakness is perhaps its growing inability to structure presidential elections so that the major-party candidates build electoral and governing coalitions broad enough for minorities and other relatively disadvantaged citizens to feel included.[40] One question is whether this weakness is great enough to overcome the many virtues of the Electoral College. A second question is whether any alternative system could overcome this limitation.

EVALUATING THE CHALLENGERS
The Popular-Plurality System

Abolishing the Electoral College and having a national popular election determined by the plurality rule is the most obvious alternative to the Electoral College. We use popular-plurality elections to select our governors and representatives, and they are a familiar, acceptable, and perhaps laudatory part of American politics.

The case for a popular-plurality system does not depend on the faulty argument that it ensures outcomes consistent with "the public will." It is a mistake to believe that the winner of a popular election has authority because his election embodies the public will. It is also a mistake to believe that such a winner necessarily has a public mandate to impose his policy agenda.[41] But in a democracy, who has a more legitimate claim to the presidency than the candidate who receives the most citizen votes? Thus, the legitimacy of a president seems as assured under the popular-plurality system as it is under the Electoral College. And having a legitimate president encourages effective governance in our separation-of-powers system.[42]

The popular-plurality system also ensures voter equality, which is perhaps its most important democratic justification. Voters are not equal under the Electoral College, as citizens of small states and large competitive states have more voting power than citizens in middle-sized states and noncompetitive large states.[43] Every vote has equal value in the popular-plurality system, and voters are not made irrelevant because their states are not "in play." Thus, by pursuing all voters, presidential campaigns could spread their resources more widely throughout the country.[44] Parties and interest groups might be more active in getting out their supporters across the nation. And the media may pay more attention to how voters react to campaigns in all regions. In the popular-plurality system, citizens would not feel that their vote is worthless because they live in a state where the outcome is preordained, even as a heated battle rages in the nation as a whole. While individual decisions to vote surely depend on many factors, citizens should be more likely to vote if they think that there is some chance (no matter how small) that their vote will make a difference.[45]

The popular-plurality system has the practical justification of being reasonably compatible with the two-party system.[46] The popular-plurality presidential scheme resembles the first-past-the-post (or single winner) legislative electoral system, which clearly promotes a two-party system. Other proposed reforms, like proportional allocation or runoffs, would encourage the more active participation of third parties in presidential elections, if only to increase their bargaining power with a majority party in need of their support to win a close election.[47] These alternative reforms would also provide supporters of third parties with greater incentives and opportunities to cast sincere votes for the candidates of their own parties, rather than casting sophisticated votes for their favored major-party candidate. But under a popular-plurality system, the electoral outcome could hinge on small vote differences between the two leading candidates, who would most likely be from the Democratic and Republican parties. Both major parties would thus retain their incentives to create broad electoral coalitions to edge out their rival. And the supporters of third parties would still have incentives to become sophisticated voters and not "waste their vote."[48] Thus, third parties may not fare much better under the popular-plurality system than under the electoral college system. In fact, regional parties that can win a few states would almost certainly do better under current electoral rules.

The popular-plurality scheme also retains the advantages of two-party politics for achieving effective governance within our separation-of-powers system. Because the entire nation, not just a few competitive states, would be "in play," the relationships between a party's candidate for the presidency and its congressional candidates would be strengthened. The president's electoral "coattails" might well help elect more members of Congress from the same party.[49] As a result, we might end up with less divided government, and thus more effective governance, under the popular-plurality system.

Still, fewer barriers to third parties would seem to exist under the popular-plurality system than under the Electoral College. The existing system creates disincentives for third parties to compete nationally, as they have little to gain by coming in second or third in states where the unit rule assures that all electoral votes will go to either Democrats or Republicans. Under the popular-plurality system, all popular votes gained in such states contribute to the national total, so third parties would be encouraged to conduct nationwide campaigns. Such increased competition could encourage the two dominant parties to campaign more inclusively by appealing to voters who could be attracted to the third parties. It could even lead to a third party becoming strong enough to replace one of the major parties as a real contender for presidential power. In short, a popular plurality scheme may make the existing party system more adaptive to the changing aspirations of voters and the emerging needs of the country.[50]

But there are dangers in this scenario. The popular-plurality system may create incentives for many new parties to form and compete for the presidency. If more parties compete nationally and peel off voters from the major parties, the realistic threshold of votes needed to win might become dangerously low. A highly fragmented party system could emerge, in which many parties run on fairly narrow platforms (e.g., an environmental party, a right-to-life party, and a flat-tax party.). If so, the two dominant parties could no longer provide the glue that makes governance possible under our separation-of-powers system.[51] Worse, the chances increase that we might elect an extremist president — someone successful at rallying a small but sufficient plurality from one segment of the population, despite being disliked by most of the electorate. Such an outcome could bring about the sort of social instability that the electoral college system has avoided.[52]

Another popular-plurality danger comes with the instability that could result if we replicated the Florida events of 2000 on a national scale. In other words, an extremely close popular vote would lead to challenges of the initial results throughout the nation, not just in a single pivotal state.[53] We could be searching for evidence of fraud or fouled ballots in every county in the country. In short, we might plunge into a futile attempt to get a "true measurement" of voter preferences, even though repeated counts would only yield different estimates of who "really won." Because of our inability to detect every instance of fraud or to avoid each mistake in counting the ballots, the "true winner" of close elections would remain obscure. Indeed, candidates' supporters would have incentives to engage in fraudulent and discriminatory activities throughout the country. Savvy operatives would know that these activities could decide the national outcome and that they would be difficult to detect, because — unlike in the Electoral College — investigations into fraud would not be focused on particular states. All this could lead to challenges to the legitimacy of whoever is declared the winner of a close popular-plurality election, resulting in social and political instability.

In addition, the popular-plurality procedure could produce other problematic outcomes. Presidential candidates might be less concerned with the particular needs of states and pursue a national agenda that undermined the autonomy of state governments and their capacity to serve as laboratories of policy experimentation.[54] The popular-plurality system would likely enhance the role of national advertising in campaigns, which would make electoral outcomes more dependent on the fund-raising capacities of parties and candidates. It could also destabilize voter choices, making them a function of last-minute demagogic attacks on opponents rather than on thoughtful considerations of which candidate best satisfies the aspirations, interests, and political principles of the voter.[55]

The National Bonus Plan
This proposed reform is a synthesis between the Electoral College and the popular-plurality system. The Electoral College would be retained but the win-

ner of a popular-vote plurality would get an additional 102 electors, which should cure the Electoral College defect of occasionally producing a president who is not "the people's choice." Thus a couple of merits of the popularly-plurality system would be achieved. The legitimacy of the president would be enhanced, in that, as the winner of the popular vote, his or her margin of victory in the Electoral College would grow. With all votes counting the same in determining the national popular winner, citizens would have more equal voting power than they would under the existing system. At the same time, the Electoral College's merits would be retained, at least formally. There would continue to be a federal aspect to our presidential elections, as states qua states would still have two electors and could still determine the rules for their allocation of electors. With the winner of the national popular vote getting a huge block of electors, there would be almost no chance of having a House contingency election, so that this system would be even more compatible with our separation-of-powers principles than the Electoral College. The two-party system — and the advantages to effective governance provided by that system — would be less threatened than by most other reforms, perhaps including the pure popular-plurality system. After all, the rules of the Electoral College that discourage voters from "wasting their votes" on third parties would still be in force.

Still, our general assessment of the national bonus plan is that it would be a de facto popular-plurality system.[56] The electoral college aspects of the system would become mere formalities. Because the winner of the national popular vote would almost assuredly pick up enough electoral votes in the states to win, attention would be focused on the national popular vote result rather than the results in particular states. Thus, it is hard to see how some of the dangers of the popular-plurality system could be avoided. There would be nationalization of the election and perhaps of government, with some possible reduction in state autonomy. An extremist candidate might capture a plurality of the national popular vote (and enough electoral votes from the states) to win. Perhaps the most likely danger is the instability that could occur in an extremely close election. As in the pure popular-plurality system, we could be engaged in an attempt to recount ballots and ascertain fraud throughout the country in a futile attempt to obtain an accurate national vote total, upon which the results of the election hinged.

Since the national bonus plan is a de facto popular-plurality system, and since the risks would be similar under both systems, there seems little reason for keeping the façade of an electoral college in an amended Constitution. Why add to our Constitutional complexity when a simple national popular-plurality system would have the same result?

The Popular-Majority System
Although a bit more complex than the popular-plurality system, most citizens would grasp the popular-majority system more easily than they would the Elec-

toral College. And its main justification is powerful: the president should win the support of a voting majority. If the initial popular vote failed to produce a candidate who is the first choice of a majority of voters, a runoff election could be held a few weeks later between the top two candidates, thus ensuring a majority.

This system has clear benefits. First, most of the advantages that the popular-plurality system has over the Electoral College would be retained by popular-majority procedures. Once again, all votes would count equally, regardless of where they were cast, and the inequalities that arise through the Electoral College putting a limited number of states in play would vanish.[57] Second, this system would likely maximize the legitimacy of the winner, who would be not only the people's choice, but also the ultimate choice of most people. Third, this scheme would provide more protection than the popular-plurality system against the possibility of electing extremist presidents and the resulting potential for instability. Should an extremist lead a fragmented field of candidates after the first round of balloting, the majority of citizens opposed to the narrow concerns and/or rigid ideology of the extremist could rally around the second-place finisher in the runoff.[58] Fourth, there may be greater protection against voter fraud in a popular-majority system than in a popular-plurality one. Local results from second-round balloting that are markedly at odds with the results from the initial round would signal the possibility of something being amiss. Efforts to detect fraud could thus be focused under a popular-majority system, discouraging such activities.[59]

Nevertheless, the popular-majority system has several defects. First, nationalizing elections and government would be a concern. Second, while this system has the potential to enhance the legitimacy of the president, it could also reduce it. If the first-round winner lost in the second round, his supporters might question the legitimacy of the elected president, as well as the runoff system itself.[60] A third and related problem is likely "voter fatigue" in the second round.[61] A significant reduction in second-round turnout could produce different outcomes in the first and second rounds of balloting. If different rules and a smaller turnout elected a different winner, legitimacy would be compromised.

But the most important deficiency of the popular-majority system is its effect on the party system.[62] While all but the two top vote-getters would be eliminated from the runoff election, many parties and candidates would have increased incentives to run major campaigns in the initial round of balloting. Citizens would see a second electoral round as providing them with the opportunity to cast a sophisticated vote for the more preferred of two candidates. Voters might well act "sincerely" in the initial round, by supporting those candidates who best represented their narrow interest or ideological orientation. Candidates would probably emerge to capture such votes, and so the first round could be cluttered with parties and candidates. Many candidates who now seek a major-party nomination but who lose in the primaries and party caucuses might bypass the major parties and simply enter the first round of the general election. There would be two incentives to do so. First, in a crowded initial field, such a candidate could finish first or second and thus get into the runoff; he or she could even be matched against another candidate with similar intense but narrow appeal, providing a chance to ascend to the presidency. Second, such a candidate could attract enough votes to broker a deal with one of the top two finishers. As in coalition governments, the top two finishers would offer policy concessions or offices in the administration to those parties and candidates who were eliminated in the first round but could deliver their voters during the second round. Even though they lost in the first round, such parties and candidates might exert disproportionate influence over the overall electoral result. We might even see much more "minority representation" — including members of extremist parties — within the administration as a result of such deals.[63] In short, the popular-majority system would probably lead to party fragmentation both in the electoral process and in governing. The chances for effective governance could thus decline from what is experienced under the current system. In the end, many of the political scientists in this project took these concerns seriously and gave a low ranking to the popular-majority system.

The Instant Runoff

Sometimes a fresh new face enters a presidential campaign, has attributes that are attractive to some voters, but simply fails to catch fire with the larger electorate and finishes out of the running in the early primaries. Such seems to be the fate of the instant runoff, at least when the electorate is comprised mainly of political scientists specializing in American politics. In chapters 4 through 11, our various groups often provided positive evaluations of the instant runoff, but when our votes were cast, this alternative received little support.

The main theoretical justification for the instant runoff is that it absolves citizens of the need to make a decision between being sincere voters and being sophisticated voters. Because citizens can rank-order their preferences among candidates, they can indicate as their top choice their sincere preference for an independent or third-party candidate who best reflects their interests or principles but who has little chance of winning. They can then indicate as their second choice their sophisticated preference for the major candidate that they prefer over the other major candidate.[64] The "transferable vote" aspect of the instant runoff ensures that, if and when their sincere preference is eliminated in the counting procedure, their sophisticated preference will be taken into account. Thus, they will not have contributed to the election of their least preferred candidate by "wasting" their vote on their sincere choice.

The instant runoff is one form of a national popular vote, and it would capture the benefits of such systems. Voters would count equally. No voters would be inconsequential because they lived in states where the results were preordained.

All candidates, third parties, and minority parties in one-party dominant states would have incentives to appeal to all voters and to get out the vote of all their supporters, regardless of their geographical location.

The instant runoff would surely increase the role of third parties and independent candidates in the presidential election process, and it might maximize the positive elements of such parties and candidates while minimizing the negatives. Voters who are now alienated from the Republicans and Democrats, or who simply see little difference between their candidates, could become mobilized and active voters by the presence of other candidates on the ballot.[65] An environmentalist may come to the polls to cast a sincere vote for Nader, decide that Gore is a more committed environmentalist than Bush, and so indicate such a preference in the rank-order ballot of this system. A social conservative could cast a sincere vote for Buchanan, and still indicate a second preference for Bush over Gore because of Bush's more conservative social policies. Thus, the instant runoff may result both in a higher voter turnout and in a set of ballots that more accurately reflects voters' preferences than occurs under the Electoral College or, arguably, other alternative electoral systems. In short, the instant runoff may minimize the distortion of voters' intents, which adds to the legitimacy of the winning candidate and reduces the threat to social stability that might follow such distortions, real or perceived.[66]

While increasing the role of third parties, the instant runoff may nevertheless maintain most aspects of the prevailing two-party system. The major parties would have incentives to be inclusive, by incorporating the goals and issues of third parties into their own platforms and speeches and by trying to avoid alienating third-party supporters. Such informal coalition building would flow from the desires of both major parties to be seen as closer to the issue positions of third-party supporters and thus receive their transferable votes.[67]

The instant-runoff system may thus be the most supramajoritarian of our alternatives.[68] A candidate would need only a slim majority of first-ranked and transferred votes to get elected. But he or she would like to be ranked as highly as possible on as many ballots as possible, because the instant runoff would reward the major candidate who is most highly supported by those who are *not* part of the candidate's own party.

The instant runoff would promote a multiparty system in which the major parties understand they lack the core of supporters to win on their own. In the electoral college system, the two main parties can take for granted or ignore voters in states where the outcome is preordained. Under the popular-plurality system candidates may be satisfied with getting a mere plurality of supporters to put them over the top. With a desire to reach the second round, candidates would initially seek enough core supporters to be one of the top two vote-getters among a number of parties and candidates that would contest the first round. Between the first and second rounds of votes, the top-ranked candidates might seek only the minimal winning coalition, making bargains with specific candidates who can deliver the needed votes.[69] In contrast, by requiring candidates to obtain a majority, the instant-runoff scheme mandates that the preferences of all voters could matter, with no last-minute bargaining for votes. Candidates would understand the need for supramajoritarian coalition building. Moreover, under the instant-runoff system, voters may feel part of the winning coalition, even if they did not list the winner as their first choice. Having ranked the winner as a second or third choice may convey a sense of having "approved" of the winner, enhancing his or her legitimacy.

The participants in this project also report other possible benefits of the instant-vote system. The comparativists, specializing in social stability, rate the system as moderately effective at limiting fraud, because having a rank-order ballot complicates its successful commission.[70] They also rank the system highly in terms of preventing extremists from ascending to the presidency, because it requires a winning candidate to command broad public support. And our experts on the media suggested that the instant runoff might do more than any other electoral system to encourage the media to engage in more citizen-oriented, substantive coverage of the campaign.[71] Under the instant-runoff system, reporting poll results on who is winning the horse race would be even more inadequate than it is now. Reporters would have to look more carefully at the messages of the candidates and how they were received by various kinds of voters. Additionally, the media might well report the efforts of candidates to appeal to voters beyond their own party, rather than focusing on attacks made by major candidates on each other. Such reporting might encourage people to see politics as a positive and inclusive coalition-building activity aimed at solving national problems rather than a negative and competitive activity aimed at tearing down adversaries.

Despite such positive qualitative assessments, the instant-vote system did not garner much support from our participants. As a national voting scheme, it would be problematic for supporters of state and local autonomy. Even if the major parties could become more inclusive, the instant runoff would certainly encourage the growth of third parties. In the long run, several parties could grow in influence and become legitimate contenders in presidential and legislative races. If this happened, gridlock between our governmental institutions might increase and make governance more difficult. Some doubts were also raised about the capacity of voters to cast meaningful rank-order ballots.[72] Many voters have difficulty determining which of two parties has orientations that best reflect their interests and principles. Could such voters cast informed ballots rank-ordering their preferences among three or more candidates?

Without doubt, the instant-runoff ballot would be a radical reform in American politics. Passing the required constitutional amendment would be difficult, as Democratic and Republican politicians tend to see few advantages in innovations that could significantly threaten their customary practices and their power.

As a foreign import that is unfamiliar to most Americans, the chances it will generate widespread support are close to nil. The instant runoff is a fresh face with attractive features that might appeal to some intellectuals in Ann Arbor, Cambridge, and other university towns. Still, political scientists are realists, and their assessment is that this reform is going nowhere.

The District Plan

Having states abolish their unit rule by dividing the states into congressional districts, allocating one elector to each district, and awarding that elector to the winner of a popular-plurality vote in the district has both positive and negative implications. As a result, some participants in the project rated this reform positively, but others were highly critical.

On the positive side, the district plan is compatible with the Constitution and its major features. The Constitution permits states to select electors in any manner they wish, so particular states could follow Maine's and Nebraska's lead and adopt the district plan without an amendment. Likewise, the district plan is compatible with federalism.[73] The electoral college system would remain in effect, with two electors going to the winner of the popular-plurality vote in each state as a whole. While national popular vote schemes would reduce federalism by enhancing the role of national organizations in the presidential election, the district plan would extend federalism to the substate level, as political organizations within districts would play increasingly important roles. The district plan might slightly reduce the impact of the separation of powers, as presidential electors and legislators would come from the same congressional districts. Presidential coattails might be longer if boundaries for presidential elections coincided with those of congressional races. Members of Congress might be more susceptible to presidential influence if a president captured electors from their districts. But such effects would probably be small and sometimes run in the reverse direction, especially for those legislators who represent districts that the president lost.

The district plan would probably have no effect on the basic structures of our two-party system. Elections for Congress in the districts are now mostly two-party affairs, because their first-past-the-post feature enhances citizen perceptions that votes for third-party and independent candidates are wasted. Elections for presidential electors in the districts would have the same features.

The district plan would certainly change the geographic calculations of conducting presidential campaigns. Many new areas would be hotly contested. Proponents of the district plan emphasize that while most states are not competitive, some districts within these states are and could no longer be ignored. Presidential campaigns would be more active in these districts, and their ads and other activities may spill over into adjoining districts.[74] Parties in competitive districts would be energized, as citizens would see that their votes could make a difference. Because of such changes, the district plan may be associated with higher voter turnout.[75] But the reverse could also occur. Presidential elections in some states may be highly competitive, with some districts within these states being dominated by one party or the other. Adoption of the district plan would probably decrease political activity in these areas.[76]

The district plan has several potential problems that concern the participants in this project. For some, the district plan is a minor reform that doesn't address the real problems of the Electoral College and may in fact exacerbate them. Take unequal voting power, for example. Small states will still get the same two extra electors that the large states get, enhancing the vote value of citizens in small states. Simultaneously, whatever advantage accrued to large states would be lost if they abolished the unit rule, which had made them so important to presidential campaigns.

The possible discrepancy between the winner of the Electoral College vote and the winner of the popular vote would also persist and might well worsen. Al Gore would have lost more decisively in an Electoral College allocating votes under the district plan than he did in the existing Electoral College, despite having won the national popular vote. The district plan would have produced similar discrepancies in 1960 and 1976. This phenomenon occurs because the boundaries of districts can be drawn so as to concede a small number of districts to one party, packing its party identifiers into these districts, while creating a larger number of other districts where the other party has a thinner but still relatively safe partisan majority. The first party may have more supporters overall in the state, but the second party would win more districts and get more electors. Currently, Democrats seem to be more highly concentrated in some congressional districts, while Republicans have thinner majorities in a larger number of districts. This enables Republicans to do better under the district plan than in the popular vote.

This feature of the district plan makes it especially inhospitable to racial minorities and the urban poor, who are often concentrated in specific districts; this dilutes their capacity to exercise voting power on behalf of their favored party and raises the problem of congressional districting.[77] For the most part, state legislatures determine the boundaries of House seats, and their highly partisan, contentious processes have historically produced districts that work to the disadvantage of racial minorities and the urban poor. As a result of these problems, the district plan is strongly opposed by political scientists whose principles support the idea that our political institutions should be particularly responsive to the interests of our least advantaged citizens.

Proportional Allocation

Absent any constitutional amendment, specific states could abolish their unit rule and allocate their electors in proportion to the number of popular votes that a candidate received within their state. Like the district plan, this reform would be consistent with federalism, though the focus of presidential elections would remain at the state level. But in other respects, the differences between the district plan and proportional allocation could be quite profound.

Under the district plan, only competitive districts would be in play. With proportional allocation, every state (and district) would be a factor, as dominant parties could not assume the capacity to win all electors; some electors could and would be peeled off by minority and third parties in the state.[78] Such parties and independent candidates would gain fresh incentives to compete aggressively for each and every elector to be proportionately distributed. Thus, states adopting proportional allocation might expect an overall increase in activity by political parties and other political organizations and an increase in citizen participation, as voters in noncompetitive states (or districts) would no longer see their vote as irrelevant to the outcome. The whole country — rather than specific localities, states, or regions — would be up for grabs; this would encourage presidential campaigns to spread their resources more equally across the nation. In this respect, proportional allocation would resemble the popular-plurality system.

Widespread adoption of proportional allocation would threaten the existing two-party system.[79] Freed from winner-take-all rules, third parties and independent candidates would seek electors in proportion to their popular success in each state. Supporters of such parties and candidates would be encouraged to cast sincere ballots for them, adding to their success. Party fragmentation would likely occur, making effective governance more difficult. To reduce such fragmentation and to limit the role of narrow or special-interest candidates and fringe parties, proportional allocation plans might require candidates to attain some minimal percentage of popular votes — typically 5 or 10 percent — to qualify for any electors. Of course, such requirements would only be important in larger states, as candidates winning 10 (or so) percent of the popular vote would not qualify for any electors unless the state had ten or more electors to allocate, at least if there was no fractional allocation of electors.

This points to the importance of allocation rules. If states seek an allocation of electoral votes that more precisely mirrors the distribution of popular votes, fractional allocation of electors would be necessary. Such distributions would provide some representation in the College for candidates getting only a small number of votes.[80] If states seek an allocation formula that avoided a fragmentation of electoral votes, they could adopt the d'Hondt formula discussed in chapter 10, which keeps electors whole and allocates seats in the College in a manner that reduces representation of minor parties and favors the major parties. In short, the d'Hondt system appears to be the preferred method of proportional allocation if the goal is to obtain a better balance between governance and representation.

In our discussion of the Electoral College above, we argued that representation within the executive branch of government was a problematic goal. As noted, presidents are not required to include members of the opposing or third parties in their administration; rather, they seek to govern effectively by developing cabinets and staff that emphasize cohesion more than representation. Proportional allocation focuses on representation in the Electoral College, rather than on the executive. Such reform seeks to select a delegation of state electors that represents the entire range of citizens within a state, as opposed to the unit rule, which excludes those citizens who voted for the losing candidate.

Four purposes or values may be served by such representation. First, it may enhance the incentives of campaigns to build supramajorities within states.[81] Under the Electoral College, dominant parties in noncompetitive states can ignore those minority interests and groupings that are too small to threaten their continued dominance. Proportional allocation would encourage parties and campaigns to attract such interests so as to maximize their number of electors.

Second, in contrast to the perceived exclusion produced by current rules, proportional allocation may enhance the sense of inclusion that citizens have about the political process, increasing both their participation in politics and their compliance with governmental authority.[82]

Third, such representation under proportional allocation may reduce the mismatch between electoral votes and popular votes. The unit rule stands as the major cause of discrepancies between popular vote totals and electoral vote totals, as the popular votes given to losing candidates within states count for nothing. Proportional allocation ensures that electoral vote totals will more closely reflect the popular vote, but this system is no guarantee against the ultimate mismatch of the 2000 election. Factors such as the overrepresentation of small states in the allocation of electors and the imperfect rounding rules of any proportional allocation scheme could result in the election of a president who has a majority of proportionally allocated electors but who has lost the popular vote.

Fourth, the kind of representation achieved by proportional allocation could lead to the greater inclusion of minority interests in the administration, though this is unlikely. Suppose that every state had adopted the d'Hondt system in 2000 and the results were as described in table 10.2 (p. 154): Gore would have had 268 electoral votes, Bush would have had 267, and Nader would have had 3. Despite his few electoral votes, Nader could have controlled the outcome, and both parties would have had huge incentives to bargain with him. Nader's electors would not be "automatic" and could be induced to switch to (say) Gore if Gore were to promise to include Nader and other Green Party members in his administration. Continuing conflict between the Greens and the Democrats might have complicated Gore's ability to govern, but the proportional allocation system and the subsequent bargaining would have resulted in wider representation of interests in the administration.

Proportional allocation rules would probably lead to far more electors being allocated to third parties and independents than has occurred historically, increasing the likelihood that neither the Republican nor the Democratic candidate would achieve an Electoral College majority on their own. If no bargain could be struck between a leading party and the array of independents and third-party candidates holding key electoral votes to produce an Electoral College majority, the selection of the president would be thrown into the House of Representatives. Many of the reservations about proportional allocation expressed by participants in this project emphasized that this reform would enable third parties to become sufficiently strong that they could become spoilers on a regular basis. Few participants welcomed the possibility that the House would even occasionally select the president.

In summary, we find all alternatives to the Electoral College to have combinations of strengths and weaknesses. No alternative commends itself as a clear improvement over the existing system. Our qualitative evaluations are perhaps most favorable to the instant-runoff system, but it fares poorly in our balloting, largely because it is unfamiliar and unlikely to be adopted. The popular-plurality system may be the best alternative, as it might enhance presidential legitimacy and minimally disrupt our two-party system. Still, it is susceptible to fraud and the possible election of extremist candidates.

Our qualitative evaluations suggest that reforming the Electoral College with a proportional allocation of electors is preferable to having electors selected in congressional districts, as this could further various aspects of representation, perhaps including a better representation of minorities. State legislatures could implement proportional allocation plans, and so some experimentation with this system is possible and perhaps desirable. State legislatures in one-party dominant states would almost certainly reject such reforms, as they would have no incentives to have the minority party peel off some electors from their winner-take-all advantage. But legislatures in smaller and more competitive states might see advantages in proportional allocation, as they may prefer a system that would deliver some electoral votes to the candidate of their party rather than incur the risks of the winner-take-all system. As political scientists, we would welcome such reforms that would permit empirical assessments of their effects.[83] However, adoption of proportional allocation would increase the chances that no candidate would receive a majority in the Electoral College, and this raises a couple of important questions. Should proportionally allocated electors be "automatic" electors (or more firmly bound human electors) who could not be used as bargaining chips to achieve an Electoral College majority? Should the House contingency procedure be abandoned or reformed?

OF ROGUE ELECTORS AND THE HOUSE CONTINGENCY RELIC

Even defenders of the Electoral College generally concede that the discretion of electors and the House contingency election are problems, but see them to be of little contemporary consequence.[84] But, on election night in 2000, as the networks began to call various states for Bush or for Gore and to project possible outcomes in other states, a tie in the Electoral College loomed as a distinct possibility. The close presidential race reminds us that the House contingency remains a constitutional necessity if no candidate receives an Electoral College majority. Moreover, when the electors' votes were counted, we learned that one elector from the District of Columbia abandoned his pledge to vote for Gore. This had no effect on the outcome, but if two electors pledged to Bush had been "faithless" and voted instead for Gore, the election would have been thrown into the House. And had three Bush electors switched, Gore would have won. In short, the chances are remote — but real — that rogue voters or the House contingency election will be decisive. We need to consider abolishing the freedom of electors and the House contingency election.

Automatic Electors

When the Electoral College was established, electors were expected to be independent, casting their ballots for the persons whom they regarded as most qualified for the presidency. But today, electors are expected to perform their ceremonial role of voting for the state's popular vote winner. Electors are selected by state party organizations, but in most states, they are neither listed nor mentioned on the ballot. State laws merely provide that the party of the candidate receiving the most popular votes gets to have its electors cast their presidential votes at a designated location in each state on a designated time in December. Electors in a few states must pledge and even take formal oaths to support their party's national nominee, and some states would fine electors who violate their pledges, but these provisions are of questionable constitutionality.[85] Given that electors are loyal partisans, these provisions have normally been unnecessary, but on a few occasions "rogue" or "faithless" electors have cast ballots that violated their pledge to support the winner of the state's popular election. Since 1824, more than 20,000 electoral votes have been cast, with only eight instances when electors clearly violated their pledge. On no occasion did this affect the outcome.[86]

The argument for eliminating the freedom of electors is simple. If an election ever turned on the faithless act of a rogue voter, the legitimacy of the outcome would be severely challenged, as would the legitimacy of the system that permitted such an outcome. After a close election, a candidate who is within an electoral vote or two of victory might approach some of his opponent's electors with inducements to switch. Indeed, a state legislature controlled by the opposing party to the winner of the popular vote may be tempted to substitute its own electors, which might well have happened if a recount had favored Gore.[87] Given the possibility of corruption and the presumed role of electors as mere delegates of the electorate, many reformers have proposed a constitutional amendment to make casting of electoral votes automatic, based entirely on the popular vote.[88]

But the case for eliminating the elector's discretion is scarcely airtight. Indeed, the political scientists in our project leaned toward "keeping the present system intact, allowing the slight possibility of rogue voters." Why so? First, the issue was thought too inconsequential to deserve a constitutional amendment. Second, our political system has always had a place of honor for the maverick — the freethinking human who refuses to succumb to the party line or popular pressure. For example, the decision of Vermont Senator James Jeffords to change his party affiliation from Republican to Independent in May 2001, and thus change control of the Senate from Republican to Democratic, resembles the action of a rogue elector. For many of us, politics is a human endeavor and humans should exercise individual judgment. Third, an amendment creating automatic electors would eliminate the possibility that a third-party candidate could request that his electors cast their ballots for another candidate to further his party's interests. Had Nader received enough electors to determine the outcome, he might have concluded that it served the interests of the Green Party to reach an agreement with Gore in the Electoral College, rather than have the decision go to the House, which would probably have chosen the less environment-friendly Bush. Again, an amendment creating automatic electors would remove the possibility of a reasonable political decision that might lead to majority-based outcomes.

Fixing the House Contingency Procedure

Having the House of Representatives elect the president if no candidate receives a majority in the Electoral College was a crucial part of the presidential selection process at its inception. Since 1824, however, this procedure has gone unused. But if several states were to create proportional allocation systems that awarded some electors to third-party candidates, the House contingency procedure could become an occasional element of the presidential election process. The majority of the participants in this project (60 percent) support constitutional changes to avoid this possibility. There are at least five problems with the House contingency procedure.

First, there is a reasonable chance of stalemate in the House. The Constitution provides for a House vote by state delegations; each delegation receives one vote, and a majority (26 states) is needed to name a winner. Given current partisan divisions and loyalties, this could lead to stalemate (as almost happened in 1824). If a state delegation is equally divided by party and no one abandons his party, the state would abstain. A majority of all states is still required. The Republicans had majorities of only 25 of the House delegations in the 106th Congress (1999–2000), and thus could not have dictated the outcome.[89] Had the responsibility of resolving the election fallen to the outgoing rather than the incoming House, it is difficult to see how stalemate could have been avoided as long as loyalty to party dominated the decision process. Nevertheless, the House must choose the president.

This points to a second, related problem: the results of the popular vote would get short shrift in any House contingency election. While partisan concerns would likely prevail if one party had a majority among the state delegations, an initial deadlock would likely result in bargaining over matters of power and policy, rather than simply deferring to popular wishes.

Third, the contingency procedure provides for Senate selection of the vice president, which raises the possibility of the president and vice president coming from different parties. This could have happened in 2000–2001. Bush would have won in the House, but the new Senate was evenly split along party lines, and thus the sitting vice president, who was still Al Gore in early January 2001 when this process would have occurred, could have cast the tie-breaking vote for Joe Lieberman, his Democratic running-mate. Although we cannot be sure how this arrangement would affect our political system (that would take another book), most participants and observers perceive it as seriously undermining executive branch cohesion.

A fourth problem is simply that invoking the House contingency would violate our contemporary conception of fairness, which includes the idea of voting equality. Despite the formal equality in providing each state with one vote, there is a real inequality in a procedure that underrepresents the citizens of populous states. The 494,782 citizens of Wyoming would have the same one vote as the nearly 34 million citizens of California.

A fifth problem is that the House contingency violates the principle of the separation of powers by making the Executive a creation of Congress.

There have been numerous proposals for correcting these problems with the House contingency process,[90] but the simplest would abolish its need by eliminating the requirement for a majority in the Electoral College.[91] The main objection to this change is that "it is feared it could produce a President with an insufficient mandate."[92] However, if there is such a thing as an electoral mandate, it is a matter of perception, and presidents without popular majorities or even popular pluralities have governed as if they had one. It is difficult to see how George W. Bush has a greater mandate with his narrow majority in the Electoral College than he would have with a larger margin of victory in the College that still fell somewhat short of a majority because a spoiler captured a few dozen votes.

Another approach to this problem is to create an alternative contingency process. For example, if one candidate held a popular vote margin of more than one percent over his closest rival (yet failed to get an electoral majority), he could be declared the winner. Or the matter could be referred to the House, but the rule of voting by House delegations could be dropped in favor of the more common practice of giving each representative one vote. The participants in this project could not agree on the best alternative to the present House contingency procedure, but they expressed widespread support for giving this issue more attention than it has thus far received.

HALT THE REVOLUTION. LET THE EXPERIMENTS BEGIN

Most revisions of our presidential election process — ranging from developing an alternative national popular vote to modifying the House contingency procedure — would require constitutional amendments. But such amendments rarely succeed, and there is no indication that any electoral reforms could overcome the formidable obstacles of modifying the Constitution. Perhaps such obstacles would be overcome if the public strongly believed that an electoral reform would greatly improve American democracy, but the participants in this project doubt that such a belief would be warranted.

Of course, electoral rules do matter, as different procedures can produce different winners of presidential elections. Different electoral procedures can also lead to other changes in our political process. But one conclusion that emerges from the assessments of our participants is that the changes wrought by just changing our electoral college procedure may not be profound. Among other things, our participants conclude that:

- the unequal voting power that the Electoral College provides to citizens of small states is not very substantial;
- the orientations of a presidential candidate toward the balance between national power and state autonomy does not depend on being elected under the electoral college system;
- any electoral system will normally provide its winner with legitimacy, but most systems can produce outcomes that reduce the winning candidate's legitimacy;
- our two-party system is a product of forces beyond the electoral college system, and would be only slightly modified under several alternative systems;
- campaign organizations allocate resources unequally under the electoral college system but they would continue to do so under any electoral system;
- imperfect media coverage of elections is primarily due to considerations independent of the Electoral College;
- electoral reform is unlikely to increase voter turnout significantly, and higher levels of voter turnout would not significantly improve the quality of American democracy;
- American elections are seldom associated with social instability, and the alternative electoral systems have both strengths and weaknesses in reducing the risks of instability; and
- minorities may not benefit from the current electoral college system, but alternate systems would not greatly enhance their power.

Over and over again, the participants in this project provide assessments that electoral reform would not fundamentally transform the things they study. They do not see in electoral reform any quick fixes to problems that occur in our political process.

Because of the institutional and structural barriers to electoral change discussed in chapter 1, reforms need broad and fairly intense public support. Such change probably requires a social movement, but most movements arise to support causes that are thought to transform social, economic, or political life. The analyses in this book indicate that there is not much here to spark the kind of social movement essential for enacting a constitutional amendment.

This is not to say that the Electoral College is without problems or cannot be improved. Some of us would suggest that the states experiment with district plans and proportional allocation — reforms that could be implemented by individual states without a constitutional amendment. State experimentation with such reforms could address two sorts of analytical problems that hinder making effective collective judgments.

First, many suspected consequences of reforms could not be adequately investigated because we lack opportunities to collect and analyze the data. The authors of chapter 9 put this point nicely: "We know little about how the Electoral College impacts citizen participation. This paucity of knowledge owes in part to the Electoral College's longevity. There has been little opportunity to experiment with other methods of electing the president."

Throughout this volume, our participants have had to speculate about the impacts of various reforms. Although theories and related empirical research could generate expectations about the consequences of various reforms, direct study to confirm or disconfirm these expectations was usually impossible. Trying out some reforms, especially in the unique American context, could contribute to our understanding of the desirability of proposed changes.

Second, some consequences of reform are simply unforeseen and perhaps unforeseeable. The concept of unintended consequences was one of the major recurring themes throughout this book. This notion is deeply imbedded in the culture and discipline of political science, making scholars leery of reforms that promise more than they deliver and that deliver problems that were unforeseen.[93] Reforms always change things, but the changes wrought may be quite different from those sought or expected. Since the implications of the electoral reforms analyzed here cannot always be foreseen, they can become apparent only through state-level experiments that can enable us to discover their unanticipated consequences.

Perhaps adoption of the district plan by some state (other than Maine and Nebraska) with significant minority populations would reveal what many of us fear — that the district plan would undermine minority influence. Better to find that out by an experiment in a few states than after a constitutional amendment imposed the system on the nation.

Proportional allocation may be the more promising method of achieving various forms of improved representation. If some states adopted this reform, such effects could be confirmed or disconfirmed. One virtue of the electoral college system is that it allows states to engage in such experiments from which the nation as a whole can learn. Absent any compelling reason for changing the system now, we have time to draw lessons from the modest experiments that the states might conduct.

In short, we find the Electoral College a flawed but acceptable method of choosing our president. We do not regard any alternatives as offering such significant gains as to be worth the risks that would accompany wholesale changes in our electoral system. Still, the issue of electoral reform should not be forgotten. Progressive reformers should continue to address the relative merits of the popular-plurality and the instant-runoff systems in their search for a consensual alternative to the Electoral College. The problems associated with rogue voters and especially the House contingency procedure warrant continued national attention. Experimentation in some states with the district plan and especially with proportional allocation of electors could enable us to better understand if such reforms could lead to modest improvements in American democracy.

Of course, such conclusions merely reflect the judgments of the political scientists involved in this project. While the theories and research of political science has contributed much to these judgments, political science is not an exact science, and different judgments can be drawn from the analyses presented here. To help us develop a more complete portrait of the views of various kinds of people about the issues presented here, we invite and encourage you to visit our website at http://raven.cc.ukans.edu/~college. There you will be provided the opportunity to express your judgments about the Electoral College and the various alternatives to it discussed in this volume.

NOTES

1. The role of approval voting in arriving at accurate collective choices is most strongly developed in the work of Steven Brams and Peter C. Fishburn, *Approval Voting* (Boston: Birkhause, 1983).
2. A related problem with approval voting is that some voters may adopt a generous conception of approval (i.e., "I guess I can live with this alternative") while others may adopt a more narrow conception (i.e., "I disapprove of this alternative in the sense that — while I can accept it — I much prefer higher-ranked alternatives"). Thus, the results of approval voting can underestimate support for those alternatives that have received "disapproval ballots" for strategic reasons.
3. The role of the Borda count in such choices is most strongly presented by Donald Saari, *The Geometry of Voting* (Berlin: Springer, 1994).
4. We use the Borda count to determine each group's choice. In all groups save one, the top choice in the Borda count was also a Condorcet winner. (In the one group without a Condorcet winner, there was a voting cycle.)
5. Would creating one southern and one northern district per group (depending on the geographical location of the university where each participant is employed) be much less arbitrary than the congressional districts created by some state legislatures?
6. Using the d'Hondt formula for allocating electors proportionally, the extra two electors provided to our social cleavage group would go to the popular-majority system, so that it would end up with five electoral votes under proportionality, tying the district plan for third under this voting system.
7. We assume that all seven systems are under consideration. Shortly, we will consider outcomes of head-to-head competition.
8. One of our participants ranked two of these options among his top choices, so his ballot was transferred to his third-ranked option.
9. Perhaps they would agree to have automatic electors or reform the House contingency procedure. Who knows what kinds of concessions our reformers would have demanded before agreeing to support the Electoral College!

10. Jonathan Levin and Barry Nalebuff, "An Introduction to Vote-Counting Schemes," *Journal of Economic Perspectives* 9 (Winter 1995): 4.

11. In chapter 5 (p. 131), our institutionalists note that public opinion polls report that "only one respondent in three backed the Electoral College."

12. National public opinion polls often produce a contrived consensus behind an alternative by simply asking respondents if they prefer a national popular election rather than the Electoral College, ignoring both the variations within popular voting schemes and the reforms of the Electoral College that are possible alternatives to it.

13. This evaluative tradition goes back to Aristotle, as employed in his *Politics*. A recent discussion of this method is found in Paul Schumaker, Dwight C. Kiel, and Thomas W. Heilke, *Great Ideas/Grand Schemes: Political Ideologies in the Nineteenth and Twentieth Centuries* (New York: McGraw-Hill, 1996): 18–20.

14. See William H. Riker, *Liberalism against Populism: A Confrontation between the Theory of Democracy and the Theory of Social Choice* (San Francisco: W. H. Freeman, 1982), 67–73.

15. See chapter 3 for a more extensive discussion of the role of the Electoral College in the Constitution and for a discussion of its effectiveness in American history.

16. In chapter 5 (p. 85), our institutionalists note that the only president failing to have sufficient legitimacy to govern effectively was Andrew Johnson, and he was not elected to the office.

17. See chapter 10 (p. 152) for a more extensive discussion of the election of 1860.

18. The authors of chapters 4 and 11 stress the unequal value of the vote for citizens in different-sized states. From the perspective of federalism, there is nothing inherently unfair about the inequalities in voting value for individuals that arise from the allocation of two electors equal to the states. From the perspective of those of us interested in equal voting power among people of different ethnic and racial backgrounds, such allocations result in troubling racial biases.

19. But such incentives may not be sufficient to ensure that presidents are very sensitive to states rights, as discussed in chapter 4 (pp. 61–63).

20. Our political theorists, in chapter 3 (especially on pp. 31–35) are most clear on the link between the Electoral College and the separation of powers.

21. This conception of effective governance derives from our comparativists. See chapter 10 (pp. 150–51).

22. Our specialists on national institutions, parties, and campaigns all discuss at some length the idea that effective governance can be harmed by a proliferation of parties. See chapters 5, 6, and 7.

23. The role of the Twelfth Amendment in the development of our two-party system is revealed by our political theorists in chapter 3 (pp. 35–40).

24. This point is made most forcefully by our comparativists in chapter 10 (pp. 152–55) and by our specialists in social cleavages in chapter 11.

25. The importance of the "median voter" in governing coalitions is emphasized in the extensive literature examining the linkages between public opinion and public policy. See, for example, Elaine Sharp, *The Sometimes Connection: Public Opinion and Social Policy* (Albany: State University of New York Press, 1999). The theory of the median voter dates from Anthony Downs, *An Economic Theory of Democracy* (New York: Harper and Row, 1956).

26. The failure of American presidents to include other parties in the executive branch is discussed in chapter 3 (pp. 38–40) and chapter 10 (p. 147).

27. If so, we should probably abolish the highly unrepresentative Senate and develop a system of proportional representation to select members of Congress.

28. This role of the Electoral College in taming extremism is discussed by our party specialists in chapter 5 and by our comparativists in chapter 10 (pp. 148–49).

29. The myth that founders were "undemocratic" is debunked by both our theorists in chapter 3 (p. 35) and by our federalists in chapter 4 (pp. 55–57).

30. In chapter 4, our federalists contrast the intents of the framers of the Electoral College (pp. 54–57), with the practices of current candidates to be satisfied with gaining thin majorities in the necessary states (pp. 63–64).

31. See, for example, Robert Dahl, *Democracy and Its Critics* (New Haven: Yale University Press, 1989), 106–18.

32. This tenet of public choice theory, discussed in chapter 2 (pp. 20–21) was never disputed by the participants in this project, even by those who supported national popular elections.
33. In chapter 9 (pp. 136–37) our experts on citizen participation stress the similarities between voters and nonvoters, but this does not mean that there are no important areas where voters and nonvoters have divergent preferences.
34. See chapter 3 (pp. 43–44) for an extended discussion of the importance of counting errors.
35. The role of fraud in distorting the public will is most extensively discussed by our comparativists in chapter 10 (pp. 145–46).
36. See chapter 10 (p. 146).
37. This is a recurring theme throughout the chapters provided by our participants. It is most directly discussed by our experts on campaigns in chapter 7 (pp. 102–16).
38. See chapter 9 (pp. 129–30).
39. These questions are raised most forcefully in chapter 11 of this volume.
40. This issue is raised by both our federalists in chapter 4 (pp. 63–64) and our experts on social cleavages in chapter 11 (pp. 163–64).
41. Even presidents who win popular elections by such large margins that their victories would be assured under any electoral system and whose victories cannot be diminished by questions of fraud, counting errors, or small and unrepresentative voter turnouts cannot safely claim a public mandate for particular policies that they wish to pursue. After all, many voters may have supported them for reasons other than because they supported the particular policy for which a president claims a mandate.
42. Our institutionalists most strongly make these points in chapter 5.
43. The importance of voter equality is most strongly asserted by our specialists on voter cleavages in chapter 11 (pp. 162–63). Data on the unequal value of the vote for citizens in various states is shown in table 4.1 and table 11.1.
44. While acknowledging the logic of this proposition, our campaign specialists are unsure that campaigns would really allocate resources much differently under a national popular vote system. See chapter 7 (pp. 103–4).
45. However, our specialists in citizen participation argue that the increase in voter turnout under a popular election system would be small and perhaps trivial. See chapter 9 (pp. 129–30).
46. See chapter 6 (pp. 93–94).
47. See chapter 7 (pp. 106–8) and chapter 6 (pp. 95–96).
48. See chapter 6 (pp. 93–94).
49. See chapter 5 (p. 81).
50. These contentions are, of course, debatable, as indicated by our party specialists in chapter 6 (pp. 93–95).
51. The centrality of the two-party system to effective governance is asserted by both our institutionalists in chapter 5 (pp. 81–82) and our party specialists in chapter 6 (pp. 92–93).
52. See chapter 10 (pp. 148–49).
53. See chapter 10 (pp. 144–45).
54. See chapter 4 (pp. 68–69).
55. This possibility is inferred from the discussion of peripheral voters who cast ballots on the basis of the most recent campaign ads. See chapter 9 (p. 139).
56. See chapter 6 (pp. 94–95).
57. This consideration weighed especially heavily with our specialists on social cleavages. Indeed, they saw the runoff as providing both parties strong incentives to appeal to minority voters who might contribute to their needed majority. See chapter 11 (pp. 172–73).
58. See chapter 10 (p. 148).
59. See chapter 10 (pp. 145–46).
60. Our institutionalists raise this concern in chapter 5 (p. 78).
61. See chapter 9 (p. 130).
62. The following discussion draws primarily from our party specialists in chapter 6 (pp. 93–95) and our experts on campaigns in chapter 7 (pp. 106–9).
63. See chapter 10 (pp. 148).

64. Of course, voters who sincerely prefer two or more minor candidates to the major candidates, would list their sophisticated choice between major candidates lower in their rankings.
65. Though generally skeptical that electoral reform would impact voter turnout, our experts on citizen participation suspect that the instant runoff would have the greatest effect on voter participation. See chapter 9 (p. 133–35).
66. For example, our comparatives believe that the instant runoff would be the best system for limiting vote distortion while providing protection against extremist candidates. See chapter 10 (p. 149).
67. However, our experts on campaigns foresee circumstances when candidates having similar ideologies and being very closely matched in the polls would turn to bitter personal attacks to finish ahead of their rivals. See chapter 7 (pp. 107–8).
68. This argument is made by our federalists in chapter 4 (pp. 69–70) and by our social cleavage specialists in chapter 11 (pp. 156–57).
69. William Riker, *The Theory of Political Coalitions* (New Haven: Yale University Press, 1962).
70. See chapter 10 (pp. 155–56).
71. While our media experts though that the instant runoff might help stimulate more substantive media coverage, they also were skeptical of such possibilities. See chapter 8 (pp. 115–16).
72. See chapter 9 (pp. 129–30).
73. See chapter 4 (pp. 65–66).
74. See chapter 7 (p. 105).
75. For a mixed assessment of whether the district plan would enhance voter turnout, see chapter 9 (pp. 131–33).
76. But such reductions might be fairly minimal as the votes' cast in safe districts within competitive states could still be decisive for the determination of electors at the state level. These matters are discussed in chapter 6 (pp. 97–98).
77. See chapter 11 (pp. 171–72).
78. See chapter 6 (p. 96).
79. See chapter 6 (pp. 95–96).
80. See chapter 2 (p. 16).
81. See chapter 4 (pp. 67–68).
82. See chapter 10 (p. 152).
83. For example, analyses could be conducted paralleling that of the effects of the district plan on voter turnout reported in Figure 9.1.
84. See Polsby and Wildavsky, *Presidential Elections*, p. 252, and Judith A. Best, *The Choice of the People?* (Lanham, Md.: Rowman and Littlefield, 1996), 45–49.
85. See chapter 10, note 12 for a list of states having restrictions on the freedom of electors.
86. Longley and Peirce, *Electoral College Primer, 2000*, 112–13.
87. Demetrios James Caraley, "Editor's Opinion: Why Americans Deserve a Constitutional Right to Vote for Presidential Electors," *Political Science Quarterly* 116: 1 (2001) 1–3.
88. Polsby and Wildavsky, *Presidential Elections,* 252
89. The Democrats had majorities in 20 state delegations. Four delegations were evenly split, and the only Representative from Vermont (Bernie Sanders) in an independent with inclinations toward socialism.
90. See Judith Best, *The Case Against the Direct Election of the President* (Ithaca, N.Y.: Cornell University Press, 1971), 83–123.
91. If the Electoral College were maintained but the majority rule requirement were dropped, a contingency for breaking a tie in the College would still be required. However, this could be done by simply devising some alternative for calculating electoral vote totals, rather than by developing some completely different system as we now have. For example, the contingent calculation procedure could involve a proportional and fractional allocation of electors. This procedure is described below.
92. Best, *Case Against the Direct Election*, 88.
93. Arthur Lupia, "Evaluating Political Science Research," *PS: Political Science and Politics* 33 (March 2000), 7–18.

The Electoral College Map at the Millennium

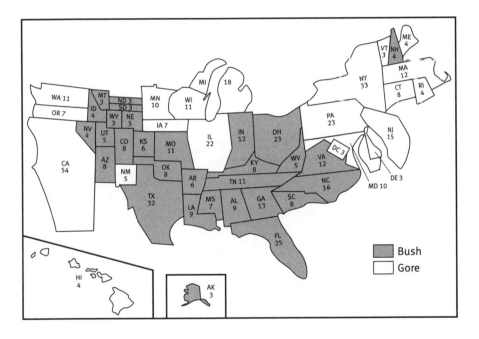

Electoral and Popular Votes for President, 1789–2000

Year	Candidate	Party	Electoral Vote[a]	Popular Vote	Percentage of Popular Vote
1789	*George Washington*		69[b]	–[c]	
	John Adams		34		
	John Jay		9		
	Others		26		
1792	*George Washington*	Federalist	132		
	John Adams	Federalist	77		
	George Clinton	Democratic-Republican	50		
	Others		5		
1796	*John Adams*	Federalist	71		
	Thomas Jefferson	Democratic-Republican	68		
	Thomas Pinckney	Federalist	59		
	Aaron Burr	Antifederalist	30		
	Others		5		
1800	*Thomas Jefferson*	Democratic-Republican	73[d]		
	Aaron Burr	Democratic-Republican	73		
	John Adams	Federalist	65		
	C. C. Pinckney	Federalist	64[e]		
1804	*Thomas Jefferson*	Democratic-Republican	162[f]		
	C. C. Pinckney	Federalist	14		
1808	*James Madison*	Democratic-Republican	122		
	C. C. Pinckney	Federalist	47		
	George Clinton	Independent-Republican	6		
1812	*James Madison*	Democratic-Republican	128		
	DeWitt Clinton	Fusion	89		
1816	*James Monroe*	Republican	183		
	Rufus King	Federalist	34		
1820	*James Monroe*	Republican	231		
	John Q. Adams	Independent-Republican	1		

Year	Candidate	Party	Electoral Vote[a]	Popular Vote	Percentage of Popular Vote
1824	John Q. Adams	No	84[g]	108,740	30.5
	Andrew Jackson	distinct	99	153,544	43.1
	Henry Clay	party	37	47,136	13.2
	W. H. Crawford	designations	41	46,618	13.1
1828	Andrew Jackson	Democratic	178	647,286	56.0
	John Q. Adams	National Republican	83	508,064	44.0
1832	Andrew Jackson	Democratic	178	64,286	56.0
	Henry Clay	National Republican	49	530,189	42.4
	William Wirt	Anti-Masonic	7 }	33,108	
	John Floyd	Nullifiers	11 }		2.6
1836	Martin Van Buren	Democratic	170	762,678	50.9
	Wm. H. Harrison	Whig	73	549,508	36.6
	Hugh L. White	Whig	26	143,352	9.7
	Daniel Webster	Whig	14	41,287	2.8
	W. P. Mangum	Anti-Jackson	11		
1840	William H. Harrison	Whig	234	1,275,016	52.9
	Martin Van Buren	Democratic	60	1,129,102	46.8
1844	James K. Polk	Democratic	170	1,337,243	49.6
	Henry Clay	Whig	105	1,299,062	48.1
	James G. Birney	Liberty	0	62,300	2.3
1848	Zachary Taylor	Whig	163	1,360,099	47.4
	Lewis Cass	Democratic	127	1,220,544	42.5
	Martin Van Buren	Free Soil	0	291,263	10.1
1852	Franklin Pierce	Democratic	254	1,601,274	50.9
	Winfield Scott	Whig	42	1,386,580	44.1
	John P. Hale	Free Soil	0	155,825	5.0
1856	James Buchanan	Democratic	174	1,838,169	45.3
	John C. Frémont	Republican	114	1,341,264	21.6
	Millard Fillmore	American	8	874,534	21.6
1860	Abraham Lincoln	Republican	180	1,866,452	39.9
	J. C. Breckenridge	Democratic	72	847,953	18.1
	Stephen A. Douglas	Democratic	12	1,375,157	29.4
	John Bell	Constitutional Union	39	590,631	12.6
1864	Abraham Lincoln	Republican	212	2,213,665	55.1
	George B. McClellan	Democratic	21	1,805,237	44.9
	Not voted		81		
1868	U. S. Grant	Republican	214	3,012,833	52.7
	Horatio Seymour	Democratic	80	2,703,249	47.3
	Not voted		23		
1872	U. S. Grant	Republican	286	3,597,132	55.6
	Horace Greeley	Democratic; Liberal Republican	66[h]	2,834,125	43.8
	Others		63	35,652	.6
1876	Rutherford B. Hayes	Republican	185	4,036,298	47.9
	Samuel J. Tilden	Democratic	184	4,300,590	51.0
	Others		0	94,935	1.1

Year	Candidate	Party	Electoral Vote[a]	Popular Vote	Percentage of Popular Vote
1880	*James A. Garfield*	Republican	214	4,454,416	48.3
	W. S. Hancock	Democratic	155	4,444,952	48.2
	James B. Weaver	Greenback-Labor	0	308,578	3.3
1884	*Grover Cleveland*	Democratic	219	4,874,986	48.5
	James G. Blaine	Republican	182	4,851,981	48.3
	John P. St. John	Prohibition	0	150,369	1.5
	Benjamin F. Butler	Greenback-Labor	0	175,370	1.7
1888	*Benjamin Harrison*	Republican	233	5,439,853	47.8
	Grover Cleveland	Democratic	168	5,540,309	48.7
	Clinton B. Fisk	Prohibition	0	249,506	2.2
	Others		0	154,083	1.4
1892	*Grover Cleveland*	Democratic	277	5,556,918	46.1
	Benjamin Harrison	Republican	145	5,176,108	42.9
	James B. Weaver	People's	22	1,041,028	8.6
	Others		0	292,672	2.4
1896	*William McKinley*	Republican	271	7,104,779	51.0
	William Jennings Bryan	Democratic	176	6,502,925	46.7
	Others		0	317,219	2.3
1900	*William McKinley*	Republican	292	7,207,923	51.6
	William Jennings Bryan	Democratic; Populist	155	6,358,133	45.5
	Others		0	396,200	2.8
1904	*Theodore Roosevelt*	Republican	336	7,623,486	56.4
	Alton B. Parker	Democratic	140	5,077,911	37.6
	Eugene V. Debs	Socialist	0	402,283	3.0
	Silas C. Swallow	Prohibition	0	258,536	1.9
	Others		0	149,357	1.1
1908	*William H. Taft*	Republican	321	7,678,908	51.6
	William Jennings Bryan	Democratic	162	6,409,104	43.0
	Eugene V. Debs	Socialist	0	420,793	2.8
	Eugene W. Chafin	Prohibition	0	253,840	1.7
1912	*Woodrow Wilson*	Democratic	435	6,293,454	41.9
	William H. Taft	Republican	8	3,484,980	23.2
	Theodore Roosevelt	Progressive	88	4,119,538	27.4
	Eugene V. Debs	Socialist	0	900,672	6.0
	Others		0	238,931	1.6
1916	*Woodrow Wilson*	Democratic	277	9,129,606	49.3
	Charles E. Hughes	Republican	254	8,538,221	46.1
	A. L. Benson	Socialist	0	585,113	3.2
	Others		0	269,812	1.5
1920	*Warren G. Harding*	Republican	404	16,152,200	60.4
	James M. Cox	Democratic	127	9,147,353	34.2
	Eugene V. Debs	Socialist	0	919,799	3.4
	Others		0	566,916	2.1
1924	*Calvin Coolidge*	Republican	382	15,725,016	54.1
	John W. Davis	Democratic	136	8,386,503	28.8
	Robert La Follette	Progressive	13	4,822,856	16.6

Year	Candidate	Party	Electoral Vote[a]	Popular Vote	Percentage of Popular Vote
1928	Herbert Hoover	Republican	444	21,391,381	58.2
	Alfred E. Smith	Democratic	87	15,016,443	40.9
1932	Franklin D. Roosevelt	Democratic	472	22,821,857	57.4
	Herbert Hoover	Republican	59	15,761,841	39.7
1936	Franklin D. Roosevelt	Democratic	523	27,751,597	60.8
	Alfred M. Landon	Republican	8	16,679,583	36.6
	William Lemke	Union	0	882,479	1.9
1940	Franklin D. Roosevelt	Democratic	449	27,244,160	54.3
	Wendell L. Willkie	Republican	82	22,305, 198	44.5
1944	Franklin D. Roosevelt	Democratic	432	25,602,504	53.4
	Thomas F. Dewey	Republican	99	22,006,285	45.9
1948	Harry S. Truman	Democratic; Liberal	303	24,105,695	49.5
	Thomas E. Dewey	Republican	189	21,969,170	45.1
	J. Strom Thurmond	States' Rights	39	1,169,021	2.4
	Henry A. Wallace	Progressive	0	1,156,103	2.4
1952	Dwight D. Eisenhower	Republican	442	33,824,351	54.9
	Adlai E. Stevenson	Democratic; Liberal	89	27,314,987	44.4
1956	Dwight D. Eisenhower	Republican	457	35,582,236	57.3
	Adlai E. Stevenson	Democratic	73	26,028,887	41.9
1960	John F. Kennedy	Democratic	303	34,220,984[i]	49.5
	Richard M. Nixon	Republican	219	34,108,157	49.3
	Others and unpledged		15	827,381	1.2
1964	Lyndon B. Johnson	Democratic	486	43,129,484	61.1
	Barry M. Goldwater	Republican	52	27,178,188	38.5
1968	Richard M. Nixon	Republican	301	31,785,148	43.4
	Hubert H. Humphrey	Democratic	191	31,274,503	42.7
	George C. Wallace	American Independent	46	9,901,151	13.5
1972	Richard M. Nixon	Republican	520	47,170,179	60.7
	George S. McGovern	Democratic	17	29,171,791	37.5
	John G. Schmitz	American	0	1,090,673	1.4
1976	Jimmy Carter	Democratic	297	48,830,763	50.1
	Gerald R. Ford	Republican	240	39,147,793	48.0
	Others		0	1,577,333	1.9
1980	Ronald Reagan	Republican	489	43,904,153	50.7
	Jimmy Carter	Democratic	49	35,483,883	41.0
	John B. Anderson	National Unity	0	5,720,060	6.6
	Ed Clark	Libertarian	0	921,299	1.1
1984	Ronald Reagan	Republican	525	54,455,074	58.8
	Walter F. Mondale	Democratic	13	37,577,137	40.6
1988	George Bush	Republican	426	48,886,097	53.4
	Michael S. Dukakis	Democratic	111	41,809,074	45.6
	Others		0	899,638	1.0
1992	Bill Clinton	Democratic	370	44,909,326	43.0
	George Bush	Republican	168	39,103,882	37.4
	Ross Perot	Independent	0	19,741,657	18.9

Year	Candidate	Party	Electoral Vote[a]	Popular Vote	Percentage of Popular Vote
1996	*Bill Clinton*	Democratic	379	47,401,054	49.2
	Bob Dole	Republican	159	39,197,350	40.7
	Ross Perot	Reformed	0	8,085,285	8.4
	Others		0	1,589,573	1.7
2000	*George W. Bush*	Republican	271	50,456,600	47.9
	Albert Gore	Democratic	266	50,997,100	48.4
	Ralph Nader	Green	0	2,830,900	2.7
	Others		0	1,043,140	1.0

Sources: Richard Hofstadler, William Mellen, and Daniel Aaron, *The United States: The History of a Republic* (Englewood Cliffs, N.J.: Prentice-Hall, 1957), 775–81; Lawrence D. Longley and Neal R. Peirce, *The Electoral College Primer, 2000* (New Haven: Yale University Press, 1999), 177–87; and www.cnn.com/election/2000/results/president/

a. Before 1804 electors voted for two candidates for president. To win, a candidate needed to be named on the ballots of more than half of the electors. Thus, more than 25 percent of the total number of electoral votes was needed.

b. During the elections of 1789 and 1792, each elector cast one of his two ballots for Washington. The electors distributed their second ballots among others as indicated.

c. State legislatures initially chose most electors. Two-thirds of the states held popular elections to select electors pledged to particular candidates and parties by 1824, and the popular vote totals are usually regarded as meaningful beginning in 1828.

d. Both Jefferson and his running mate, Burr, received the necessary number of votes to win, but the fact that they were tied required that the election be decided in the House.

e. The Electoral College totals reported in certain years may be incomplete as we do not list instances when a person received a single vote or when one elector did not cast his/her ballot.

f. The Twelfth Amendment took effect in 1804, requiring electors to cast one ballot for president and a second distinct ballot for vice president. Electoral vote totals from 1804 forward are just the votes cast for president.

g. Because no candidate received a majority in the Electoral College, John Quincy Adams was selected through the House contingency procedure.

h. Greeley died between the national popular election and the casting of electoral ballots. The electors pledged to him scattered their votes among four others.

i. In 1960 Alabama voters did not vote directly for Kennedy but instead cast multiple ballots for electors, some pledged to Kennedy and some unpledged. This has led to questions about the number of popular votes that should be credited to Kennedy. We report the conventional attribution, but an alternate method yields only 34,049,976 votes for Kennedy. By this calculation method, Nixon won the national popular vote. See Longley and Peirce, *Electoral College Primer,* 46–59.

Bibliography

Abbott, David W., and James P. Levine. *Wrong Winner: The Coming Debacle in the Electoral College.* New York: Praeger, 1991.

Abramson, Paul R., and John H. Aldrich. "The Decline of Electoral Participation in America." *American Political Science Review* 76 (September 1982): 502–21.

Abramson, Paul R., John H. Aldrich, Phil Paolino, and David W. Rohde. "Third-Party and Independent Candidates in American Politics: Wallace, Anderson and Perot." *Political Science Quarterly* 110 (Fall 1995): 363.

Aldrich, John H. *Why Parties?* Chicago: University of Chicago Press, 1995.

———. "Rational Choice and Turnout." *American Journal of Political Science* 37 (March 1993): 246–78.

Alford, John R., Keith Henry, and James Campbell. "Television Markets and Congressional Elections." *Legislative Studies Quarterly* 15 (March 1985): 665–78.

Alger, Dean. *Megamedia: How Giant Corporations Dominate Mass Media, Distort Competition, and Endanger Democracy.* Boulder, Colo.: Rowman & Littlefield, 1998.

Almond, Gabriel, and Sidney Verba. *Civic Culture: Political Attitudes and Democracy in Five Nations.* Princeton: Princeton University Press, 1963.

Amy, Douglas. *Real Choices/New Voices: The Case for Proportional Representation Elections in the United States.* New York: Columbia University Press, 1993.

Atkeson, Lonna Rae, "From the Primaries to the General Election: Does a Divisive Nomination Race Affect a Candidate's Fortunes in the Fall?" In *In Pursuit of the White House 2000: How We Choose Our Presidential Nominees,* edited by William G. Mayer. New York: Chatham House, 2000.

Atkeson, Lonna Rae, and Randall W. Partin. "Economic and Referendum Voting: A Comparison of Gubernatorial and Senatorial Elections." *American Political Science Review* 89 (March 1995): 99–107.

Bachrach, Peter, and Morton Baratz. *Power and Poverty.* New York: Oxford University Press, 1970.

Barber, Benjamin. *Strong Democracy.* Berkeley: University of California Press, 1983.

Bartels, Larry M. "Partisanship and Voting Behavior." *American Journal of Political Science* 43 (September 1999): 35–50.

———. "Resource Allocation in a Presidential Campaign." *Journal of Politics* 47 (August 1985): 928–36.

Bass, Loretta E., and Lynne E. Cooper. "Are There Differences in Registration and Voting Behavior between Naturalized and Native-Born Americans?" Bureau of the Census Working Paper No. 28, February 1999.

Beard, Charles. *An Economic Interpretation of the Constitution of the United States.* 1913. Reprint, New York: Free Press, 1986.

Beitz, Charles. *Political Equality: An Essay in Democratic Theory.* Princeton: Princeton University Press, 1989.

Bennett, Stephen, and D. Resnik. "The Implications of Nonvoting for Democracy in the United States." *American Journal of Political Science* 72 (November 1990): 314–33.

Bensen, Clark. "Presidential Election 2000 Congressional District Preliminary Study." At www.polidata.org.

Berelson, Bernard, Paul F. Lazarsfeld, and William N. McPhee. *Voting: A Study of Opinion Formation in a Presidential Election.* Chicago: University of Chicago Press, 1954.

Best, Judith A. *The Choice of the People? Debating the Electoral College.* Lanham, Md.: Rowman & Littlefield, 1996.

———. *The Case against the Direct Election of the President: A Defense of the Electoral College.* Ithaca, N.Y.: Cornell University Press, 1971.

Bibby, John F., and L. Sandy Maisel. *Two Parties — or More?* Boulder, Colo.: Westview, 1998.

Black, Gordon S., and Benjamin D. Black. "Americans Want and Need a New Political Party." *Public Perspective* 4 (November/December 1992): 3–6.

Blais, André, Louis Massicotte, and Agnieszka Dobrzynska. "Direct Presidential Elections: A World Summary." *Electoral Studies* 16 (December 2000): 441–55.

Brams, Steven J., and Morton D. Davis. "The 3/2's Rule in Presidential Campaigning." *American Political Science Review* 68 (March 1974): 113–34.

Brams, Steven J., and Peter C. Fishburn. *Approval Voting.* Boston: Birkhause, 1983.

Brooks, Clem, and Jeff Manza. "Social Cleavages and Political Alignments: U.S. Presidential Elections, 1960 to 1992." *American Sociological Review* 62 (December 1997): 937.

Browne, William. *Cultivating Congress.* Lawrence: University Press of Kansas, 1995.

Bryans, Craig Leonard, and Bernard Grofman. "Election Day Registration's Effect on U.S. Voting Turnout." *Social Science Quarterly* 82 (March 2001).

Buell, Emmett H., Jr. "Divisive Primaries and Participation in Fall Presidential Campaigns: A Study of 1984 New Hampshire Primary Activists." *American Politics Quarterly* 14 (October 1986): 376–90.

Burnham, Walter Dean. *The Crisis in American Politics.* New York: Oxford University Press, 1982.

Caraley, Demetrios James. "Editor's Opinion: Why Americans Deserve a Constitutional Right to Vote for Presidential Electors." *Political Science Quarterly* 116, no. 1 (2001): 1–3.

Carey, George, and James McClellan, eds. *The Federalist.* Dubuque, Iowa: Kendall/Hunt, 1990.

Colantoni, Claude S., Terrence J. Levesque, and Peter C. Ordeshook. "Campaign Resource Allocation under the Electoral College." *American Political Science Review* 69 (March 1975): 141–54.

Connelly, William F., Jr., and John J. Pitney. *Congress' Permanent Minority?* Lanham, Md.: Rowman & Littlefield, 1994.

Conway, Margaret. "Gender and Political Participation." In *Gender and American Politics,* edited by Sue Tolleson-Rinehart and Jyl J. Josephson. Armonk, N.Y.: M. E. Sharpe, 2000.

Cook, Rhodes. *The Rhodes Cook Newsletter,* March 2001.

Cox, Gary. *Making Votes Count.* New York: Cambridge University Press, 1997.

Dahl, Robert A. "The Myth of the Presidential Mandate." *Political Science Quarterly* 105 (Fall 1990): 355–72.

———. *Democracy and Its Critics.* New Haven: Yale University Press, 1989.

Denardo, James. "Turnout and the Vote: The Joke's on the Democrats." *American Political Science Review* 74 (June 1980): 406–20.

Dionne, E. J., Jr. *Why Americans Hate Politics.* New York: Simon and Schuster, 1991.

Donald, David Herbert. *Lincoln.* New York: Simon and Schuster, 1995.

Downs, Anthony. *An Economic Theory of Democracy.* New York: Harper & Row, 1957.

Durand, Jorge, Douglas S. Massey, and Fernando Charvet. "The Changing Geography of Mexican Immigration to the United States, 1910–96." *Social Science Quarterly* 81 (March 2000): 1–16.

Duverger, Maurice. *Political Parties,* translated by Barbara and Robert North, 2d ed. London: Methuen, 1959.

Epstein, Leon D. *Political Parties in the American Mold.* Madison: University of Wisconsin Press, 1986.

Fishkin, James. *The Voice of the People: Public Opinion and Democracy.* New Haven: Yale University Press, 1995.

Franklin, Mark. "Electoral Participation." In *Comparing Democracies: Elections and Voting in Global Perspective,* edited by Lawrence LeDuc, Richard G. Niemi, and Pippa Norris. Thousand Oaks, Calif.: Sage, 1996.

Frey, William. "Regional Shifts in America's Voting-Aged Population: What Do They Mean for National Politics?" Report no. 00-459, Population Studies Center, Institute for Social Research, University of Michigan, 2000.

Frye, Timothy. "A Politics of Institutional Choice: Post-Communist Presidencies." *Comparative Political Studies* 30 (October 1997): 523–52.

Gaines, Brian J. "Popular Myths About Popular Vote–Electoral College Splits." *PS: Political Science and Politics* 34, no. 1 (March 2001): 71–75.

Gans, Herbert. *Deciding What's News.* New York: Random House, 1979.

Garand, James C., and T. Wayne Parent. "Representation, Swing, and Bias in U.S. Presidential Elections, 1872–1988." *American Journal of Political Science* 35 (October 1991).

Gelman, Andrew, and Jonathan Katz. "How much does a vote count? Voting power, coalitions and the Electoral College." Available at www.polmeth.ufl.edu/papers/01/gelman01.pdf.

Gibson, James L., Cornelius P. Cotter, John F. Bibby, Robert J. Huckshorn. "Whither the Local Parties? A Cross-Sectional and Longitudinal Analysis of the Strength of Party Organizations." *American Journal of Political Science* 29 (February 1985): 139–60.

Giles, Michael G., and Marilyn K. Dantico. "Political Participation and Neighborhood Social Context Revisited." *American Journal of Political Science* 26 (February 1982): 144–50.

Graber, Doris A. *Mass Media and American Politics.* Washington, D.C.: CQ Press, 1998.

Grofman, Bernard, and Arend Lijphart, eds. *Electoral Laws and their Political Consequences.* New York: Agathon, 1986.

Gunther, Richard, and Anthony Mughan. "Political Institutions and Cleavage Management." In *Do Institutions Matter? Government Capabilities in the United States and Abroad,* edited by R. Kent Weaver and Bert A. Rockman. Washington, D.C.: Brookings Institution, 1993.

Hagen, Michael G., and William G. Mayer. "The New Politics of Presidential Selection: How Changing the Rules Really Did Change the Game." In *In Pursuit of the White House 2000: How We Choose Our Presidential Nominees,* edited by William G. Mayer. New York: Chatham House, 2000.

Hansen, John Mark. "How Federalism Put W. in the White House." Unpublished paper, Department of Political Science, University of Chicago.

Hardaway, Robert. *The Electoral College and the Constitution: The Case for Preserving Federalism.* Westport, Conn.: Praeger, 1994.

Hayek, Friedrich. *Constitution of Liberty.* Chicago: University of Chicago Press, 1969.

Herrnson, Paul S. "The Revitalization of National Organizations." In Sandy Maisel, *The Parties Respond: Changes in American Parties and Campaigns.* 2d ed. Boulder Colo.: Westview, 1994.

Hershey, Marjorie Randon. "The Campaign and the Media." In *The Elections of 2000,* edited by Michael Nelson. Washington, D.C.: CQ Press, 2001.

———. "The Campaign and the Media." In *The Election of 2000,* edited by Gerald M. Pomper. New York: Chatham House, 2001.

Hibbing, John, and Elizabeth Theiss-Morse. "Popular Preferences and American Politics: What Americans Want Government to Be." *American Political Science Review* 95 (March 2001): 145–54.

———. *Congress as Public Enemy.* New York: Cambridge, 1995.

Hicks, Alexander, and Duane H Swank. "Politics, Institutions and Welfare Spending in Industrialized Democracies." *American Political Science Review* 86 (September 1992): 658–74.

Hill, Kim Quaile, and Jan E. Leighley. "The Policy Consequences of Class Bias in State Electorates." *American Journal of Political Science* 35 (May 1992): 351–65.

Horowitz, Donald L. *A Democratic South Africa? Constitutional Engineering in a Divided Society.* Berkeley: University of California Press, 1991.

Huckfeldt, Robert, and John Sprague. "Political Parties and Electoral Mobilization: Political Structure, Social Structure, and the Party Canvass." *American Political Science Review* 86 (March 1992): 70–86.

———. "Networks in Context: The Social Flow of Political Information." *American Political Science Review* 81 (December 1987): 1197–1216.

Jacobson, Gary C. *The Politics of Congressional Elections.* New York: Longman, 2001.

Jones, Mark P. "Electoral Laws and the Effective Number of Candidates in Presidential Elections." *Journal of Politics* 61 (February 1999): 171–84.

———. *Electoral Laws and the Survival of Presidential Democracies.* South Bend, Ind.: Notre Dame University Press, 1995.

Just, Marion, et al. *Crosstalk.* Chicago: University of Chicago Press, 1996.

Keech, William. *Winner Take All: Report of the Twentieth Century Fund Task Force on Reform of the Presidential Election Process.* New York: Holmes and Meier, 1978.

Kelley, Stanley, Jr. "The Presidential Campaign." In *The Presidential Election and Transition 1960–1961,* edited by Paul T. David. Washington, D.C.: Brookings Institution, 1961.

Kerbel, Matthew R. "The Media: Old Frames in a Time of Transition." In *The Elections of 2000,* edited by Michael Nelson. Washington, D.C.: CQ Press, 2001.

———. *Edited For Television: CNN, ABC, and American Presidential Elections.* Boulder, Colo.: Westview, 1998.

King, David C. "The Polarization of American Parties and Mistrust of Government." In *Why People Don't Trust Government,* edited by Joseph S. Nye Jr., Philip D. Zelikow, and David C. King. Cambridge, Mass.: Harvard University Press, 1997.

Kymlicka, Will. *Contemporary Political Philosophy.* New York: Oxford Press, 1990.

Leighley, Jan E. "Attitudes, Opportunities and Incentives: A Field Essay on Political Participation." *Political Research Quarterly* 48 (March 1995): 181–209.

Lengle, James I. "Divisive Presidential Primaries and Party Electoral Prospects, 1932–1976." *American Politics Quarterly* 8 (July 1981): 261–77.

Levin, Jonathan, and Barry Nalebuff. "An Introduction to Vote-Counting Schemes." *Journal of Economic Perspectives* 9 (Winter 1995).

Lijphart, Arend. "Unequal Participation: Democracy's Unresolved Dilemma." *American Political Science Review* 91 (March 1997): 1–13.

———. *Electoral Systems and Party Systems: A Study of 27 Democracies, 1945–1990.* Oxford: Oxford University Press, 1994.

Linz, Juan J. "Presidential or Parliamentary Democracy: Does it Make a Difference?" In *The Failure of Presidential Democracy,* edited by Juan J. Linz and Arturo Valenzuela. Baltimore: Johns Hopkins University Press, 1994.

Longley, Lawrence D., and Alan G. Braun. *The Politics of Electoral College Reform.* New Haven: Yale University Press, 1972.

Longley, Lawrence D., and Neal R. Peirce. *The Electoral College Primer, 2000.* New Haven: Yale University Press, 2000.

Lowi, Theodore J. "Toward a Responsible Three-Party System: Plan or Obituary?" In John C. Green and Daniel M Shea, *The State of the Parties,* 3d ed. Boulder, Colo.: Rowman & Littlefield, 1999.

Lupia, Arthur. "Evaluating Political Science Research." *PS: Political Science and Politics* 33 (March 2000): 7–18.

McDonald, Forrest. *States' Rights and the Union.* Lawrence: University Press of Kansas, 2000.

———. *The American Presidency: An Intellectual History.* Lawrence: University Press of Kansas, 1994.

Madison, James. *Notes of Debates in the Federal Convention of 1787.* New York: Norton, 1987.

Magleby, David B., ed. *Election Advocacy: Soft Money and Issue Advocacy in the 2000 Congressional Elections.* Center for the Study of Elections and Democracy, Brigham Young University. www.byu.edu/outsidemoney/2000general/contents.htm

Mebane, Walter R., Jr. "Fiscal Constraints and Electoral Manipulation in American Social Welfare." *American Political Science Review* 88 (March 1994): 77–94.

Menefee-Libey, David. *The Triumph of Campaign-Centered Politics.* New York: Chatham House, 2000.

Mermin, Jonathan. *Deliberating War and Peace: Media Coverage of U.S. Intervention in the Post-Vietnam Era.* Princeton, N.J.: Princeton University Press, 1999.

Mikhailov, Valentin. "Kolichestvo demokratii [The Quantity of Democracy]." *Armageddon* 3 (May-June 1999): 134–53.

Milbrath, Lester W. *Political Participation.* Chicago: Rand McNally, 1965.

Milkis, Sidney, and Michael Nelson. *The American Presidency: Origins and Development, 1776–1998.* 3d ed. Washington, D.C.: CQ Press, 1999.

Milnor, A. J. *Elections and Political Stability.* Boston: Little, Brown, 1969.

Mishler, William, and Anne Hildreth. "Legislatures and Political Stability." *Journal of Politics* 46 (February 1984): 25–59.

Newman, Russell. "The Global Impact of New Technologies." In *The Politics of News, The News of Politics,* edited by Doris Graber, Denis McQuail, and Pippa Norris. Washington, D.C.: CQ Press, 1998.

Owen, Diana. "The Press' Performance." In *Toward the Millennium: The Elections of 1996,* edited by Larry J. Sabato. Boston: Allyn and Bacon, 1997.

Page, Benjamin. *Who Deliberates: Mass Media in Modern Democracy.* Chicago: University of Chicago Press, 1996.

Patterson, Samuel C., and Gregory A. Caldeira. "Mailing In the Vote: Correlates and Consequences of Absentee Voting." *American Journal of Political Science* 29 (November 1985): 766–88.

———. "Getting Out the Vote: Participation in Gubernatorial Elections." *American Political Science Review* 77 (September 1983): 675–89.

Patterson, Thomas E. *Out of Order.* New York: Knopf, 1993.

Peirce, Neal R., and Lawrence D. Longley. *The People's President: The Electoral College in American History and the Direct Vote Alternative.* New Haven: Yale University Press, 1981.

Pfiffner, James P. "Reevaluating the Electoral College." Unpublished manuscript, George Mason University, 1 January 2001.

———. *The Modern Presidency.* New York: St. Martin's, 1994.

Polsby, Nelson W. *Consequences of Party Reform.* New York: Oxford University Press, 1983.

Polsby, Nelson W., and Aaron Wildavsky. *Presidential Elections: Strategies and Structures of American Politics.* 10th ed. New York: Chatham House, 2000.

Pomper, Gerald M. "The Presidential Election." In *The Election of 2000,* edited by Gerald M. Pomper. New York: Chatham House, 2001.

———. "Parliamentary Government in the United States." In *The State of the Parties,* edited by John C. Green and Daniel Shea. 3d ed. (Lanham, Md.: Rowman & Littlefield, 1999.

Powell, G. Bingham, Jr. *Elections as Instruments of Democracy: Majoritarian and Proportional Visions.* New Haven: Yale University Press, 2000.

———. "American Voter Turnout in Comparative Perspective." *American Political Science Review* 80 (March 1986): 17–44.

———. "Party Systems and Political System Performance: Voting Participation, Government Stability and Mass Violence in Contemporary Democracies." *American Political Science Review* 75 (December 1981): 861–79.

Putnam, Robert. *Bowling Alone.* Cambridge, Mass.: Harvard University Press, 2000.

———. "The Prosperous Community: Social Capital and Public Life." *American Prospect* 72 (Spring 1993): 35–42.

Rabinowitz, George, and Stuart Elaine MacDonald. "A Directional Theory of Issue Voting." *American Political Science Review* 83 (March 1989): 93–121.

———. "The Power of the States in U.S. Presidential Elections." *American Political Science Review* 80 (March 1986): 65–87.

Rae, Douglas. *The Political Consequences of Electoral Laws.* New Haven: Yale University Press, 1967.

Ragsdale, Lyn, and Jerrold G. Rusk. "Who Are Nonvoters? Profiles from the 1990 Senate Elections." *American Journal of Political Science* 37 (August 1993): 721–46.

Ranney, Austin. "Nonvoting Is Not a Social Disease." *Public Opinion* (October/ November 1983): 16–20.

———. "Political Parties, Reform and Decline." In *The New American Political System,* edited by Anthony King. Washington, D.C.: American Enterprise Institute, 1980.

Rawls, John. *A Theory of Justice.* Cambridge, Mass.: Harvard University Press, 1971.

Reiter, Howard. *Selecting the President: The Nominating Process in Transition.* Philadelphia: University of Pennsylvania Press, 1985.

Richie, Robert, and Steven Hill. *Reflecting All of Us: The Case for Proportional Representation.* Boston: Beacon Press, 1999.

Riker, William H. *The Theory of Political Coalitions.* New Haven: Yale University Press, 1962.

———. *The Art of Political Manipulation.* New Haven: Yale University Press, 1986.

———. *Liberalism against Populism: A Confrontation between the Theory of Democracy and the Theory of Social Choice.* San Francisco: W. H. Freeman, 1982.

———. *Federalism: Origin, Operation, Significance.* Boston: Little, Brown, 1964.

Roche, John P. "The Founding Fathers: A Reform Caucus in Action." *American Political Science Review* 55 (December 1961).

Rorty, Richard. *Achieving Our Country.* Cambridge, Mass.: Harvard University Press, 1998.

Rose, Gary. *Controversial Issues in Presidential Selection.* Albany: State University of New York Press, 1991.

Rosenstone, Steven J., and John Mark Hansen. *Mobilization, Participation, and Democracy in America.* New York: Macmillan, 1993.

Saari, Donald. *The Geometry of Voting.* Berlin: Springer, 1994.

Sayre, Wallace S., and Judith H. Parris. *Voting for President.* Washington, D.C.: Brookings Institution, 1968.

Schattschneider, E. E. *Party Government.* New York: Holt, Rinehart and Winston, 1967.

Schudson, Michael. "The Public Journalism Movement and Its Problems." In *The Politics of News, The News of Politics,* edited by Doris Graber, Denis McQuail, and Pippa Norris. Washington, D.C.: CQ Press, 1998.

Schumaker, Paul, Dwight Kiel, and Thomas Heilke. *Great Ideas/Grand Schemes.* New York: McGraw-Hill, 1996.

Shachar, Ron, and Barry Nalebuff. "Follow the Leader: Theory and Evidence on Political Participation." *American Economic Review* 89 (June 1999).

Sharp, Elaine. *The Sometimes Connection: Public Opinion and Social Policy.* Albany: State University of New York Press, 1999.

Shaw, Daron R. "The Methods Behind the Madness: Presidential Electoral College Strategies, 1988–1996." *Journal of Politics* 69 (November 1999): 893–913.

———. "The Effect of TV Ads and Candidate Appearances on Statewide Presidential Votes, 1988–96." *American Political Science Review* 93 (June 1999): 359–60.

Shepsle, Kenneth A. "Representation and Governance: The Great Legislative Tradeoff." *Political Science Quarterly* 103 (Fall 1988): 461–84.

Shugart, Matthew Soberg, and John M. Carey. *Presidents and Assemblies: Constitutional Design and Electoral Dynamics.* Cambridge: Cambridge University Press, 1992.

Sindler, Allen P. "Presidential Election Methods and Urban-Ethnic Interests." *Law and Contemporary Problems* 27 (Spring 1972): 213–33.

Smith, Eric R. A. N., and Peverill Squire. "Direct Election of the President and the Power of the States." *Western Political Quarterly* 40 (March 1987): 29–44.

Southwell, Priscilla L. "The Politics of Disgruntlement: Nonvoting and Defection among Supporters of Nomination Losers, 1968–1984." *Political Behavior* 8 (1986): 81–95.

Spilerman, Seymour, and David Dickens. "Who Will Gain and Who Will Lose Influence under Different Electoral Rules." *American Journal of Sociology* 80 (June 1974): 443–77.

Stanley, Harold W., and Richard G. Niemi. *Vital Statistics in American Politics, 1999–2000.* Washington, D.C.: CQ Press, 2000.

Stein, Robert M. "Early Voting." *Public Opinion Quarterly* 62 (Spring 1998): 57–70.

———. "Economic Voting for Governor and U.S. Senator: The Electoral Consequences of Federalism." *Journal of Politics* 52 (February 1990): 29–53.

Stein, Robert M., and Patricia Garcia-Monet. "Voting Early, But Not Often." *Social Science Quarterly* 78 (September 1997): 657–77.

Stepan, Alfred, and Cindy Skach. "Constitutional Frameworks and Democratic Consolidation: Parliamentarism versus Presidentialism." *World Politics* 46 (October 1993): 1–22.

Subcommittee on the Constitution, Committee of the Judiciary, U.S. House of Representatives. "Proposals for Electoral College Reform." 4 September 1997. Serial 87.

Sundquist, James. *Politics and Policy.* Washington, D.C.: Brookings Institution, 1968.

Taagepera, Rein, and Matthew Shugart. *Seats and Votes.* New Haven: Yale University Press, 1989.

Tabarrok, Alexander, and Lee Spector. "Would the Borda Count Have Avoided the Civil War?" *Journal of Theoretical Politics* 11 (April 1999).

Taylor, Michael, and V. M. Herman. "Party Systems and Government Stability." *American Political Science Review* 65 (March 1971): 28–37.

Teixeira, Ruy. *The Disappearing American Voter.* Washington, D.C.: Brookings Institution, 1992.

Teske, Paul, Mark Schneider, Michael Mintrom, and Samuel Best. "Establishing the Micro Foundations of a Macro Theory: Information, Movers, and the Competitive Local Market for Public Goods." *American Political Science Review* 87 (September 1993): 702–13.

Tidmarch, Charles M., Lisa J. Hyman, and Jill E. Sorkin. "Press Issue Agendas in the 1982 Congressional and Gubernatorial Election Campaigns." *Journal of Politics* 46 (November 1984): 1226–42.

Underwood, Doug. "Market Research and the Audience for Political News." In *The Politics of News, The News of Politics,* edited by Doris Graber, Denis McQuail, and Pippa Norris. Washington, D.C.: CQ Press, 1998.

Uslaner, Eric. "Is the Senate More Civil than the House?" In *Esteemed Colleagues: Civility and Deliberation in the Senate,* edited by Burdett A. Loomis. Washington, D.C.: Brookings Institution, 2000.

———. *The Decline of Comity in Congress.* Ann Arbor: University of Michigan Press, 1993.

Verba, Sidney, Norman Nie, and J. Kim. *Participation and Political Equality: A Seven Nation Comparison.* Cambridge: Cambridge University Press, 1978.

Verba, Sidney, Kay L. Schlozman, Henry Brady, and Norman Nie. "Resources and Political Participation." Paper prepared for the annual meeting of the American Political Science Association, 1991.

Wayne, Stephen J. *The Road to the White House, 2000.* Boston: Bedford/St. Martin's, 2000.

West, Darrell. "Constituencies and Travel Allocations in the 1980 Presidential Campaign." *American Journal of Political Science* 27 (August 1983): 515–29.

Wildenthal, John. "Consensus after LBJ." *Southwest Review* 53 (Spring 1968): 1113–30.

Wolfinger, Raymond E., and Steven J. Rosenstone. *Who Votes?* New Haven: Yale University Press, 1980.

Wolfinger, Raymond E., David P. Glass, and Peverill Squire. "Residential Mobility and Voter Turnout." *American Political Science Review* 81 (March 1987): 45–66.

Wright, John. *Interest Groups and Congress.* Boston: Allyn and Bacon, 1996.

Zaller, John. "The Myth of Massive Media Impact Revived: New Support for a Discredited Idea." In *Political Persuasion and Attitude Change,* edited by Diana C. Mutz, Paul M. Sniderman, and Richard A. Brody. Ann Arbor: University of Michigan Press, 1996.

———. *The Nature and Origins of Mass Opinion.* Cambridge: Cambridge University Press, 1992.

Index

suffrage
　male-only, 125
　universal, 21
supramajority, 3, 56, 63, 67
Supreme Court, 46, 162, 170. *See also*
　specific cases
swing counties, 119
swing states, 98–99, 167
swing voters, 131, 167

Taiwan, 146
technology, 19, 121–22, 169
television networks, 25
third parties, 22, 78, 88, 90–91, 106
　barriers to, 91, 94, 108, 150
　electoral reform and, 94, 97, 116, 118, 134,
　173
three-fourths state ratification rule, 46
Tilden, Samuel J., 40
Truman, Harry, 41
Twelfth Amendment, 14, 34–35, 37, 40
Twenty-third Amendment, 12
two-party system, 23, 88, 152, 153, 162, 173
　development of, 14, 57
　maintenance of, 63, 92, 106, 156
two-thirds majority, 46
tyranny, 20, 35

utilitarianism, 21–22

vice presidency, 36, 38
Virginia Plan, 31–32, 35
voter fatigue, 19
voter fraud, 7, 42, 43, 143–45
vote swapping, 122
vote value, 167–69
voting, 7, 25, 119, 128, 167–69, 171
　effects of mobilization on, 127–28
　error, 42, 43–44
　and minorities, 91, 164–69
　patterns and methods of, 8, 19, 43, 36,
　162
　restrictions and laws on, 6, 128, 153,
　166–67, 169
　turnout, 25, 60, 90, 93

Wallace, George, 62, 89
Washington, George, 13, 84
wasted votes, 94, 106, 150, 188
Wesberry v. Sanders, 162
Whig Party, 151
white flight, 91
White House, 104, 107
Wilson, James, 32
Wilson, Woodrow, 41
women voters, 64, 152, 162, 163
World Wide Web. *See* Internet

"yellow dog" partisans, 105